RECONFIGURATIONS OF CLASS AND GENDER

RECONFIGURATIONS OF CLASS AND GENDER

Edited by Janeen Baxter and Mark Western

STANFORD UNIVERSITY PRESS
STANFORD, CALIFORNIA
2001

Stanford University Press
Stanford, California
© 2001 by the Board of Trustees of the
Leland Stanford Junior University

Printed in the United States of America on acid-free,
archival-quality paper.

Library of Congress Cataloging-in-Publication Data
Reconfigurations of class and gender / edited by Janeen
    Baxter and Mark Western.
        p. cm. — (Studies in social inequality)
    Includes bibliographical references and index.
    ISBN 0-8047-3841-6 (alk. paper)
        1. Social classes.   2. Sex role.   3. Social
    history—1970–   4. Economic history—1971–
    1990.   5. Economic history—1990–   I. Baxter,
    Janeen.   II. Western, Mark, 1962–   III. Series.

    HT609 .R423 2001
    305.5—dc21   2001018403

Original printing 2001

Last figure below indicates year of this printing:
09   08   07   06   05   04   03   02   01

Typeset by G&S Typesetters in 10/14 Sabon

CONTENTS

Janeen Baxter is an associate professor in the Department of Sociology, School of Social Science, at the University of Queensland in Brisbane.

Gunn Elisabeth Birkelund is a professor of sociology at the University of Oslo.

Wallace Clement is the director of the Institute of Political Economy and a professor of sociology at Carleton University in Ottawa.

Rosemary Crompton is a professor of sociology at City University in London.

Paula England is a professor of sociology and the director of Women's Studies and the Alice Paul Research Center at the University of Pennsylvania.

Siv Øverås is a researcher at the Fafo Institute for Applied Social Science in Oslo.

Rachel A. Rosenfeld is a professor and chair of the Department of Sociology at the University of North Carolina at Chapel Hill.

Mark Western is a senior lecturer in the Department of Sociology, School of Social Science, at the University of Queensland in Brisbane.

Erik Olin Wright is Vilas Professor of Sociology at the University of Wisconsin, Madison.

Tables

Figures

ACKNOWLEDGMENTS

The initiative for this book stems from the Reconfigurations of Class and Gender Conference held at the Australian National University in Canberra in August 1997. This conference also incorporated the final meeting of the Comparative Project on Class Structure and Class Consciousness initiated by Erik Olin Wright at the University of Wisconsin, Madison. At this meeting, members of the various national class project teams and chapter contributors came together to exchange ideas and present drafts of papers. The conference was jointly funded by the Reshaping Australian Institutions Project and the Research School of Social Sciences at the Australian National University with additional support from members of the Comparative Project. We would particularly like to thank Geoff Brennan, John Braithwaite, Frank Jones, and Frank Castles for their support and encouragement. Margrit Davies was instrumental in helping to make the conference a success, and we thank her for her work in bringing everyone together.

We would also like to acknowledge the support of the School of Sociology and Social Work at the University of Tasmania, where much of the work in editing this volume was carried out. Kay Wagland, Diane Fenwick, Colleen Bassett, and Amanda Knight provided invaluable research and editorial assistance. We also owe thanks to Mike Hout for suggesting that we approach Stanford University Press; David Grusky, the series editor, for his support; and Laura Comay, Anna Eberhard Friedlander, Sumathi Raghavan, and Theresa Moran for their assistance in seeing the volume through to completion. Finally, we owe our greatest thanks to the chapter authors. We thank them for their willingness to be part of this volume and for helping us to realize our goal of bringing this volume to completion.

RECONFIGURATIONS OF CLASS AND GENDER

CHAPTER ONE

Introduction

Mark Western and Janeen Baxter

As the title suggests, this is a book that argues that class and gender processes in contemporary societies are currently being transformed. It is also a book that asserts the basic empirical interconnectedness of social relations of class and gender. Both the transformation of class and gender relations and their empirical interconnections have their origins in a basic shift in the institutional characteristics of the advanced societies, a shift that is captured by the move from talking about industrial societies to postindustrial ones.

As several commentators have argued (e.g., Block 1990: chap. 1; Esping-Andersen 1993b), much social analysis of the nineteenth and twentieth centuries was underwritten by a master concept of "industrial society" or "industrial capitalism" within which social processes were played out. From this perspective, industrial society provided the organizing context for undertaking sociological analysis, and the characteristics of industrial society informed the development of concepts and theories within sociological research. The industrial society framework had a number of characteristics that implicitly informed orthodox Marxist and Weberian class analysis. Economic activity was based on the production of goods, not services. Work was organized along Fordist lines, with mass production, a hierarchical division of labor, and highly routinized blue- and white-collar jobs with predictable careers and life chances. Male participation in wage labor was almost universal, and the male life course consisted of an orderly progression of education, full-time continuous employment, and eventual retirement. Within the household, women were responsible for the private provision of services and the reproduction of wage labor (Esping-Andersen 1993b; see also Clement and Myles 1994: chap. 1).

Within a theoretical framework defined by the concept of industrial society, it was reasonable to pursue class analysis in a highly specific way. Most notably, the "industrial society model" of class analysis tended to focus only on those who were currently in paid work, to emphasize the experiences and attributes of men rather than women, to use blue- and white-collar or manual and nonmanual distinctions to index differences between the working and middle classes, and to treat work and family as distinct and nonoverlapping realms of social life. Men carried out public sphere activities in the world of paid work while women were responsible for the private sphere. For our purposes, probably the most pertinent attribute of this industrial society model is that it allows class analysis unproblematically to ignore gender (and, more particularly, women). Within industrial capitalism, women do not "work," at least to any significant extent, and therefore can be safely ignored in class-analytic accounts of social action and inequality.

Industrial society was clearly the economic and social context informing class analysis throughout the nineteenth century and most of the twentieth. However, residues of this approach still persist today. When researchers argue that class membership can be defined solely in terms of a snapshot of current job characteristics of the "head of household" or that a white-collar/blue-collar distinction maps directly onto a middle-class/working-class one, they are drawing on ideas that made sense within the institutional framework of industrial society. However, the advanced capitalist societies today are characterized not by the social and economic conditions of industrialism but by the conditions of postindustrialism. For this reason, class analysis can no longer assume the economic and social conditions of industrial society as a basis for social analysis. For our purposes, postindustrial societies contain a number of key features that problematize aspects of traditional class analysis. These features include the shift by core economies from manufacturing to services, the increasing entry of married women into the labor market, the rise of part-time employment and the associated polarization of working hours, changing patterns of family formation and an increasingly diverse range of household types, and enduring persistent unemployment. Some of the chapters that follow describe these trends in more detail, and all are concerned with clarifying the implications of these processes for class and gender relations.[1]

The impact of postindustrial social change has been reflected in a number of recent theoretical and empirical debates in class analysis. In the 1970s and early 1980s, many class theorists were preoccupied with the so-called boundary debate, namely, how to theorize the class structure of advanced capitalism in response to the proliferation of new-middle-class jobs associated with postindustrial service-based economies. Although there were earlier attempts to theorize the nature and role of the middle class (e.g., Dahrendorf 1959; Weber 1982), the boundary debate focused specific attention on these issues (see, e.g., Abercrombie and Urry 1983; Carchedi 1979; Ehrenreich and Ehrenreich 1979; Goldthorpe 1982; Poulantzas 1978; Wright 1978, 1985) precisely because the middle class was proving to be much more durable and socially significant than traditional class analysis predicted. Prior to the boundary debate, both Marxist and non-Marxist class analysis tended to focus on the working class (Savage 1995) and to treat white-collar middle-class employees as an essentially residual category that was probably becoming proletarianized (Lockwood 1995).

With the boundary debate, class theorists began for the first time to take seriously the possibility that the middle class was an enduring feature of capitalist societies rather than a temporary residual category that was destined to disappear. The boundary debate signaled a general recognition that professional, technical, and managerial employees are emerging groups rather than transitional ones who occupy particular locations within the class structure that empower them in distinctive sorts of ways. While managerial jobs emerged as a consequence of the separation of formal legal ownership from effective control that was associated with industrial capitalism (Hill 1981: chap. 2), the growth of technical and professional occupations that mobilize socially rewarded expertise is fundamentally associated with postindustrialism and the shift to an information or service economy (Bell 1976; Esping-Andersen 1993a).

The other sense in which the boundary debate is an accommodation to postindustrial social change lies in the general acceptance among class theorists that the working class no longer consists solely of blue-collar workers in manufacturing—the archetypal industrial proletariat—but that nonsupervisory employees in semi- and unskilled clerical, sales, and service occupations are also included in this grouping (see, e.g., Erikson and Goldthorpe 1993; Wright 1985). The shift from goods to service production leads to the development of a postindustrial working class of routinized nonsupervisory white-collar employees that complements older working-class fractions in primary and secondary industry (see, e.g., Erikson and Goldthorpe 1993;

Goldthorpe and Payne 1986; Marshall et al. 1989; Wright 1978, 1985). Most distinctively, this new fraction of the working class is predominantly female (Clement and Myles 1994: chap. 2; Esping-Andersen et al. 1993b), while the industrial working class remains predominantly male.

The boundary debate in class analysis was not effectively resolved in favor of one universal conception of "the postindustrial class structure." Nonetheless, the two most influential accounts of class structure to have emerged from the debate, proposed by John Goldthorpe (Erikson and Goldthorpe 1993; Goldthorpe 1995) and Erik Wright (Wright 1985, 1997), focus theoretical attention on postindustrial middle- and working-class groupings. For Goldthorpe, the preeminent class of postindustrial societies is the service class, that group of professional and managerial employees whose employment is constructed in terms of a "service relationship" between themselves and their employers rather than a purely contractual one. Service-class employees exercise delegated authority and expertise in the interests of their employers, and their organizational commitment must therefore be secured through the service nature of the employment relationship. The defining features of the service relationship that promote organizational loyalty are the existence of stable career structures and relatively guaranteed systems of remuneration over the working life and afterward. The employment relations defining the service class can be contrasted against those of manual and nonmanual or blue- and white-collar fractions of the working class, whose employment is typically organized in terms of a fixed labor contract in which wages are exchanged for specifically defined tasks, often over a specific time period (Erikson and Goldthorpe 1993; Goldthorpe 1995).

For Wright (1997: chap. 1), the postindustrial class structure of advanced capitalism is defined in terms of social relations of production with respect to three productive resources: productive property, organizational authority, and occupational skills/expertise. Relationships of ownership and control with respect to these resources distinguish different class locations, most notably capitalists and petite bourgeoisie among the owners of productive property and managers, experts, and workers among employees. Managers and experts control or mobilize authority and occupational expertise, respectively, and along with the petite bourgeoisie represent the "middle class" in contemporary capitalism. The working class is defined in terms of employees in blue- and white-collar occupations who lack both organizational authority and significant levels of occupational expertise.[2]

The second recent debate in class analysis that represents a specific response to postindustrial social change is the debate around the "unit of class analysis" or the "gender-class debate." This debate was sparked by John Goldthorpe's "defense" of conventional practice in class and stratification research of allocating women a class location not on the basis of their own economic activity but on that of a male breadwinner, such as a husband or father (Goldthorpe 1983). Goldthorpe argued that women's comparatively limited labor force participation meant that a woman's class circumstances were better indexed by the economic activity of a male breadwinner such as a father and husband than by her own job. Because the economic activity of the man more strongly shaped the material circumstances of the household, class-dependent outcomes for both women and men were better predicted by assigning individuals within a household class membership on the basis of the job of the male breadwinner. Goldthorpe's initial paper led to a number of theoretical and empirical analyses that attempted to specify conceptually the appropriate unit of class analysis—family or household—and to determine how married women's labor force participation mattered for individual and family class outcomes such as class identification or voting behavior (see, e.g., Baxter 1988, 1991, 1994; Dale, Gilbert, and Arber 1985; Goldthorpe 1983, 1984; Heath and Britten 1984; Stanworth 1984; Wright 1989).

More recently, however, feminist sociologists (Crompton 1986, 1996; Witz 1995) have argued that Goldthorpe's conception of a homogeneous service class as a stable set of managerial and professional positions organized in terms of a predictable firm-specific career is predicated on a particular gendered division of labor. The service class depends on women being responsible for social reproduction of the family and household while men carry out paid work. The existence of the postindustrial service class, as Goldthorpe understands it, therefore causally depends on gender relations associated with industrialization that shaped distinct male and female life courses. Other British research (Crompton and Jones 1984; Savage 1992) links the historical emergence of the service class to gender-specific career tracks for women and men in particular industries such as banking, with restrictions on promotion for women but not men, and female exclusion from higher education that restricted women's access to professional jobs.

The debate about the appropriate unit of class analysis and the subsequent recognition that certain kinds of class relations may causally depend on gender relations are significant in two respects. First, the debate concerning the appropriate unit of class analysis has salience only because the increasing employment of married women and changes in processes of family formation associated with rising divorce and remarriage rates and increased diversity of household types undermine what Goldthorpe (1983) refers to as the conventional view in class analysis. Under this postindustrial reorganization of gender relations, it makes sense to ask what criteria should be used to determine women's class locations and what implications arise for describing the class structure and addressing outcomes such as economic inequality by taking an individual or household view. Conversely, if the typical female life course involves schooling, limited paid employment, marriage, and child rearing, with permanent withdrawal from the labor market on marriage or the birth of children, allocating women class locations on the basis of their husbands' jobs is a defensible strategy. By problematizing the idea that women and men have distinctly different life courses, with only men's directly intersecting the class structure, the postindustrial transformation of gender relations increasingly draws attention to empirical interrelationships between gender and class relations. These interrelationships matter for how we conceptualize the class structure and think about the ways gender and class impact on people's lives.

Second, however, arguments that the development of the service class can be understood only by referring to a gendered division of labor involving work in the labor market and work in the family (e.g., Crompton 1986, 1996, Chapter 4 in this volume; Witz 1995) illustrate the need to examine labor market and family processes in tandem rather than in isolation. Traditional class analysis tended to focus primarily on what occurred in labor markets, and labor market processes were theorized largely independently of the private sphere. With postindustrialism and the rise of two-earner households, people's needs to accommodate work in the family and work in the labor market are much more obvious, thereby drawing further attention to the way class and gender relations intersect.

Like the boundary debate, the gender-class debate was not so much resolved as superseded. There is still no clear consensus about whether individuals or households are the basic "units" of class analysis, although, as Wright argues in Chapter 3, there are various ways of dealing with these issues that acknowledge that individuals are simultaneously located in gender and class relations and that these structures will jointly impact on their lives. England's analysis of U.S. trends in gender gaps in poverty and earnings in Chapter 8 provides a stark example of this process. Similarly, despite arguments about the causal impact of gender relations on the existence of particular class locations, there is still disagreement about how important these factors were for the emergence of the service class (Goldthorpe 1995; Witz 1995) or whether they are even legitimate questions for sociological inquiry (Crompton 1995; Goldthorpe 1990, 1995; Witz 1995).

However, although the gender-class and boundary debates were not unanimously resolved, they clearly sensitized researchers to changes occurring in the institutions of the economy, work, and family that would have to be accommodated in analyses of gender and class relations in postindustrial societies. Most class analysts, for example, now recognize that the petit bourgeois old middle class is much more durable than Marxist theory predicts, that professional/technical and managerial occupations make up core elements of the "new middle class" (however we specifically define this group), and that the working class comprises both blue- and white-collar fractions. Similarly, many researchers would accept that the economic welfare and sociopolitical attitudes and behavior of married women (and men) potentially reflect both their own and their partners' labor force participation and that the relative weight of these factors varies for different dependent variables, for individuals at different stages of the life course, and so on. Most researchers would arguably also accept that social practices within households and social practices within labor markets impact jointly on one another so that these institutional spheres need to be analyzed together rather than independently. Clement's chapter illustrates this by showing how labor market regimes in different countries reflect social understandings about the nature of work and who is or is not included within the labor market.

One outcome of the debates we have just described is that researchers are probably much more circumspect about the usefulness of purely theoretical answers to questions about how gender and class relations interrelate (cf. Crompton, Chapter 4 in this volume; Wright, Chapter 3 in this volume). Detailed empirical analyses of the ways that gender and class relations jointly matter in postindustrial societies are necessary for sociological work to progress because class and gender processes are embedded in concrete institutional contexts whose effects cannot be abstractly theorized a priori. In our view, it is not surprising that the most enduring class analyses to have emerged from the boundary debate are those that are linked to empirical research programs rather than those that specified purely theoretical solutions to the question of the middle class. Goldthorpe's employment relations conception is the basis for an international comparative study of class mobility (Erikson and Goldthorpe 1993), while Wright's conception informs the Comparative Project on Class Structure and Class Consciousness, an international research project investigating the significance of class in a range of different countries (Wright 1997). Empirical research is necessary because gender and class processes are institutionally embedded within empirical contexts defined by labor markets, welfare state regimes, and family institutions, among others. Such institutions vary from country to country, and cross-national comparative research strategies are thus exceptionally well suited for examining how institutional variations in these factors impact on class and gender processes and are influenced by them.

Class theorists believe that a class framework is essential for understanding how economic welfare and economic opportunities are shaped in advanced capitalist societies (Hout, Brooks, and Manza 1993). Locations in the class structure are defined with respect to the basic productive resources (productive property, occupational skills and expertise, and managerial authority) and employment relations (employment status and nature of the labor contract) out of which economic welfare emerges. At the same time, however, family and labor market institutions contextualize or "overdetermine" relationships between class, gender, and economic outcomes. Labor market institutions, such as the mode of wage setting (e.g., highly centralized versus highly decentralized); the nature of labor and management organizations and the rules governing labor relations; and the mandated rights and benefits that workers are entitled to (Freeman 1994) all impact on class and gender processes. Family institutions such as the nature of household types; laws governing marriage, divorce, and cohabitation; and social policies directed toward supporting or discouraging particular kinds of family structures similarly matter. Another key set of institutions that moderate or contextualize class and gender effects are those of the welfare state.

Welfare state institutions matter for class and gender relations because, like class and gender relations, welfare states determine social and economic well-being. More important, however, as with labor market and family institutions, the way the welfare state operates organizes class and gender relations (cf. Esping-Andersen 1990: 23–26). In his well-known typology of welfare-state regimes, Esping-Andersen (1990) illustrates how some of these processes occur. In liberal, residualist welfare states, such as the United States, Canada, and Australia, the state acts primarily to supplement the market through modest needs-based social welfare programs. Social welfare programs are typically means tested and targeted on the basis of need, but the liberal welfare regime assumes that participation in the capitalist labor market fundamentally determines economic well-being. The liberal welfare state does not undermine class mechanisms as a cause of economic welfare because liberal welfare policies aim to reinforce and supplement the market rather than replace it (Esping-Andersen 1990: chap. 3).

In social democratic welfare regimes, such as are found in the Scandinavian countries, social welfare programs are universalistic and tied to citizenship rather than particularistic and tied to participation in the labor market, as in the liberal welfare state. There is a strong emphasis on decommodification—the state guarantees welfare through income protection independently of labor market participation—but there is an equally strong commitment to full employment (Esping-Andersen 1990: 27–28). In social democratic welfare states, then, we might expect class inequalities to be less pronounced than in liberal welfare regimes because universalistic social policy undermines the market as a means of allocating welfare and because much state policy is directed expressly toward ameliorating such inequalities. There is some evidence from other research (e.g., Grusky and Hauser 1984; Western 1994; Western and Wright 1994) that social democratic welfare states show higher levels of social mobility than liberal ones and that levels of earnings and income inequality are less in countries with social democratic regimes than in liberal ones (Freeman 1994; Freeman and Katz 1994).

In corporatist welfare states, as in social democratic ones, the state plays a central role in providing welfare, but benefit levels are inegalitarian and linked to preexisting class and status differences. Thus, the corporatist regime is not redistributive, in contrast to the social democratic one. In addition, in corporatist states, such as Italy, France, Austria, and Germany, the Church strongly influences welfare policy, particularly around issues relating to the family. Corporatist welfare policy is particularly concerned with maintaining the family as the site of social reproduction; thus, initiatives such as child care tend to be underdeveloped, while family benefits encourage motherhood and discourage female employment participation (Esping-Andersen 1990).

Esping-Andersen's (1990) typology is useful because it draws attention to the principles underlying the provision of social rights in different welfare regimes. These principles may undermine or enhance class mechanisms, and they may rigidify or open up the boundaries between the labor market and the family in ways that impact on class and gender relations. Liberal and corporatist welfare regimes potentially enhance or at least fail to ameliorate class inequalities, while social democratic regimes potentially undermine them. Similarly, liberal and corporatist regimes may shape interconnections between class and gender relations differently—from each other and from social democratic regimes—because of the different emphases regime types place on markets, families, and the state and on sources of economic welfare. Many of the following chapters take up these issues and rely on Esping-Andersen's account of welfare states to contextualize their own analyses of class and gender.

Following this chapter, this volume presents two theoretical chapters by Erik Wright that set the agenda for the contributions that follow. In Chapter 2, Wright lays out what is at stake in a Marxist version of class analysis. By defining the key concepts of Marxist class analysis and specifying its normative and explanatory aims, Wright provides an account and a defense of Marxist class analysis. At the same time, he provides a more general overview of the conceptual, explanatory, and normative similarities and differences between Marxist and Weberian approaches to class analysis.

In Chapter 3, Wright takes up directly the central theme of the volume: the interconnection between class and gender relations. Beginning with the observation that class analysis and feminism can be reconciled only by undertaking detailed empirical analyses of the interconnections between class and gender relations, he attempts to clarify conceptually exactly what it means to say that class and gender are interconnected. This results in a "conceptual menu" of the various ways that class and gender relations might intersect. For example, class and gender relations may causally influence one another if one set of relations is causally necessary for the existence of the other. The gender-class debate that linked the emergence of the service class to the unpaid domestic labor of women is one example of this type of interconnection. Alternatively, gender may sort individuals into class locations, as in conventional analyses of class and occupational sex segregation. In another "menu item," people's locations to the class structure may be mediated by gender relations. Individuals who do not work in the labor market, for example, may have a mediated link to the class structure through the labor market activity of a spouse. Gender relations typically organize how this type of mediated location operates. From the point of view of mediated class locations, Goldthorpe's defense of the conventional approach in class analysis is a defense that says that a married woman's mediated class location, as defined by her husband's job, captures everything that is causally salient about class for that individual. Finally, in Wright's conceptual menu, class and gender may interact to jointly determine social outcomes. This kind of interconnection occurs when class and gender mechanisms do not work independently of one another. Empirically, interactions between class and gender mean that gender differences in some outcome variable, such as consciousness or economic well-being, are not the same across classes or, equivalently, that class differences in outcomes themselves vary for men and women. The finding that, for example, class differences in earnings are larger for men than women (Western 1991) illustrates an interaction between class and gender that arises from the joint operation of gender and class relations in shaping earnings.

Wright's chapters provide some theoretical contours with which to situate the remaining ones. In Chapter 4, Crompton engages directly with what she describes as the "employment aggregate" approach to class analysis of Wright, Goldthorpe, and others. The "employment aggregate" approach (Crompton 1995) defines class locations structurally in terms of relations occurring in the labor market, allocates individuals to class locations on the basis of their jobs, and then examines how these classes and class locations so defined matter in contemporary societies. Crompton reviews the feminist criticisms of this approach, some of which we have already mentioned, and then focuses on how class and gender relations have causally impacted on one another to shape the historical emergence of professional middle-class occupations. In so doing, she provides a theoretical critique of class-analytic approaches, such as those of Wright and Goldthorpe, that treat class and gender relations as conceptually distinct although empirically interrelated.

The remaining empirical chapters address various other forms of the interconnection between class and gender. Within the industrial society framework, gendered male and female life courses meant that the family provided the institutional setting within which gender relationships were constructed, while the paid labor market was the institutional setting for interactions between classes. One residue of the industrial society model of class analysis, then, is to treat the institutions of family and labor market as separate and nonoverlapping social spheres. In contrast, the empirical chapters, along with Crompton's, deliberately emphasize how family and labor market institutions and gender and class relations are interconnected in postindustrialism.

In Chapter 5, Clement undertakes a detailed empirical analysis of labor market definitions and practices in six countries. By looking at labor force participation, unemployment, low-paid employment, employee leaves, and the impact of the age structure, he shows that postindustrial labor markets vary from one country to another in ways that reflect the impact of family institutions and the causal effects of class and gender relations. The result is a variety of postindustrial labor market regimes that complement Esping-Andersen's (1990) typology of welfare state regimes. In Chapter 6, Western and Baxter examine the mutual interconnections between work in the family and work in the labor market and how these relationships are shaped particularly by gender relations and different types of social policies in Australia and Sweden. Interconnections between family and labor market institutions and their effects on class, gender, and ethnic relations are further examined by Rosenfeld in Chapter 7. By looking at employment flexibility in the United States, she shows how different forms of flexibility are shaped by class and gender relations and also how they advantage or disadvantage employees in different class, gender, and ethnic groups. In Chapter 8, England examines the paradox that, in the United States, female poverty rates tended to rise just at the time that the gender gap in earnings began to close in favor of women. She develops an explanation that hinges on changing gender relations reorganizing social processes occurring in labor markets and families. In the final chapter, Birkelund and Øverås examine how rising female labor force participation in Scandinavia is related to the fragmentation of the Scandinavian labor movement and associated class disorganization.

It is increasingly common to announce the "death of class" as a source of social inequality and social conflict (Pakulski and Waters 1996). One aspect of this argument is that other bases of inequality and conflict, such as gender, have assumed preeminence. It is also sometimes argued that the shift from industrial society to postindustrialism also implies the decline of class, or at least the fragmentation of the working class, by divisions of skill, political interest, and life chances (Grusky and Sørensen 1998). It is hoped that this volume will illustrate a viable alternative view. In contemporary societies, new institutional arrangements redefine relations between class and gender in ways that undermine traditional or orthodox accounts of these structures, but the new institutional context also points to the continued importance of gender and class relations in the patterning of social inequality and conflict.

CHAPTER TWO

Foundations of Class Analysis
A Marxist Perspective

Erik Olin Wright

If "class" is the answer, what is the question? The word "class" is deployed in a wide range of explanatory contexts in sociology, and, depending on that explanatory context, different concepts of class may be needed. Three broad kinds of questions are particularly common for which the word "class" figures centrally in the answer. First, the word "class" sometimes figures in the answers to questions such as "How do people locate themselves within a social structure of inequality?" Class is one of the possible answers to the question. In this case, the concept would be defined something like "a social category sharing a common set of subjectively salient attributes within a system of stratification." Second, class is offered as part of the answer to the question "What explains inequalities in economically defined standards of living?" Here, typically, the concept of class would not be defined by subjectively salient attributes of a social location but rather by the relationship of people to income-generating resources or assets of various sorts. Third, class plays a central role in answering the question "What sorts of struggles have the potential to transform capitalist economic oppressions in an emancipatory direction?" This is the distinctively Marxist question. Marxists may share with Weberians the second question concerning the explanation of economic inequalities, and, as we will see, the Marxist concept of class shares much with the Weberian concept in terms of its role in explaining such inequality. Marxists may also use the concept of class in the account of people's subjective understandings of their location in systems of stratification, as in the first question. However, it is the third question that imparts to the Marxist concept of class a distinctive explanatory and normative agenda. It suggests a concept of class that is not simply defined in terms of relations to economic resources but that elaborates these relations in terms of mechanisms of economic oppression. The problem of specifying the theoretical foundations of the concept of class, therefore, crucially depends on what explanatory work the concept is called on to do.

In these terms, the concept of class has greater explanatory ambitions within the Marxist tradition than in any other tradition of social theory, and this, in turn, places greater burdens on its theoretical foundations. In its most ambitious form, classical historical materialism argued that class—or very closely linked concepts such as "mode of production" or "the economic base"—constituted the primary explanation of the epochal trajectory of social change as well as social conflicts located within concrete time and place, and of the macro-level institutional form of the state along with the micro-level subjective beliefs of individuals. Expressions such as "class struggle is the motor of history" and "the executive of the modern state is but a committee of the bourgeoisie" captured this ambitious claim of explanatory primacy for the concept of class.

Most Marxist scholars today have pulled back significantly from the grandiose explanatory claims of historical materialism (if not necessarily from its explanatory aspirations). Few today defend stark versions of "class primacy." Nevertheless, it remains the case that class retains a distinctive centrality within the Marxist tradition and is called on to do much more arduous explanatory work than in other theoretical traditions. Indeed, a good argument can be made that this, along with a specific orientation to radically egalitarian normative principles, is a large part of what defines the remaining distinctiveness and vitality of the Marxist tradition as a body of thought, particularly within sociology. It is for this reason that I have argued that "Marxism as class analysis" defines the core agenda of Marxist sociology (see Wright, Levine, and Sober, 1992: chap. 8).

The task of this chapter is to lay out the central analytical foundations of the concept of class in a way that is broadly consistent with the Marxist tradition. This is a tricky business, for within Marxism there is no consensus on any of the core concepts of class analysis. What defines the tradition is more a loose commitment to the importance of class analysis for understanding the conditions for challenging capitalist oppressions and the language within which debates are waged—what Alvin Gouldner (1970) aptly called a "speech community"—than a precise set of definitions and propositions. Any claims about the analytical foundations of Marxist class analysis that I make, therefore, will reflect my specific stance within that tradition rather than an authoritative account of "Marxism" in general or of the work of Karl Marx in particular.

I proceed in the following manner. First, I lay out a series of conceptual elements that underlie the kind of Marxist class analysis that I have pursued. Many of these elements apply, perhaps with some rhetorical modification, to Weberian-inspired class analysis as well as Marxist, although as a package they reflect the background assumptions characteristic of the Marxist agenda. Some of the points I make here may be quite obvious, but nevertheless I think it is useful to lay these out step by step. Second, I specify what I feel is the core common explanatory claim of class analysis in both the Marxist and the Weberian tradition. Third, I identify what I believe to be the distinctive hallmark of the Marxist concept, which differentiates from its Weberian cousins and anchors the broader theoretical claims and agenda of Marxist class analysis. This involves, above all, elaborating the specific causal mechanisms through which Marxists claim that class relations generate social effects. Finally, I briefly lay out what I see as the advantages of the Marxian-inspired form of class analysis.

CONCEPTUAL ELEMENTS

Five conceptual elements need to be clarified in order to give specificity to the Marxist approach to class analysis: (1) the concept of social relations of production, (2) the idea of class as a specific form of such relations, (3) the problem of the forms of variation of class relations, (4) the meaning of a "location" within class relations, and (5) the distinction between micro and macro levels of class analysis.

Relations of Production

Any system of production requires the deployment of a range of assets or resources or factors of production: tools, machines, land, raw materials, labor power, skills, information, and so forth. This deployment can be described in technical terms as a production function—so many inputs of different kinds are combined in a specific process to produce an output of a specific kind. The deployment can also be described in social relational terms: The individual actors that participate in production have different kinds of rights and powers over the use of the inputs and over the results of their use. Rights and powers over resources, of course, are attributes of social relations, not descriptions of the relationship of people to things as such: To have rights and powers with respect to land defines one's social relationship to other people with respect to the use of the land and the appropriation of the fruits of using the land productively. The sum total of these rights and powers constitutes the "social relations of production."

Class Relations as a Form of Relations of Production

When the rights and powers of people over productive resources are unequally distributed—when some people have greater rights/powers with respect to specific kinds of productive resources than do others—these relations can be described as class relations. The classic contrast in capitalist societies is between owners of means of production and owners of labor power since "owning" is a description of rights and powers with respect to a resource deployed in production.

Let us be quite precise here: The rights and powers in question are not defined with respect to the ownership or control of things in general but only of resources or assets insofar as they are deployed in production. A capitalist is not someone who owns machines but someone who owns machines, deploys those machines in a production process, hires owners of labor power to use them, and appropriates the profits from the use of those machines. A collector of machines is not, by virtue of owning those machines, a capitalist. To count as a class relation, it is therefore not sufficient that there be unequal rights and powers over the sheer physical use of a resource. There must also be unequal rights and powers over the appropriation of the results of that use. In general, this implies appropriating income generated by the deployment of the resource in question.

Variations in Class Relations

Different kinds of class relations are defined by the kinds of rights and powers that are embodied in the relations of production. For example, in some systems of production, people are allowed to own the labor power of other people. When the rights accompanying such ownership are absolute, the class relation is called "slavery." When the rights and powers over labor power are jointly owned by the laborer and someone else, the class relation is called "feudalism."[1] In capitalist societies, in contrast, such absolute or shared ownership of other people is prohibited.

Because of the specific role that class analysis played in historical materialism, Marxists have traditionally limited the range of variation of types of class relations to a very few abstract forms, slavery, feudalism, and capitalism being the main types. Once the restrictions of historical materialism are relaxed, the basic concept of class relations allows for a much richer array of variations. The rights and powers that constitute "ownership" can be decomposed, with different rights and powers going to different actors. Just as feudalism is characterized by a decomposition of rights and powers over labor power—some belonging to feudal lords, others to serfs—so too can there be a decomposition of the rights and powers over means of production. Government restrictions on workplace practices, union representation on boards of directors, codetermination schemes, employee stock options, delegations of power to managerial hierarchies, and so on all constitute various ways in which the property rights and powers embodied in the idea of "owning the means of production" are decomposed and redistributed. Such redistribution of rights and powers constitutes a form of variation in class relations. To be sure, such systems of redistributed rights and powers are complex and move class relations away from the simple, abstract form of perfectly polarized relations. One of the objectives of class analysis is to understand the consequences of these forms of variation of class relations. Such complexity, however, is still complexity in the form of class relations, not some other sort of social relation, since the social relations still govern the unequal rights and powers of people over economically relevant assets.

The sum total of the class relations in a given unit of analysis can be called the "class structure" of that unit of analysis. One can thus speak of the class structure of a firm, of a city, of a country, and perhaps of the world. A class structure generally does not consist of a single type of class relation. Typically, a variety of forms of class relations are combined in various ways, further adding to the complexity of class structures.[2]

Class Locations within Class Relations

"Class locations" can be understood as the social positions occupied by individuals—and, in some contexts, families—within class relations. Again, these class locations need not be polarized—locations in which there is an absolute disjuncture between the rights and powers of the different locations within relations. A characteristic feature of many class structures is the existence of what I have termed "contradictory locations within class relations." The claim of a class analysis of such social locations is that the specific pattern of rights and powers over productive resources that are combined in a given location defines a set of real and significant causal processes. Contradictory locations are like a chemical compound in which its properties can best be explained by uncovering the specific way in which different elements—different rights and powers with respect to the various assets used in production—are combined rather than treating such locations as unitary, one-dimensional categories.

Micro- and Macro-Class Analysis

The micro level of class analysis attempts to understand the ways in which class impacts on individuals. At its core is the analysis of the effects of class locations on various aspects of individual lives. Analyses of labor market strategies of unskilled workers or political contributions of corporate executives would be examples of micro-level class analysis as long as the rights and powers of these actors over economic resources figured in the analysis. The macro level of analysis centers on the effects of class structures on the unit of analysis in which they are defined. The analysis of how the international mobility of capital constrains the policy options of states, for example, constitutes a macro-level investigation of the effects of a particular kind of class structure on states.

THE EXPLANATORY CLAIMS:
THE FUNDAMENTAL METATHESIS OF CLASS ANALYSIS

The fundamental metathesis of class analysis is that class, understood in the way described here, has systematic and significant consequences for both the lives of individuals and the dynamics of institutions. One might say "class counts" as a slogan. At the micro level, whether one sells one's labor power on a labor market, whether one has the power to tell other people what to do in the labor process, whether one owns large amounts of capital, whether one possesses a legally certified valuable credential, and so on have real consequences in the lives of people. At the macro level, it is consequential for the functioning of a variety of institutions whether the rights over the allocation and use of means of production are highly concentrated in the hands of a few people, whether certain of these rights have been appropriated by public authority or remain privately controlled, whether there are significant barriers to the acquisition of different kinds of assets by people who lack them, and so on. To say that class counts, then, is to claim that the distribution of rights and powers over the basic productive resources of the society have significant, systematic consequences.

What, then, are the specific mechanisms through which these effects are generated? By virtue of what are class relations, as defined here, explanatory? At the most general and abstract level, the causal processes embedded in class relations help explain two kinds of proximate effects: what people get and what they have to do to get what they get. The first of these concerns, above all, the distribution of income. The class analysis claim is, therefore, that the rights and powers that people have over productive assets constitute a systematic and significant determinant of their standards of living: What you have determines what you get. The second of these causal processes concerns, above all, the distribution of economic activities. Again, the class analysis thesis is that the rights and powers over productive assets constitute a systematic and significant determinant of the strategies and practices in which people engage to acquire their income: whether they have to pound the pavement looking for a job, whether they make decisions about the allocation of investments around the world, whether they have to worry about making payments on bank loans to keep a farm afloat, and so on. What you have determines what you have to do to get what you get. Other kinds of consequences that are linked to class—voting patterns, attitudes, friendship formation, health, and so on—are second-order effects of these two primary processes.

These are not trivial claims. It could be the case, for example, that the distribution of the rights and powers of individuals over productive resources has relatively little to do with their income or economic activities. Suppose that the welfare state provided a universal basic income to everyone sufficient to sustain a decent standard of living. In such a society, what people get would be significantly, although not entirely, decoupled from what they own. Similarly, if the world became like a continual lottery in which there was virtually no stability either within or across generations to the distribution of assets, then, even if it were still the case that relations to such assets statically mattered for income, it might make sense to say that class did not matter very much. Or, suppose that the central determinant of what you had to do to get what you get was race or sex or religion and that owner-ship of economically relevant assets was of marginal significance in explain-ing anyone's economic activities or conditions. Again, in such a society, class might not be very explanatory (unless, of course, the main way in which gen-der or race affects these outcomes was by allocating people to class positions on the basis of their race and gender). The sheer fact of inequalities of in-come or of domination and subordination within work is not proof that class counts; what has to be shown is that the rights and powers of people over productive assets have a systematic bearing on these phenomena.

MARXIST CLASS ANALYSIS

As formulated above, there is nothing uniquely Marxist about the explana-tory claims of class analysis. "What people get" and "what people have to do to get what they get" sounds very much like "life chances." Weberian class analysts would say very much the same thing. It is for this reason that there is a close affinity between Marxist and Weberian concepts of class (al-though less affinity in the broader theoretical frameworks within which these concepts figure or in the explanatory reach class is thought to have).

What makes class analysis distinctively Marxist is the account of specific mechanisms that are seen as generating these two kinds of consequences. Here the pivotal concepts are exploitation and domination. These are the conceptual elements that anchor the Marxist concept of class in the distinc-tive Marxist question of class analysis.

Exploitation is a complex and challenging concept. It is meant to desig-nate a particular form of interdependence of the material interests of people, namely, a situation that satisfies three criteria: [3]

1. *The inverse interdependent welfare principle*: The material welfare of exploiters causally depends on the material deprivations of the exploited.
2. *The exclusion principle*: This inverse interdependence of welfares of exploiters and exploited depends on the exclusion of the exploited from access to certain productive resources.
3. *The appropriation principle*: Exclusion generates material advantage to exploiters because it enables them to appropriate the labor effort of the exploited.

Exploitation is thus a diagnosis of the process through which the in-equalities in incomes are generated by inequalities in rights and powers over productive resources: The inequalities occur, at least in part, through the ways in which exploiters, by virtue of their exclusionary rights and powers over resources, are able to appropriate surplus generated by the effort of the exploited. If the first two of these principles are present, but not the third, economic oppression may exist, but not exploitation. The crucial difference is that in nonexploitative economic oppression, the privileged social category does not itself need the excluded category. While their welfare does depend on the exclusion, there is no ongoing interdependence of their activities. In the case of exploitation, the exploiters actively need the exploited: Exploiters depend on the effort of the exploited for their own welfare.

This deep interdependence makes exploitation a particularly explosive form of social relation for two reasons. First, exploitation constitutes a social relation that simultaneously pits the interests of one group against another and that requires their ongoing interactions. Second, it confers on the disadvantaged group a real form of power with which to challenge the interests of exploiters. This is an important point. Exploitation depends on the appropriation of labor effort. Because human beings are conscious agents, not robots, they always retain significant levels of real control over their expenditure of effort. The extraction of effort within exploitative relations is thus always to a greater or lesser extent problematic and precarious, requiring active institutional devices for its reproduction. Such devices can become quite costly to exploiters in the form of the costs of supervision, surveillance, sanctions, and so on. The ability to impose such costs constitutes a form of power among the exploited.

Domination is a simpler idea. It identifies one dimension of the interdependence of the activities within production itself rather than simply the interdependence of material interests generated by those activities. Here the issue is that, by virtue of the relations into which people enter as a result of their rights and powers that they have over productive resources, some people are in a position to control the activities of others—to direct them, to boss them, to monitor their activities, to hire and fire them, or to advance or deny them credit.[4] The Marxist class analysis thesis, therefore, is not simply that "what you have determines what you have to do to get what you get" but, rather, "what you have determines the extent to which you are dominated or dominating when you do what you have to do to get what you get."

In Weberian class analysis, just as much as in Marxist class analysis, the rights and powers that individuals have over productive assets define the material basis of class relations. However, for Weberian-inspired class analysis, these rights and powers are consequential primarily because of the ways they shape life chances, most notably life chances within market exchanges, rather than the ways they structure patterns of exploitation and domination. Control over resources affects bargaining capacity within processes of exchange, and this in turn affects the results of such exchanges, especially income. Exploitation and domination are not centerpieces of this argument.

This suggests the contrast between Marxist and Weberian frameworks of class analysis illustrated in figure 2.1. Both Marxist and Weberian class analysis differ sharply from simple gradational accounts of class in which class is itself directly identified within inequalities in income since both begin with the problem of the social relations that determine the access of people to economic resources. In a sense, therefore, Marxist and Weberian definitions of class in capitalist society share the same definitional criteria. Where they differ is in the theoretical elaboration and specification of the implications of this common set of criteria: The Marxist model sees two causal paths being systematically generated by these relations—one operating through market exchanges and the other through the process of production itself—whereas the Weberian model traces only one causal path; and the Marxist model elaborates the mechanisms of these causal paths in terms of exploitation and domination as well as bargaining capacity within exchange, whereas the Weberian model deals only with the last of these. In a sense, then, the Weberian strategy of class analysis is contained within the Marxist model.

Of course, any Weberian can include an analysis of class-based domination and exploitation within any specific sociological inquiry. One of the charms of the Weberian analytical framework is that it is entirely permissive about the inclusion of additional causal processes. Such an inclusion, however, represents the importation of Marxist themes into the Weberian model; the model itself does not imply any particular importance to these issues. Frank Parkin (1979) once made a well-known quip in a book about class theory: "Inside every neo-Marxist is a Weberian struggling to get out." The argument presented here suggests a complementary proposition: "Inside every leftist neo-Weberian is a Marxist struggling to stay hidden."

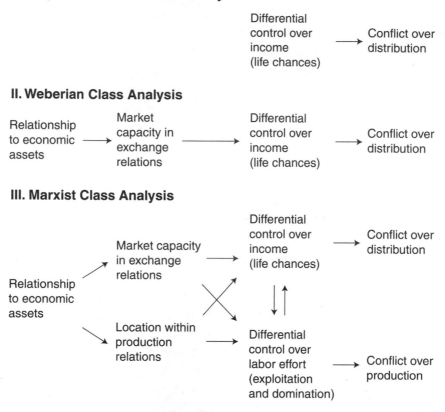

I. Simple Gradational Class Analysis

Differential control over income (life chances) ⟶ Conflict over distribution

II. Weberian Class Analysis

Relationship to economic assets ⟶ Market capacity in exchange relations ⟶ Differential control over income (life chances) ⟶ Conflict over distribution

III. Marxist Class Analysis

Relationship to economic assets

Market capacity in exchange relations ⟶ Differential control over income (life chances) ⟶ Conflict over distribution

Location within production relations ⟶ Differential control over labor effort (exploitation and domination) ⟶ Conflict over production

Figure 2.1.   Three Models of Class Analysis

THE PAYOFF: WHAT ARE THE ADVANTAGES
OF THE MARXIST STRATEGY OF CLASS ANALYSIS?

Elaborating the concept of class in terms of exploitation and domination clearly facilitates its analytical relevance to the agenda embedded in the distinctive Marxist question: "What sorts of struggles have the potential to challenge and transform capitalist economic oppressions in an emancipatory direction?" Class struggles have this potential because of the way class relations shape the interests and capacities of actors with respect to those oppressions. Saying this, of course, does not define the conclusion of the Marxist agenda but only its starting point. It does not prejudge the problem of what social conditions enable or impede such struggles or determine their effectiveness, of how class struggles are linked to other kinds of social conflicts, whether class compromises are possible within such struggles, or even of the historically possible extent to which capitalist economic oppressions can be eliminated. I am claiming, however, that the answer to these questions is facilitated when class is understood in terms of exploitation and domination.

However, what if one is not particularly interested in the foundational Marxist question? What if one believes that emancipatory transformations of capitalism, however morally attractive, are utopian fantasies? Or, even more critically, what if one believes that capitalism is not especially oppressive? If one rejects the relevance of the Marxist question, does this necessarily imply a complete rejection of the Marxist conceptualization of class as well? I think not. There are a number of reasons that elaborating the concept of class in terms of exploitation and domination has theoretical payoffs beyond the specific normative agenda of Marxist class analysis itself:

1. *Linking exchange and production.* The Marxist logic of class analysis affirms the intimate link between the way in which social relations are organized within exchange and within production. This is a substantive, not a definitional, point: The social relations that organize the rights and powers of individuals with respect to productive resources systematically shape their location both within exchange relations and within the process of production itself. This does not mean, of course, that there is no independent variation of exchange and production, but it does imply that this variation is structured by class relations.

2. *Conflict.* One of the standard claims about Marxist class analysis is that it foregrounds conflict within class relations. Indeed, a conventional way of describing Marxism in sociological textbooks is to see it as a variety of "conflict theory." This characterization, however, is not quite precise enough, for conflict is certainly a prominent feature of Weberian views of class as well. The distinctive feature of the Marxist account of class relations in these terms is not simply that it gives prominence to class conflict but that it understands conflict as generated by inherent properties of those relations rather than simply contingent factors. Exploitation defines a structure of interdependent interests in which advancing the interests of exploiters depends on their capacity to impose deprivations on the exploited. This is a stronger antagonism of interests than simple competition, and it underwrites a strong prediction within Marxist class analysis that class systems will be conflict ridden.

3. *Power*. At the very core of the Marxist construction of class analysis is the claim not simply that class relations generate deeply antagonistic interests but that they also give people in subordinate class locations forms of power with which to struggle for their interests. As already noted, since exploitation rests on the extraction of labor effort and since people always retain some measure of control over their own effort, they always confront their exploiters with capacities to resist exploitation.[5] This is a crucial form of power reflected in the complex counterstrategies that exploiting classes are forced to adopt through the elaboration of instruments of supervision, surveillance, monitoring, and sanctioning. It is only by virtue of this inherent capacity for resistance—a form of social power rooted in the interdependencies of exploitation—that exploiting capacities are forced to devote some of their resources to ensure their ability to appropriate labor effort.

4. *Coercion and consent*. Marxist class analysis contains the rudiments of what might be termed an endogenous theory of the formation of consent. The argument is basically this: The extraction of labor effort in systems of exploitation is costly for exploiting classes because of the inherent capacity of people to resist their own exploitation. Purely coercively backed systems of exploitation will often tend to be suboptimal since under many conditions it is too easy for workers to withhold diligent performance of labor effort. Exploiting classes will therefore have a tendency to seek ways of reducing those costs. One of the ways of reducing the overhead costs of extracting labor effort is to do things that elicit the active consent of the exploited. These range from the development of internal labor markets that strengthen the identification and loyalty of workers to the firms in which they work to the support for ideological positions that proclaim the practical and moral desirability of capitalist institutions. Such consent-producing practices, however, also have costs attached to them, and thus systems of exploitation can be seen as always involving trade-offs between coercion and consent as mechanisms for extracting labor effort.

This argument points to a crucial difference between systems of non-exploitative oppression and exploitative class relations. In nonexploitative oppression, there is no dependency of the oppressing group on the extraction of labor effort of the oppressed and thus much less need to elicit their active consent. Purely repressive reactions to resistance—including genocidal repression—are therefore feasible. This is embodied in the abhorrent nineteenth-century American folk expression that "the only good Indian is a dead Indian," an expression that reflects the fact that Native Americans were generally not exploited, although they were certainly oppressed. The comparable, if less catchy, expression for workers would be that "the only good worker is an obedient worker"; it would make no sense to say that "the only good worker is a dead worker." This contrast points to the ways in which an exploitation-centered class analysis suggests an endogenous understanding of the construction of consent.

5. *Historical/comparative analysis.* As originally conceived, Marxist class analysis was an integral part of a sweeping theory of the epochal structure and historical trajectory of social change. However, even if one rejects historical materialism, the Marxist exploitation-centered strategy of class analysis still provides a rich menu of concepts for historical and comparative analysis. Different kinds of class relations are defined by the specific mechanisms through which exploitation is accomplished, and these differences in turn imply different problems faced by exploiting classes for the reproduction of their class advantage and different opportunities for exploited classes to resist. Variations in these mechanisms and in the specific ways in which they are combined in concrete societies provide an analytically powerful road map for comparative research.

These are all reasons why a concept of class rooted in the linkage between social relations of production on the one hand and exploitation and domination on the other should be of sociological interest. Still, the most fundamental payoff of these conceptual foundations is the way in which it infuses class analysis with moral critique. The characterization of the mechanisms underlying class relations in terms of exploitation and domination focuses attention on the moral implications of class analysis. Exploitation and domination identify ways in which these relations are oppressive and create harms, not simply inequalities. Class analysis can thus function as part not simply of a scientific theory of interests and conflicts but also of an emancipatory theory of alternatives and social justice. Even if socialism is off the historical agenda, the idea of countering the exploitative logic of capitalism is not.

CHAPTER THREE

A Conceptual Menu for Studying the Interconnections of Class and Gender

Erik Olin Wright

Both Marxism and feminism are emancipatory theoretical traditions. Both identify and seek to understand specific forms of oppression in the existing world—gender oppression, particularly of women, in the case of feminism; class oppression, particularly of workers, in the case of Marxism.[1] Both theoretical traditions explore the consequences of the oppression on which they focus for other social phenomena, and both seek to understand the conditions that contribute to the reproduction of the oppression in question. Both believe that these forms of oppression should be and can be eliminated. Both see the active struggle of the oppressed groups at the core of their respective theories as an essential part of the process through which such oppression is transformed: The struggles of women are central to the transformation of gender oppression, the struggles of workers are central to the transformation of class oppression. Intellectuals working within both traditions believe that the central reason for bothering to do social theory and research is to contribute in some way to the realization of their respective emancipatory projects.

Given these parallel moral and intellectual commitments, one might have thought that Marxists and feminists would work closely in tandem, mutually seeking to understand the complex ways in which class and gender interact. With some notable exceptions, this has not happened. Indeed, far from trying to forge a close articulation of Marxist analyses of class and feminist analyses of gender, in many ways the most sustained challenge to class analysis as a central axis of critical social theory in recent years has come from feminists. Feminists have argued that class analysts, especially in the Marxist tradition, have generally implied that class was a "more important" or "more fundamental" dimension of social structure than gender.[2] Even when such claims were not overtly defended by Marxists, the relative inattention to gender in the Marxist tradition has often been taken by feminist commentators as a de facto denigration of gender as a significant causal factor. As a result, most feminists have distanced themselves from class analysis.

These criticisms had some force when it was the case that most Marxist class analysts accepted the core theoretical ideas of classical historical materialism. Within historical materialism, class, but not gender, was at the center of the dynamic processes that imparted to history a definable trajectory of development. While the centrality of class in explaining large-scale historical trajectories does not logically entail any kind of explanatory primacy with respect to gender relations within a given kind of society, nevertheless there was a tendency in much Marxist writing for this dynamic primacy to spill over to a more diffuse explanatory primacy. Feminists interested in understanding gender oppression and its conditions of transformation, therefore, were justifiably wary of Marxist class analysis.

Times have changed. Relatively few class analysts, even those still explicitly identifying with the Marxist tradition, strictly adhere to the tenets of classical historical materialism any longer. Virtually no one defends strong functionalist versions of the base/superstructure image of society, even for the specific task of explaining historical trajectories of economic structures. In addition, while most Marxists continue to see class as being central to the dynamics of capitalism, few give class transhistorical primacy in the explanation of historical change. While it remains the case that Marxists generally do try to place class analysis in a historical context, this usually has at best a tenuous relation to a materialist theory of the overall trajectory of human history as such. In practice, then, to be "historical" has generally come to mean "to be historically specific" rather than "to be embedded in a theory *of* history."[3] Marxist class analysis is thus now generally closer to what might be loosely termed "sociological materialism," a framework of analysis in which class, because of its linkage to exploitation and the control of economic resources, has a presumptive importance for a broad range of social problems but is not invariably viewed as the most important determinant. As a result, the debate over what was once called "class reductionism" or "economic determinism" has waned considerably in recent years.

If one accepts this way of understanding the explanatory project of class analysis, then the central task for a reconciliation of Marxism and feminism is to sort out for specific explananda the forms of interaction between class and gender as causal processes. Class may indeed turn out to be "more important" than gender for certain problems, but equally gender may be more important than class for others. Advances in the class analysis of gender *and* the gender analysis of class depend on research that will clarify these interactions.

As a preliminary task for empirical investigations of class and gender, it is useful to lay out a conceptual menu of the various ways that class and gender might be interconnected. This list is not meant to be exhaustive, and it certainly does not constitute a *theory* of class and gender. Rather, it is an agenda of issues that need to be considered within empirical research and theory construction.

1. *Gender as a form of class relations*. While the concepts of class and gender are analytically distinct, there are empirical situations in which gender relations themselves are a form of class relation (or, equivalently, a situation in which class relations are themselves directly organized through gender relations). Friedrich Engels (1884), in his classic essay on the family and private property, formulates the relationship between class and gender in early civilizations this way: "The first class antagonism which appears in history coincides with the development of the antagonism between man and woman in monogamian marriage, and the first class oppression with that of the female sex by the male." Gerda Lerner (1986) elaborates a rather different argument about the confluence of class and gender in early civilizations. She argues that one of the earliest forms of male domination consisted of men effectively *owning* women and by virtue of this appropriating the surplus produced by women. The most important form of this surplus was new people—children—who were a valuable resource in early agrarian civilizations. Control over the capacity of women to produce new labor power was thus a pivotal form of property relations. If this account is correct, then this would constitute a specific form of gendered slavery in which gender and class are melded into a single relation.[4]

2. *Gender relations as having a causal impact on class relations and class relations having a causal impact on gender relations*. Certain kinds of class positions may exist only by virtue of the fact that specific forms of gender relations are present. The classic example is domestic services: Gender

relations play a crucial role in making possible maid and child care services (Glenn 1992). It is not just that gender sorts people into these jobs; if gender relations were dramatically more egalitarian, the jobs themselves might not exist. The availability of single, unmarried farm girls in nineteenth-century New England who were not needed on the farm and who were not in line to inherit the farm was important for the development of the textile industry and the accompanying emergence of the early industrial working class. In many parts of the Third World, gender plays a critical role in making available a supply of cheap, vulnerable labor employed in various kinds of manufacturing. Again, it is not just that gender distributes people into an independently created set of class positions; the structure of gender relations helps explain why jobs with particular characteristics are available.

Equally, class relations can have an impact on gender. The physical demands of many blue-collar, industrial working-class jobs put a premium on toughness, which in turn may help to reinforce a macho gender culture among working-class men. The competitive, high-pressure career demands of many managerial and professional occupations help reinforce a specific kind of domestic gender relations in which housewives are available for managing the personal affairs of their husbands. As it is often quipped by women in such careers, what they need is a wife.

One of the most important ways in which class relations and gender relations have shaped each other centers on the problem of the "family wage." Johanna Brenner and Maria Ramas (1984) have argued that the material constraints of working-class life in the nineteenth century were a major force in shaping the development of the working-class family form and thus gender relations. Because of high infant mortality and the need for high rates of fertility among workers (since having adult, surviving children was crucial for old-age security for parents), it was in the interests of working-class families for the wife to stay at home and the husband to work in the paid labor force. This was not feasible, however, until the "family wage" was instituted. The family wage, in turn, became a powerful material force for keeping women in the home and reinforcing gender differences in pay. These gender differentials in pay, in turn, made it rational for families to orient their economic strategies around the class and job interests of the "male breadwinner," further marginalizing women's paid work. It is only in the last several decades, as the male-breadwinner family wage has begun to decline, that this system has begun to erode.[5]

Particular class relations may also facilitate the transformation of gender or gender relations in more egalitarian directions. As a professor, I occupy a quite privileged class location as a relatively affluent "expert" with high levels of control over my own work. Of particular importance to many professors is the way in which professorial work confers tremendous control over scheduling and time. Professors may work many hours per week, but they often have considerable discretion over when and where they put in the hours. Furthermore, at various times I have had grants that enabled me to buy off teaching and thus have even greater flexibility in organizing my time. This has made it possible within my family for me to play a major role in all aspects of parenting from the time when my children were infants. It has also changed the domestic terrain on which struggles over the domestic division of labor have been waged. The result is a relatively egalitarian division of labor around most domestic chores. This does not imply that class determines the gender division of labor. Far from it. My research on housework demonstrates that class location does not have a powerful overall impact on the gender division of labor in the home. Nevertheless, the specific properties of class positions transform the *constraints* within which people struggle over gender relations in their own lives, and under certain conditions this facilitates forging more egalitarian gender relations.

3. *Gender as a sorting mechanism into class locations.*[6] The way in which gender sorts people into class locations is probably the most obvious aspect of the interconnection of class and gender. One does not need to do high-powered research to observe that men and women in the labor force have very different occupational and class distributions, and most people would explain these differences by referring to gender in one way or another. It is less obvious, of course, precisely what gender mechanisms are at work here. Relatively few social scientists now believe that biological differences between men and women are the primary cause of occupational sex segregation, but such views are undoubtedly still common in the general population. Typically in social science discussions of these issues, two kinds of factors linked to gender relations are given central stage in explanations of gender differences in occupational and class distributions: (1) gendered socialization processes that shape the occupational aspirations and skills of men and women and thus affect the kinds of jobs they are likely to get and (2) various forms of inequality, domination, and discrimination that either

directly affect the access of men and women to various kinds of jobs or indirectly affect access by affecting their acquisition of relevant resources. As feminists have often noted, inequalities in the sexual division of labor in the household constrain the labor market strategies of many women and thus the kinds of jobs for which they can realistically compete. Discrimination in credit markets may make it more difficult for women to become capitalists. Traditionally, discrimination in admissions to certain kinds of professional schools made it more difficult for women to acquire the credentials necessary to occupy the expert locations within class structures. My research with Janeen Baxter on the gender gap in authority has shown that gender discrimination in promotions within authority hierarchies directly affects the probabilities of women becoming managers (Wright and Baxter 1995). In each of these instances, the distribution of power and resources within gender relations affects the likelihood of men and women occupying certain kinds of class locations.

4. *Gender as mediated linkage to class location.* Individuals are linked to class structures through a variety of relations other than their direct location in the social relations of production. The class locations of children are derived from the social relations within families that tie them to the class of their parents, not their own "jobs." Gender relations constitute one of the pivotal ways in which such "mediated linkages" to the class structure are organized, especially through marriages. One of the ways in which class and gender are interconnected, then, is via the way in which gender relations within families and kinship networks link people to various locations within the class structure. These mediated class locations affect both the gender interests of men and women—the interests they have by virtue of their location within the specific gender relations in which they live—and their class interests.

5. *Gender as a causal interaction with class in determining outcomes.* Gender and class are interconnected not merely through the various ways they affect each other but also through their mutual effects on a wide range of social phenomena. Of particular interest are those situations in which class and gender have interactive effects, for the presence of interaction effects indicates that the causal processes represented by the concepts "class" and "gender" are intertwined rather than operating simply as independent mechanisms.

One way of formally representing the interaction of class and gender is with a simple equation of the sort used in multiple regression analysis. Suppose that we were studying the effects of class and gender on political consciousness. The interaction of class and gender could then be represented in the following equation:

$$\text{Consciousness} = a + B_1(\text{Class}) + B_2(\text{Gender}) + B_3(\text{Class} \times \text{Gender})$$

The coefficients B_1, B_2, and B_3 indicate something about the magnitude of the effects of each term in the equation on consciousness. The interaction term, B_3, indicates the extent to which the effects of class vary by gender or, equivalently, the extent to which the effects of gender vary by class. An example would be a situation in which the ideological difference between capitalists and workers was greater among men than among women.

In a model of this sort, it could turn out that the additive terms were negligible (i.e., B_1 and B_2 would be zero). This would imply that both class and gender have effects on this dependent variable only when they are combined in a particular way. This would be the case, for example, if male and female capitalists and male workers all had indistinguishable attitudes but female workers were significantly different. In such a situation, the two independent variables in our equation—class and gender—could in practice be replaced by a single variable that would have a value of one for female workers and zero for everyone else. The effects of class and gender would thus function like hydrogen and oxygen in water. When the amount of water given to plants is varied, there is no "additive effect" of the amount of hydrogen and the amount of oxygen on plant growth; the effects are entirely a function of the amount of the "interaction" compound, H_2O. If class and gender behaved this way, then perhaps it would be useful to introduce a new concept, "clender," to designate the interaction term itself. In general, however, the claim that class and gender "interact" in generating effects does not imply that there are no additive effects. This means that some of what is consequential about gender occurs independently of class and that some of what is consequential about class occurs independently of gender. The task of class analysis, then, is to sort out these various kinds of effects.

The comparative class analysis project has proven to be a fruitful venue for exploring most of these different ways in which class and gender are interconnected. Let me very briefly summarize a few of the most interesting findings.[7]

THE EFFECTS OF CLASS RELATIONS
ON GENDER RELATIONS

One of the most famous predictions in classical Marxism about the effects of class on gender is Friedrich Engels's prediction that male domination would wither away in the fully proletarianized household. If, as he believed, property ownership was the material foundation for male domination, then in the long run the condition of propertylessness should lead to greater gender egalitarianism. To explore this, as well as other hypotheses about the effects of class on gender, I conducted a study of the variations in the proportion of housework performed by men across households with different class compositions. The results are striking: In both the United States and Sweden, class appears to have almost no effect on the level of inequality in housework. This result affirms the general claim that class and gender constitute distinct causal processes: Variations in class do not explain variations in this particular aspect of gender.

GENDER AS A MECHANISM FOR
SORTING PEOPLE INTO CLASS LOCATIONS

I have examined the role of gender in allocating people to class locations in two contexts: intergenerational class mobility and the gender gap in authority. In the mobility research, done with Mark Western (Western and Wright 1994), the most interesting finding was that the intergenerational mobility of women across the property boundary was significantly greater than for men. One possible explanation for this is that marriage constitutes a stronger channel for mobility across the property boundary for women than for men.

In the research on the gender gap in authority, done with Janeen Baxter and Gunn Elisabeth Birkelund, three results stand out (Wright and Baxter 1995). First, in all seven of the countries we studied—the United States, Canada, Britain, Australia, Sweden, Norway, and Japan—there was a large and significant gender gap in authority, even after controlling for a wide range of personal attributes and employment characteristics. Gender clearly affects the ways in which people are sorted into authority positions. Second, there was little evidence for the existence of what is popularly known as the "glass ceiling"—the idea that discrimination against women is concentrated at the top of hierarchies. At least within the constraints of our data, the gender gap in authority appears to be as great at the bottom of hierarchies as in the upper levels. Third, there is considerable cross-national variation in the magnitude of the gender gap in authority: The gap is significantly smaller in the English-speaking countries than in the two Scandinavian countries in our sample and significantly greater in Japan than in any other country. The effect of gender on the sorting of people into class locations is thus not a constant feature of developed capitalist societies but, rather, a variable one. We interpret these variations as at least in part the result of the differences in the effects of the women's movement in liberal democratic countries, where the focus is on equal rights, and in social democratic countries, where the focus is on the decommodified provision of services.

MEDIATED CLASS LOCATIONS

The concept of mediated class locations figures in debates over how to conceptualize the class location of married women. According to one school of thought, every member of a household necessarily occupies the same class location that should be identified with the "head of household," typically the male breadwinner. The class location of married women, therefore, is derived from their husbands, whether or not they themselves work in the paid labor force. The concept of mediated class locations, in contrast, argues that in dual earner households, both husbands and wives have direct and mediated class locations: a direct class location based on their own paid jobs and a mediated class location based on the gender relations within families. If this is an appropriate way of conceptualizing class location, then it should be possible to identify the separate effects of these two dimensions on various aspects of individual lives. To do this, I examined the effects of direct and mediated class locations on class identity for husbands and for wives in dual earner households in the United States and in Sweden. The results were striking: In Sweden, but not in the United States, the class identity of both wives and husbands was affected by both their direct class location and their mediated class locations. That is, the probability of having a working-class identity depended on both the class character of their own paid jobs (their direct class) and the class character of their spouse's class (their mediated class location). In the United States, in contrast, only the husband's class had a systematic relationship to class identity. This suggests that the relative causal importance of direct and mediated class locations on particular outcomes—in this case, class identity—is itself variable. In this particular comparison, I interpreted the Swedish/U.S. contrast as reflecting the different ways in which class identities are forged in the two countries: In the United States, class identities are much more strongly centered within the sphere of consumption, whereas in Sweden class identities are formed within production as well. A consumption-centered process of class identity formation would underwrite a more significant impact of husbands' class and the class identity of both husbands and wives, whereas a production-centered process would create more scope for the class character of women's jobs to have an independent impact on their own identities.

THE CAUSAL INTERACTION OF CLASS AND GENDER

Many of the specific studies in the class analysis project explore the causal interactions of class and gender in various ways. The study of mediated class locations is an example of such research: The effects on consciousness of being in a household with a specific class composition is different for men and women. In the more general analyses of class consciousness, the principle general finding is that once one controls for a wide range of class and class-related factors, gender itself has very little additive effect on class consciousness regardless of how consciousness is measured. There was one analysis, however, in which I found an especially interesting pattern of interactions among class, gender, and race in predicting values on an anticapitalism attitude scale: Among black Americans, there were no gender differences on this scale within the working class or within a broadly defined "middle class"; among white Americans, in contrast, there were significant differences in the attitudes of men and women within the middle class but not within the working class. White middle-class males were significantly more procapitalist than white middle-class females, but white working-class males did not differ at all from white working-class women. My guess is that this is the result of white men within the middle class being more concen-

trated than are women within the more privileged "contradictory class locations" that comprise the middle class.

The central problem of emancipatory social theory, of whatever sort, is to
identify forms of oppression in society and seek to understand the conditions for their transformation. Class and gender oppression remain two of
the most salient axes of such theoretical efforts: class because of its centrality to the problem of economic exploitation and gender because of its centrality to the problem of the subordination of women. Marxism and feminism are the two theoretical traditions that have devoted the most attention
to understanding these oppressions. In the past, a great deal of theoretical
energy has been devoted to metatheoretical debates over the general priority
to be given to one or the other of these clusters of causal processes. One of
the accomplishments of the theoretical progress of recent years has been to
move beyond such preoccupations. This does not mean that we must slide
into the postmodernist mush of everything causing everything (or nothing
causing anything). The rejection of grand metatheory means that the relative
causal importance of class and gender depend on the specific explananda under discussion. The agenda now is to get on with the messy business of empirically examining the ways in which class and gender intersect across a
wide spectrum of social questions.

CHAPTER FOUR

The Gendered Restructuring
of the Middle Classes

Rosemary Crompton

INTRODUCTION

The level of academic interest in debates relating to gender and class has, to put it mildly, declined somewhat over the last decade. In part, this trend is an outcome of the problems and weaknesses of approach within class analysis identified by the feminist critique, important aspects of which are reviewed by Wright in the previous chapter. However, although Wright is correct to conclude that it is necessary to get on with "the messy business of empirically examining the ways in which class and gender intersect" (p. 38), it may be argued that his preferred strategy of "class analysis"—the employment-aggregate approach—is not, in fact, the only way of studying these intersections. Indeed, it may be suggested that his "conceptual menu" is lacking a dessert—or even, perhaps, the main course.

   In this chapter, I first review feminist criticisms and locate them with reference to the different approaches to class analysis that have been developed by sociologists. I will then argue that one of the most fruitful ways ahead for studying the empirical intersection of gender and class lies at the meso (or occupational) level—rather than at the aggregate employment level, which is Wright's preferred strategy. At this meso level, moreover, recent developments suggest the possibility of a blurring of the boundaries between "gender" and "class" as well as a decline in the significance of class as "lived experience."

DEBATES ON "CLASS ANALYSIS," WOMEN, AND GENDER

The employment structure has long been used as a proxy for the empirical investigation of class. Indeed, "class structure" and "employment structure" are often discussed as if they were one and the same thing. With considerable oversimplification, two broad methodological strategies of class analysis in respect to employment may be identified. First, there is the study of the processes of class formation within the employment structure. In this approach, classes (or their fractions) are implicitly treated as the dependent variable. Thus, the structuring of labor markets and developments impinging on work and employment are explored with reference to class-related processes. Examples here would include Braverman's (1974) analysis of the "deskilling" and routinization of the labor process together with the subsequent "proletarianization" of the resulting jobs, Lockwood's (1958) analysis of the fragmentation of class identities among the clerical labor force of the 1950s, and the extended debate relating to the proletarianization or downgrading of particular categories of professionals (Friedson 1986). These investigations have often taken the form of case studies and employ a variety of research methods.

In contrast, the second methodological strategy using the employment structure as a proxy for class is characterized by a single research method: the large-scale sample survey. In this approach, the sociologist's class scheme is used to group together aggregates of jobs or occupations that are then labeled as different "classes." Wright has described this approach to class analysis as an "independent variable" enterprise, and in this chapter the term "employment aggregate class analysis" is used to describe sociological approaches modeled on this strategy. Wright, who has developed a Marxist class scheme, would be regarded as the major practitioner of employment aggregate class analysis in the United States. In the United Kingdom, Goldthorpe's work (Erikson and Goldthorpe 1993) provides the leading example, although the class scheme that Goldthorpe has developed is rather different from Wright's.

However, there are a number of difficulties associated with the use of employment to describe the class structure within the employment-aggregate approach (Crompton 1998: 56–58). First, there is the problem of allocating a "class situation" to those not in employment. Second, there is the fact that the employment structure bears the imprint of other social processes besides class—most notably gender, race, and age—and disentangling the impact of these processes from class processes is often a complex matter. Third, the employment structure does not give any indication of capital or wealth holdings. Fourth, as Wright has argued, the employment structure (as described by occupational titles) does not provide a systematic indication of class relations—of domination and exploitation, ownership, and control. Even more important, perhaps, is the fact that employment aggregates do not correspond to social classes in either a Marxist or a Weberian sense in that it cannot be assumed that the groupings identified by the sociologist's categorizations relate to any sense of community or consciousness of a class nature (Pahl 1989).

These problems of using employment as a proxy for class have, to varying degrees, been addressed in the work of the leading practitioners of the "employment aggregate" approach to class analysis. Indeed, the work of both Goldthorpe and Wright has developed and changed over the years, and feminist criticisms have been very important in bringing about these modifications.

Feminist criticisms of employment aggregate class analysis derive from the observation that, because the primacy of women's family responsibilities has been explicitly or implicitly treated as "natural" and men have been dominant in the employment sphere, this approach has effectively excluded women from any systematic consideration in "class analysis." Two major strands of criticism may be identified:

1. That the primary focus on paid employment does not take into account the unpaid domestic labor of women. Thus, women's contribution to production (and thus their consequent "exploitation") is not examined or analyzed.[1] In addition, the expansion of married women's paid employment has, apparently, rendered problematic the practice of taking the "male breadwinner's" occupation as a proxy for the "class situation" of the household.

2. That the "class" (i.e., employment) structure is in fact "gendered." This fact makes it difficult to construct universalistic "class schemes" (i.e., classifications equally applicable to men and women). The crowding of women into lower-level occupations, as well as the stereotypical or cultural "gendering" of particular occupations (such as nursing and teaching, for example), results in patterns of occupational segregation that give very different "class structures" for men and women when the same scheme is applied.

Even more problematic, it may be argued, is the fact that the same occupation (or "class situation") may be associated with very different "life chances" as far as men and women are concerned.[2]

The second point here emphasizes the de facto intertwining of class and gender within the employment structure. The occupational structure emerging in many industrial societies in the nineteenth and early twentieth centuries was grounded in a division of labor in which women took the primary responsibility for domestic work whilst male "breadwinners" specialized in market work (Bradley 1989). Today this is changing in that married women have taken up market work (and may even specialize in it), and this has very important consequences for employment aggregate class analysis. In the previous chapter, Wright recognizes the reciprocal relations of gender and class but emphasizes that "class" and "gender" should be regarded as distinct causal processes. While this assumption might be appropriate for particular kinds of empirical investigations, it does not enable us to fully capture the intertwining of class and gender in the actual genesis of employment structures and thus "classes" that has been emphasized by feminist historians (e.g., Davidoff and Hall 1987; Glucksmann 1995). Moreover, the separation of "class" and "gender" means that the genesis and development of the employment structure itself (which is being used as a proxy for class) is not addressed directly. Wright's own account of the structuring of employment is couched in abstract Marxist terms. It has been argued elsewhere that, despite his best efforts to operationalize a Marxist conceptualization of class, Wright has not been successful in this regard, and thus his measure is an incomplete one (Crompton 1998: 102). If his measure of class is not particularly rigorous (Wright himself notes that his class categories can be "interpreted in a Weberian or hybrid manner" [1997: 3]), his measure of gender—biological sex—is similarly approximate.

Much of Wright's analysis, therefore, focuses on the reciprocal relationship between employment categories and biological sex, and, using these categories, a number of interesting and important findings have resulted (see Wright 1997). However, it will be argued in this chapter that developments within the employment structures of the advanced service economies suggest the continuing need for investigations at the meso level (Wright 1997: 376). This strategy recognizes the complexities of both class and gender rather than simply using the proxies of employment and biological sex. Furthermore, investigations at the meso level of occupational, household, and organizational structuring suggest that the significance of the "lived experience" of class as employment is in decline—despite the fact that class structures continue to have a measurable impact on people's lives.

THE OCCUPATIONAL STRUCTURE
OF THE ADVANCED SERVICE ECONOMIES[3]

In today's advanced service economies, employment is still a significant, although not the only, determinant of "life chances" and access to them. In this very important sense, therefore, class still counts. The last twenty years, however, have seen two major and related developments that have restructured the impact of the lived experience of employment class: the shift to service work and the growth and development of married women's employment.

The shift to service employment has been associated with changes in employment relations and practices that have weakened the possible associations between the experience of employment and class attitudes, particularly those likely to generate "working class" consciousness. These associations were initially identified by Marx (and others) and further developed by twentieth-century sociologists such as Bendix and Lipset (1967), Braverman (1974), Goldthorpe et al. (1969), and Lockwood (1958). The nature and possibility of the class consciousness and action of industrial workers was often the major focus of such studies. The basic insight that these authors developed was that the "lived reality" of the employment experience of particular groups of workers was more (or less) likely to generate class-related consciousness and practices (see Wright 1997: 389–91). Employment experiences, therefore, have been an important basis for the identification of different categories (or "classes") of employee.

In particular, "traditional" employment in manufacturing (which is itself becoming a thing of the past) was seen as likely to generate "solidaristic" attitudes and behavior (see Lockwood 1966). In contrast, however, much service employment is flexible and often transitory. Service jobs frequently incorporate the personality, rather than only the labor power or technical skills, of the employee. A lack of employment concentration, together with individualized employee controls, has long been identified as being less likely to generate collective "class" types of identities and actions (Crompton 1996; Lockwood 1958; Mills 1951). Many of the new service jobs are low level in, for example, caring or the leisure industry. Esping-Andersen (1993a) has raised the important question of whether a new "service proletariat" has emerged as a consequence of these developments.[4] However, even if such a service proletariat could be identified, recent survey evidence relating to these employees suggests that this kind of low-level "people work" is not associated with conflictual attitudes—whatever the "objective" level of exploitation of the worker might be (Gallie et al. 1998).

As has been noted previously, in a number of very important national instances (e.g., Britain, the United States, and Germany), the "industrial society," which was consolidated from the second half of the nineteenth century onward, was developed on the "male breadwinner" model, in which married women were excluded from paid work (i.e., became "housewives") on the assumption that the male "breadwinner" was paid a "family wage" (see Glucksmann 1995).[5] As a consequence, the "Fordist" occupational hierarchy (where "Fordism" is used as a shorthand term to describe an industrial society based on mass manufacturing) became increasingly masculine. The growth of male-dominated industrial employment, however, was paralleled by the increasing development of social protections, notably those associated with the welfare state. Welfare state institutions, such as occupational pensions and other social benefits, were in many countries explicitly created on the assumption that the male breadwinner model was the norm. Thus, women received social benefits via their "breadwinner" (Esping-Andersen 1990; Pateman 1989). In countries without extensive state welfare protections, such as the United States, there has been an extensive development of marketized personal services.

However, the expansion of welfare state–led service provision (as well as the expansion of other state-provided services, such as education and health) was a major source of employment growth for women. Similarly, marketized personal services are also female dominated. Thus, the basis of the male breadwinner model was being eroded even as its principles were being consolidated in national institutions and policies. Other factors were also leading to the growth of women's employment, including "push" factors, such as rising levels of education, effective fertility controls, and the growth of "second wave" feminism, as well as "pull" factors, including the buoyant labor markets of the 1950s and 1960s. Service expansion was fueled not only by state expenditure and job creation but also by the growth of financial, leisure, and business services.

Esping-Andersen's comparative analysis of the consequences of the expansion of services and women's employment emphasizes cross-national differences in class (i.e., employment) structures. These reflect the varying impacts of different national institutional filters, including welfare states, educational systems, and industrial relations systems. Nevertheless, he also identifies important cross-national continuities. These include the fact that the "postindustrial" (i.e., services) job hierarchy is composed largely of women. He also argues that there will be polarization between households as the two-earner household becomes increasingly common (1993a: 22).[6]

As far as the higher levels of the occupational structure are concerned, feminist critics have focused on two rather different themes in their discussions of the gendered structuring of the middle classes: (1) the essential interdependence of men's and women's paid and unpaid work and its impact on the occupational structure and (2) the cultural "gendering" of particular occupations. In respect of (1), it is the case that, historically, women's domestic work has supported the typical "middle class" career (Finch 1983), while in the employment sphere, women have been employed in supporting roles to male managers and professionals (Crompton 1986). In respect of (2), it has been argued that particular occupations and professions are "male" in that they draw on specifically "masculine" characteristics, such as rationality, detachment, extraordinary levels of commitment, and so on (Craib 1987; Davies 1996; Witz 1992). Thus, with reference to (1), the increasing entry of women into higher-level occupations raises the question of who will be responsible for the domestic work once largely carried out by middle-class wives, and with reference to (2), as more women move into jobs that were once male preserves, such as medicine and the legal professions, will the nature of these occupations be transformed? Before examining these issues further, in the next section I will briefly describe the increase in the number of women in managerial and professional occupations.

THE GROWTH OF WOMEN IN MANAGEMENT AND THE PROFESSIONS

There have been real advances in gender equality of access to the labor market, although inequality still persists and is being reinforced in some countries.[7] In the West, much of the growth of women's employment in the decades after World War II was in low-level and subordinate jobs—reflecting

TABLE 4.1
Women in Middle-Class Employment, 1980s and 1990s

	UNITED STATES		BRITAIN	
	% Increase Women, 1983–1995	*% Women, 1995*	*% Increase Women, 1981–1991*	*% Women, 1991*
Women in total labor force	2.4	46.1	5.0	44.0
Teachers	3.8	74.7	5.6	68.8
Engineers	2.6	8.4	4.0	6.6
Public servants	11.3	49.8	20.0	52.0
Financial managers	11.7	50.3	11.4	21.0
Marketing and sales managers	14.1	35.7	16.5	28.9
Law professionals	10.4	26.2	12.5	27.5
Doctors	8.6	24.4	6.5	30.6

SOURCES: U.S. Bureau of the Census (1996); HMSO, Census Tables, 1981, 1991.

not only direct discrimination but also the relatively low level of formal qualifications and skills among women entering the labor force at this time. Although women had been granted formal access to professional training during the interwar period (e.g., in medicine and law), many formal barriers to their full labor market participation were not removed in many countries, including Britain, until the 1960s. Indirect discrimination persisted through the 1970s. However, over the last ten years, women have been steadily increasing their representation in managerial and professional occupations, as is illustrated in table 4.1, which gives details of the increase of women in professional and managerial occupations in Britain and the United States (for comparative purposes, figures relating to total employment are also given).

The problems with occupational classifications and the difficulties of making cross-national occupational comparisons are well known. Indeed, both of the major practitioners of employment aggregate class analysis have generated their own data as a consequence of these difficulties. Nevertheless, table 4.1 suggests that we can make some broad generalizations about trends in women's employment at the higher levels of the occupational structure. The proportion of women in professional and managerial occupations is increasing at a faster rate than the proportion of women in the labor force as a whole. However, this increase is not evenly distributed. The level of increase of women's representation in some heavily feminized professions, such as teaching, is relatively low, suggesting that these professions might be nearing female saturation. In other professions, such as engineering, the increase of female representation is again only modest, but in these instances from a very low base. Well above average rates of increase in the numbers and proportions of women are to be found in public service, the financial and legal professions, and in "people centered" management, such as personnel, marketing, and advertising, and above-average rates in previously male-dominated medical professions, such as medicine. In broad outline, therefore, these figures support Esping-Andersen's assertion that whereas the industrial job hierarchy remains male dominated, the postindustrial (or service) job hierarchy is becoming increasingly feminized.

It might be argued, however, that the entry of women into middle-class occupations does no more than reinforce existing patterns of gender segregation within the upper levels of the occupational structure. Thus, women are clustering in the "softer," more people-centered middle-class jobs, whereas men are still concentrated in the "harder," more scientific occupations. This kind of argument can by no means be dismissed altogether. However, it should also be noted that many of the professions that women are entering, such as medicine, pharmacy, and architecture, require a high level of scientific expertise. Both finance and law were once male-dominated preserves and were assumed to require numeric abilities and/or a high level of abstract reasoning. The gendered reconstruction of the middle classes, it would seem, is a complex process.

THE CONSEQUENCES OF THE FEMINIZATION OF THE MIDDLE CLASSES: DOMESTIC AND EMPLOYMENT CAREERS

The feminization of the middle classes would appear to be a universal trend. This means that growing numbers of women are earning sufficient income to enable them to support a household. On the whole, however, this does not mean that there has been an increase in the proportion of female heads of household or "main breadwinners." Rather, there has been an increase in the proportion of "dual breadwinner" households. One outcome of this trend, as has been noted, has been growing social polarization at the level of the household as the gap between two-income and no-income households widens (Rowntree Foundation 1995). Another major outcome of the increase of women in managerial and professional occupations has been a decline in fertility levels, particularly among well-educated women (Chafetz and Hagan 1996; Dale 1996). In Europe, total fertility rates (TFRs) had declined to 1.43 by the mid-1990s (a TFR of less than 2.1 is generally regarded as below replacement level) and were lowest of all in relatively traditional, historically child-centered countries, such as Italy, where the rate was 1.17 (see Crompton 1999: chap. 1).

These demographic trends serve to illustrate, in a rather dramatic fashion, the de facto intertwining of employment and domestic life that was one of the major points emphasized by "second wave" feminism. However, recent research suggests that, within the middle classes, there is considerable variability in the kinds of employment/family interface characteristic of particular occupations. Across a range of very different countries, women in a traditionally "professional" occupation (medicine) have been demonstrated to be more likely to develop domestic and employment careers in which family life has been accommodated or prioritized than have women in a managerial occupation (medium- and high-level managers in retail banking).[8] This has been reflected in fertility rates. Women bankers are likely to have had no children or only one; women doctors are (statistically significantly) more likely to have more children than are bankers. If they are living in a partnership, women doctors are more likely to take the main responsibility for the domestic division of labor and child care, and women bankers are more likely to share domestic responsibilities or, more usually, to pay someone else to do them.[9] These differences are reflected in the levels of part-time and flexible working among women in the two occupations.

One explanation of these findings might be individual occupational selection. While this explanation cannot be discounted by any means, a greater explanatory emphasis may be placed on the fact that the two occupations studied have different and particular characteristics, linked to the long-established sociological contrast between "professional" and "managerial" occupations. These characteristics, it may be argued, are more or less likely to facilitate particular family and employment combinations among these contrasting occupational groups.

The classic "profession" is characterized by a formal and extensive body of knowledge and expertise that is acquired through a long period of training. Professional standards are nationally (and usually internationally) recognized. Once the training and registration period has been completed, the professional is in possession of a "license to practice." Professionals may sell their skills directly to the consumer (e.g., as doctors in private practice), or they may be employed by organizations such as hospitals and clinics. During their careers, professionals may move into work situations in which there are extensive "managerial" elements. For the purposes of our argument, however, the point being emphasized is that "professional" work, such as medicine, is concerned largely with the application of a recognized body of skills and expertise. This gives the professional considerable autonomy in the management of their employment—and family—career.

There has been a massive expansion of management training, as represented in qualifications such as the Masters of Business Administration (MBA), but nevertheless managers, unlike professionals, do not require a "license to practice." Managerial careers are forged in an organizational context. In the classic bureaucratic model of organizations, the bureaucratic hierarchy provides a series of graded occupational slots to which managers can aspire. Recent trends, including "delayering" and organizational "downsizing," have had a considerable impact on the traditional bureaucratic career (Kanter 1986). However, this has not transformed the fundamental difference between classic professional and managerial occupations that is being emphasized here, that is, that professional knowledge and expertise is regulated by an external standard, whereas managerial expertise is directly evaluated by the employing organization. Thus, the manager has less career autonomy and is more dependent than the professional on an "organizational" career validation.

These differences in the nature of "professional" and "managerial" occupations are systematically reflected in the employment and family patterns of bankers and doctors. Although there have been many upheavals in the way in which medical services are supplied, there is nevertheless an underlying continuity in the content of medical training and specialization (Crompton and Le Feuvre 1997). The long period of training required of doctors means that the domestic career also has to be planned, and many women doctors "choose" medical specialties offering regular hours. Thus, existing

conventional assumptions about domestic work (i.e., that it will be organized by the woman) tend to be reproduced, a strategy that is reinforced by
the wide availability of flexible and part-time work in medicine.[10]

In contrast, in banking there is no long period of formal training before
taking up employment; rather, expertise is acquired while in employment.
Changes in the organization of banking services have (unlike medicine)
changed the content of managerial jobs.[11] The rapidity of organizational
change means that women in bank management have not, historically, been
able to contemplate the long-term forward planning of their employment
and family careers to the same extent as doctors. Rather, their employment
situation has tended to encourage "reflexive" behavior. In retail banking,
part-time working is found only among nonmanagerial staff. Employment
flexibility, therefore, is problematic for women managers, and, as we have
seen, women bank managers are less likely than doctors to have children.

Thus, although more and more women are going into middle-class
occupations, this trend has been accompanied by continuing gender differ-
entiation within the middle class as a whole. This is reflected in patterns of
family building and the domestic division of labor in different occupations
(Crompton and Harris 1999). These differences can be related to a broad
professional/managerial occupational contrast. To the extent that women
tend to cluster in occupations requiring high levels of expertise that can be
flexibly applied, the gendered restructuring of middle-class employment is
not likely to have a significant impact on the broad contours of conventional
gender roles. In contrast, the domestic pressures on women in organization-
ally based managerial jobs have resulted in more (actual and potential)
strains and tensions at the individual level. These can, of course, be negotiated and resolved on an individual basis, but there is also the possibility that
the cumulative pressures felt by individuals and households might lead to
changes in the organization of this kind of employment (shorter hours, more
flexibility, and so on).

THE CONSEQUENCES OF THE FEMINIZATION OF THE
MIDDLE CLASSES: THE GENDERING OF PROFESSIONS

To turn to the second, rather different theme identified by feminist commentators on the middle classes: the "gendering" of occupations. It has been

argued that professions are "masculine" not only because of their historical domination by the male sex but also because that "profession" itself is
deeply "gendered." In a parallel with Bologh's analysis of bureaucracy,
Davies argues that "profession . . . celebrates and sustains a masculinist vi-
sion" (1996: 669). Bologh (1990) argued that in a public world comprised
of "hostile strangers," bureaucracy regulates aggression and competition
among men and provides a necessary stability. The detached, unemotional
(and masculine) bureaucratic leader controls by maintaining distance (Davies 1996: 666). On this reading, bureaucracy is seen as embodying a rejection and denial of "feminine" qualities, such as understanding, connected-
ness, empathy, and so on (see also Craib 1987).[12]

Davies argues that professional knowledge is gained by dint of "lengthy
and heroic individual effort," creates specialisms, and sustains expertise.
Like bureaucracy, it is rational, impersonal, and impartial. Masculine professional autonomy is sustained by the preparatory and follow-up work of
others—nurses, cleaners, secretaries, and so on—who are usually women.
Gender, therefore, is constitutive of professional relations in the sense of embodying both the masculine "profession" itself and the "feminized" groups
it subordinates. However, Davies suggests that as more women enter the
professions, there is the possibility of "transformation from within." Feminization might lead to a "challenge to professional hegemony" and a "ques-
tioning of masculinity and masculine identity" (1996: 673). As professions
feminize, so the "masculinist" aspect of their constitution might be eroded.

However, an in-depth comparative study of the medical profession
(Crompton and Le Feuvre 1997; Crompton, Le Feuvre, and Birkelund 1999)
demonstrates that, despite the increasing feminization of medicine, patterns
of gender segregation within it mean that the most prestigious and best-paid
specialties—particularly surgery—remain male dominated, as, indeed, does
the profession as a whole. As these particular specialties decisively shape
medical culture in general, we should be extremely cautious concerning the
possibilities of a radical transformation of the profession and/or a challenge
to "professional" hegemony.

In summary, comparative empirical research focusing on the entry of
women into middle-class occupations suggests both increasing gender polarization within the middle classes as women and men "sort" into different
occupational slots and increasing pressures to change employment practices

in a more family-friendly direction for both men and women. The concentration of middle-class women into particular professional or skilled "niches," it may be argued, will not radically transform existing structures of control and domination within the "middle classes." Our cross-national study of doctors suggests that even in occupations that are undergoing a process of feminization, men still retain the most important positions. Nevertheless, the potential bifurcation of the middle classes into female "skilled" and male "power position" occupations might yet have important consequences, and the process of change is not yet complete by any means. Finally, the domestic labor of the middle classes will increasingly be undertaken by growing numbers of service workers and servants. Such people may be oppressed and exploited, but these occupations are not associated with the kinds of employment experiences giving rise to "class" consciousness and behavior.

Do these developments mean, therefore, that there will have been a gender revolution in employment but no real change in "class" structures or domestic relationships? This outcome might, indeed, prove to be the case. However, one important trend working against this conclusion are the pressures toward more family-friendly employment practices (Lewis and Lewis 1996). The further sharing out of employment among men and women, which would be one consequence of "family-friendly" policies, would restrain somewhat current tendencies toward employment polarization. Paradoxically, however, these pressures to modify employment practices would have originated in domestic (or household) conflicts and tensions rather than those of class. Increasingly, it is being recognized that caring is not simply a "woman's problem," and, as Bradley notes in her recent study, "the provision of childcare for employees may be seen as a class and not just a gender issue" (1998: 188). Thus, changes in class interests and objectives may follow on the restructuring of gender relations and the gender division of labor and vice versa.

DISCUSSION AND CONCLUSIONS

In this chapter, I have argued that the recognition of and research on the interaction of class and gender, for which Wright correctly argues, requires us to focus on the meso level of occupational, organizational, and household and family structuring rather than on the interaction of nominally defined employment and sexual categories alone. The intertwining of class and gender, as manifest in the occupational structure, has been the starting point. I have focused in particular on the middle classes, where a process of rapid feminization has been under way over the last two decades.

Although the entry of women into middle-class occupations has indeed been a major social change, the impact on the balance of power and influence between the sexes, broadly conceived, has been less dramatic than might have been anticipated. For the moment, the pattern of gendered resegregation within middle-class employment suggests that masculine dominance in both the employment and the domestic sphere (where "dominance" is taken to mean that women remain largely responsible for domestic tasks) is likely to persist. However, this in-depth investigation of particular occupations suggests that some kinds of work, particularly managerial work, create particular tensions in combining employment and domestic life if both partners are in employment. At the macro level, it may be suggested that these kinds of tension are reflected in the declining birth rate, and indeed some authors have suggested that conflicts between the sexes will be the major social conflict in coming decades (Beck and Beck-Gernsheim 1995).

Finally, we may raise the question as to the wider implications of these changes. It is very unlikely that there will be any "rollback" as far as women's employment is concerned. Thus, the breadwinner compromise is unlikely to become a realistic option in the advanced service economies. It has also been noted that, at the aggregate level, the increase in married women's employment has been accompanied by growing social polarization. The increasing demand for domestic servicing has created low-level jobs that, if left unregulated, are fraught with dangers on both sides. The dangers are greatest for employees, who are likely to be women. They may be migrant workers (legal or illegal) or young people. However, employers and their dependants also face potential problems if employees are particularly vulnerable and/or untrained.

The kinds of trends discussed here indicate that the relationship between market and domestic work is undergoing a process of transformation, at least as far as the middle classes are concerned. Middle-class women are moving into market work, and, as a consequence, domestic caring is becoming commodified. Thus, the household and the market are becoming even more intimately bound up with each other, and we might even begin to speak of the "reembedding" of the household and economic life. This trend, it may be argued, means that the employment experience approach to class (or, rather, class consciousness) might be becoming even less relevant today, even though "class," in the broad sense of positioning in relation to property, power, and markets, still remains as the major determinant of an individual's fate.

CHAPTER FIVE

Who Works?

Comparing Labor Market Practices

Wallace Clement

What is a labor market? A simple question, but one with profound theoretical, methodological, and practical implications. The answers involve practices of inclusion and exclusion, the terms of labor force participation, and the qualities of work that are valued. Who is inside and who is outside the "labor market"? Who is "available for work": What does "available" mean, and what does "for work" mean? Included are the treatment of part-time workers, students, "retired" workers (many of whom reappear as "self-employed" consultants at the top end of the job structure and others who can be found in "McJobs"), and especially women "in reserve" outside paid labor. Labor markets are aged and gendered quite distinctly in various advanced industrial societies. These differences have implications for how class analysis is conducted and especially for the way in which sex is incorporated in comparative analysis (Clement and Myles 1994).

There is nothing more crucial to understanding what a society values and how it provides for its members than how jobs are placed in its priorities. We should ask, What makes people available for work and work available for people? Availability for work must take into account the costs of entry. There are rigidities, especially for women, that include such diverse conditions as child care, taxation policies, and the expected experience of work. It may be, for example, that Japanese women do not wish to return to paid employment after their children are born in part because work *as they experience it* is unattractive; an equally plausible explanation is the complex character of their family structures.

Labor markets everywhere are socially constructed, not simply based on an abstract supply and demand for labor. Countries vary enormously for student work—both during the school year and during "vacations"—and the practice of retirement. Important variations also occur in paid versus unpaid work, especially child care and care of the elderly, and the use of low-paid workers. Addressing these issues is fundamental to calculations of "unemployment" rates, working time, work-life transitions, and youth and women's labor force experiences. They form part of a nation's work life regime.

Working time, who works, and the conditions under which one works have become newly recontested issues under postindustrial capitalism. During this period of major transformations in work life regimes, it is particularly important that we understand how work is organized and distributed. Of interest is understanding the conditions (such as class formations, gender relations, the influence of age, race and ethnicity, immigration policies, and labor market policies) on which different labor market outcomes are contingent. To what extent are the national categorizations of welfare-state regimes—such as Gøsta Esping-Andersen's (1990) divisions into social democratic regimes (Sweden), Anglo-Saxon liberal welfare states (Canada, United States and Australia), and continental European corporatist welfare states (Germany)—valid and useful for locating countries' work regimes?

Regime types are not always fully coherent (O'Connor and Olsen 1998; Olsen 1994). According to Esping-Andersen, Canada is characterized by a liberal regime type and Sweden by a social-democratic regime, using a summarized index of decommodification in three income transfer areas: old-age pensions, sickness benefits, and unemployment insurance. Sweden scores very much higher on old-age pensions and sickness benefits than Canada, but when it comes to unemployment insurance, Canada scores higher than Sweden (Esping-Andersen 1990: 50). For unemployment insurance, Canadian institutions and practices are more decommodifying than those in Sweden. This means that the unemployment insurance in Sweden makes people more market dependent than in Canada. Sweden's labor market policy is much closer to the labor market and to the employers than corresponding Canadian arrangements (Ahrne and Clement 1992).

Are there distinct, identifiable regimes of capital, labor, and state relations? And how have they experienced change in this era of restructuring near the end of the twentieth century? What effects do they have on labor market regimes? This means, for example, understanding not only a social democratic model as exemplified by Sweden but how the social democratic regime itself is being transformed and what its implications are for work (Clement 1994). The goal of this chapter is to begin to specify the character of the labor markets in six countries and from that identify their labor market regimes.

Work life regimes are clusters of power, including institutions, practices, and ideologies; labor market profiles are a combination of factors influencing who works and the conditions under which one works. Included in labor market profiles are the relationship between school and work (when people leave school, whether they work while in school either part time or part year), the relationship between home and work (especially relevant for part-time work, the careers of women workers), the age of retirement and whether retired workers continue to work, restrictions on workers by citizenship requirements, the recruitment of labor forces through immigration practices, systems of unemployment compensation, discouraged workers, and others. Age has become a key labor market factor, including child labor (minimum age) and "retirement" as parameters of the labor market. Child labor spans "baby-sitting" minimum ages (say 12 years) to exploited child labor in sweatshops or sweat fields.

The point is to take a holistic approach to the world of work—people's lives are 24 hours a day for their full lifetimes—and embedded in the entire social formation. Feminism has taught us that "unpaid" work is crucial to understanding the *relationship* between home and paid work. We can now see that the labor force is itself a constructed entity, and one's relationship to the labor force is crucial to understanding life outside paid work. For example, retirement benefits are understood in relationship to work life, but so too are entitlements to parental leave, training, vacations, and domestic demands to care for others. The divide between school and work is blurring for training, part-time work for school attendees, and seasonal work during vacation times. In Japan, life stage is key since even core jobs may involve early retirement into lower jobs before full retirement. Retirees' incomes are predicated on care provided by adult daughters, themselves often disadvantaged in the paid labor force.

The selection of six countries is based on the three major economies of advanced capitalism (the United States, Germany, and Japan) plus three countries that are marginal to but part of their domain (Canada within the North American Free Trade Agreement [NAFTA], Sweden within the European Union, and Australia within the Asia Pacific Rim).

LABOR FORCE PARTICIPATION: WHO WORKS?

Important to remember is just how dramatic the changes in who works for pay have been in recent times. In 1946, nearly 9 of 10 adult Canadian men were employed; by 1995, this had fallen to 2 of 3. At the same time, the employment rates for adult women tripled, from 18 percent to over half the population (52 percent). When talking about labor force participation, however, it soon becomes clear that age and sex are still important qualifiers for making comparisons.

Swedish women have exceptionally high labor force participation rates (table 5.1). When combined with Swedish men's relatively low rates, the sex gap in that country has almost disappeared. As will be seen, Swedish women "balance" family and paid work mainly through a special form of part-time work combined with labor force leave entitlements. In Japan and Germany, the two countries most consistently unequal in sex differences, the combination of high participation rates by men (in Japan) and exceptionally low rates by women (in Germany) produce the greatest sex gaps. The tension of reconciling family responsibilities and the labor force in these two countries is addressed mainly by women withdrawing from paid labor. Canada, Australia, and the United States are similar in their labor force participation rates, but the United States has the highest overall rates.

When age is factored into the labor force participation rates, some major national differences emerge (table 5.2): Teenagers in Canada, the United States, and Australia have much higher rates than in Germany, Sweden, or especially Japan, where rates are very low. In the prime age-group (25 to 54 years), Japanese women record the lowest rates.

Japan's highly gendered work regime merits specific comment. Japanese labor market policies have stressed both the requirements for women's paid work and the fulfillment of "family responsibilities" by women. In 1963, government policy encouraged women's "reentry" into "part-time employment" for those who had full-time employment before marriage but were forced to quit. As Kathleen S. Uno says, "Tax incentives discouraged married women from full-time entry into the labor force, while the 1972 Working Women's Welfare Law emphasized the need to help women 'harmonize' their home and work responsibilities, a problem that it assumed men did not face" (1993: 305). Japanese women are encouraged to work but to "work

TABLE 5.1
Employment/Population Ratios, 1995

	Men	*Women*	*Sex Gap*
Canada	74	61	−13
United States	80	67	−13
Australia	78	60	−18
Japan	88	60	−13
Germany	75	55	−20
Sweden	72	70	−2

SOURCE: Based on OECD (1996: 186, table A).

NOTE: Data are total employed population divided by working-age population, 15 to 64.

around" their extraordinarily burdensome family obligations. Few Japanese women are hired as *sogoshoku*, that is, "women expected to be faithful employees and do the same work as men." Employers group entrants into a dual path system—those in line for promotion to management (*sogoshoku*) and others with limited career paths and pay increases (*ippanshoku*). Only 28 percent of firms who hired for *sogoshoku* positions in 1996 included females among their recruits. Moreover, the experience is that many women hired as *sogoshoku* workers quit (Government of Japan 1994). Beyond the immediate workplace experiences of Japanese women, they are further restricted by "a weak boundary between work and leisure that characterizes Japanese employment. Even time nominally available for leisure is colonized by the corporation, especially in core-sector firms. Male employees are expected to socialize with colleagues and bosses in order that the ethic of commitment that binds people together in their daily work is reinforced outside the sphere of work proper" (Hinrichs, Roche, and Siranni 1991: 9). Work pressures on men shape women's work at home as well as their opportunities within paid labor. Given the strict division of labor around family responsibilities, women are unable to fulfill the informal obligations of core-sector work, and men are not in a position to take on anything resembling equal shares of domestic responsibilities. As Christoph Deutschmann (1991) points out, worker's social duties extend to weekends and companies intervening in employees private lives.

TABLE 5.2

Labor Force Participation Rates by Age, 1994

	15–19	20–24	25–54
Canada			
Men	50.5	79.5	91.4
Women	48.1	72.2	75.7
United States			
Men	54.1	83.1	91.7
Women	51.3	71.0	75.3
Australia			
Men	53.3	86.5	91.4
Women	54.4	76.0	67.4
Japan			
Men	18.3	74.9	97.5
Women	17.0	74.2	65.3
Germany			
Men	37.1	74.3	89.2
Women	32.8	72.0	71.0
Sweden			
Men	25.5	66.8	89.8
Women	29.0	64.8	86.0

SOURCE: Based on OECD (1996: 111, table 4).

In Japan, a special category of "family workers" remains important (table 5.3). In 1996, there were still nearly 3 million women in this group, increasing by 10,000 from the previous year. While this is a declining type for Japanese men, their self-employment continues to grow, to nearly five and a half million in 1996. As Yukichi Takahashi reports, Japan has an exceptionally high rate of self-employed and family enterprise employees "who remain on the pay roll even when the level of activity declines as business conditions change" (1997: 57). It should also be added that many members of core Japanese firms remain on the payrolls even if they no longer "work." Labor hoarding is described as "a lower labor density and maintenance of employment within a firm even amidst production decrease resulting from fluctuations of the business cycle" (Government of Japan 1995: 17). Age and

TABLE 5.3
Japan's Labor Force Changes during 1996

	MEN		WOMEN	
	Numbers	*Annual Change*	*Numbers*	*Annual Change*
Employees	32,600	+480	20,990	+320
Self-employed	5,440	+220	2,110	−30
Family workers	630	−50	2,960	+10
Unemployed	1,370	0	970	+50
Not employed	11,530	−170	27,540	+120
Labor force participation	77.6%		49.6%	

SOURCE: Based on Japan Information Network (1997).

NOTE: Data expressed in thousands of persons, population age 15 and over.

sex matter for characterizing work regimes everywhere but most strongly in Japan. For the other countries, Germany shares some features with Japan, but it is Sweden that is most distinctive with exceptionally high participation by women. Among young people, it is Canada, the United States, and Australia that are distinctive from the other three countries in their high labor force participation.

UNEMPLOYMENT: THE SCOURGE OF POSTINDUSTRIAL CAPITALISM

Canada and Australia have consistently high unemployment rates, while Japan has had consistently low ones. The United States has shown a pattern of decreasing unemployment over the past two decades, while Germany and Sweden became high-unemployment countries during the 1990s. Changes in Germany and Sweden are reflective of broader changes within OECD (Organization for Economic Cooperation and Development) European countries that averaged 11 percent unemployment in 1995 contrasted to 3 percent from 1960 to 1973 (table 5.4).

Disguised by these figures are changes in the base figures of the labor force, namely, those working or looking for work. In Canada between 1990

TABLE 5.4
Unemployment as a Percentage of the
Labor Force, 1985–1995 and 1997

	1985–1995	1997
Canada	11.1	12.7
United States	6.3	4.9
Australia	8.5	8.6
Japan	2.5	3.4
Germany	7.8	11.4
Sweden	4.0	8.0

SOURCE: OECD (1998: 5, table 1.3).

and early 1997, the proportion of working-age Canadians in the labor force fell by three percentage points, reflecting the withdrawal of young people who remained in school longer, early retirees, and workers discouraged from looking for work by the jobless recovery.

For Germany, Jörg Huffschmid claims that there was a shortfall of seven million jobs for 1996, based on his calculations of 3.6 million officially unemployed plus 1.1 million "looking for a job and temporarily participating in various government-financed labor market measures" and what he calls a "silent reserve" who are "too discouraged to seek a job actively and get no unemployment benefits; their number is estimated at about 50 percent of the official count" (1997: 67–68).

Unemployment in Japan is highly disguised because of "labor hoarding" (i.e., keeping people on the payroll—whether in family enterprises or core firms—even if they are not required) but also by the discouraged worker effect, which takes many women out of the labor force. Japanese women withdraw from the labor force at twice the rate for men rather than remain unemployed. As the Ministry of Labor's annual report explains, "Many jobless women have been voluntarily unemployed, and behind this lie many cases where they are obliged to quit their job for domestic reasons such as child care or care for elderly parents and other family members" (Government of Japan 1995: 48). Moreover, Japan's system of rewarding continuous em-

TABLE 5.5
Unemployment by Age, 1995

	*Teenagers**	*20–24 Years*	*25 Years or Over*
Canada	18.5	13.7	8.3
United States	17.3	9.1	4.3
Australia	20.6	12.0	6.6
Japan	8.4	5.7	2.7
Sweden	21.1	19.5	7.7

SOURCE: Based on U.S. Department of Labor (1996: 34, table 9).

NOTE: Data expressed as percentages. Teenagers are defined as 15 to 19 years of age in Canada, Australia, and Japan but 16 to 19 in the United States and Sweden. In Germany, where these data are unavailable, the official definition is 14 to 19 years of age.

ployment (conversely punishing those who take leaves or change employers) impacts most strongly on women who are compelled to "leave employment" for domestic reasons. Mature women are unable to reenter as "regular workers," further removing them to the margins of the labor market. There is clearly an absence of fluidity in the Japanese labor market.

Ginsburg et al. provide an interesting reading of the U.S. unemployment figures, reporting that 5.6 percent or 7.5 million people were officially unemployed but that an additional 5.7 million "wanted jobs but were not actually searching for them, as well as 4.5 million forced to work part-time because they could not find full-time work . . . the US imprisonment rate is about ten times Europe's. The rapidly rising US prison population, 1.6 million in 1995, has doubled in a decade . . . public jobs in criminal justice absorb 2 percent of US employment and that does not include huge private security forces" (1997: 24). What is known as the "incarceration factor" (including over eight million men on parole) has a major effect on jobless rates in the United States.

Teenagers are particularly vulnerable to unemployment, but less so in Japan and very much so in Sweden, where high youth unemployment now continues into the early adult years, as it does to a lesser extent in Canada and Australia (table 5.5).

There are no consistent differences between the sexes when controlling for age, with the notable exception of Germany, where women 25 to 54 years of age (at 10.3 percent) are considerably more unemployed than men of the same age (6.9 percent).

Even in the United States, where the unemployment rate of 4.8 percent in 1997 is at its lowest since 1973, there are still large untapped pools of available labor. Katharine Abraham, commissioner of the Bureau of Labor Statistics, recently told a congressional committee that "there are more than 66 million people aged 16 or older who are not working or actively seeking work" in the United States (*New York Times*, June 7, 1997).

Unemployment should be seen as a particular failure to match labor markets with available workers. It is a particular status socially constructed within the entire matrix of the labor market. That matrix is complex: discouraged workers, underemployed workers, women hidden in the household, students stored in schools beyond their usual leaving times, involuntary part-time workers, underutilized disabled people, those excused from work because of leaves, and so on. Also notable is a possible lack of fit between newly emerging job competencies and the people to fill them. This can occur at both ends of the skill hierarchy (e.g., service cleaning jobs in Sweden or skilled craft workers in Canada). Conservative thinkers also claim a shortage of entrepreneurs (in Canada, Australia, and the United States); immigration officials have responded with a special entrepreneur category, opening access to those with money. Therefore, we are concerned more about making a labor force (and its failures or successes) than about unemployment per se. Put otherwise, we are attempting to locate unemployment within the overall matrix of making a labor force that includes its numbers and qualities (who is included and excluded) and how this might be changing under different regimes.

Nonregular employment has come to account for nearly half the employees in Australia, Sweden, and Japan; the share is about one-third in the other three countries (table 5.6). The largest contributors to the increases are from part-time work in Canada, Australia, Japan, and Germany. In Sweden and the United States, the use of part-time work has remained stable. The most notable change in Australia is in the greater use of temporary workers over the last two decades. In Canada, the rise in part-time employment is accompanied by a greater share who wanted to work full time—from 11 percent in 1975 to 35 percent in 1994; moreover, 40 percent of involuntary part-time workers are the primary earners in their families (Schellenberg 1996).

TABLE 5.6
Nonregular Forms of Employment, 1973 and 1993

	SELF-EMPLOYED[a]		PART TIME		TEMPORARY		ALL NONREGULAR	
	1973	*1993*	*1973*	*1993*	*1973*	*1993*	*1973*	*1993*
Canada	6.2	8.6	9.7	17.2	7.5	8.3	23.4	34.1
United States	6.7	7.7	15.6	17.5	—	—	22.3	25.2
Australia	9.5	12.9	11.9	23.9	15.6	22.4	37.0	49.2
Japan	14.0	10.3	13.9	21.1	10.3	10.8	38.2	42.2
Germany	9.1	7.9	10.1	15.1	9.9	10.2	29.1	33.2
Sweden	4.8	8.7	23.6	24.9	12.0	11.9	40.4	45.5

SOURCE: Based on Standing (1997: 20, table 3).

NOTE: Data are percentage of employees.

[a]Self-employed as a percentage of nonagricultural employees.

Considerable care needs to be exercised in interpreting part-time work in Sweden compared to elsewhere where the hours are shorter and the benefits next to nonexistent. As Rianne Mahon reminds us, "Swedish part-time workers put in what amounts to three-quarters of the 'normal' day and fewer than 16 percent of part-time workers work fewer than 20 hours a week—the point where access to social insurance benefits begins to be adversely affected. Moreover, in Sweden, part-time workers tend to be unionized: at 80 percent, their unionization rate is just under that for full-time workers" (1996: 555). Until the early 1990s, private labor exchanges were prohibited in Sweden. Since they were permitted for the first time, temporary-help agencies have expanded into the extensive leave market (parental, study, vacation, and so on), but "most of the larger agencies operate under collective agreements with appropriate unions" (574).

Throughout the OECD countries, *involuntary* part-time workers (accounting for 15 million in 1993) are much more common than discouraged workers (about 4 million), with the notable exception of Japan, where there are more discouraged workers (OECD 1995: 43, 45). For Japan, Brinton reports that "measuring the number of unemployed women in the Japanese economy is nearly impossible because most women did not go on unemployment insurance, rather were absorbed into their parents' or husbands'

TABLE 5.7

Alternative Unemployment Indicators for Six Countries by Sex,
Average Rates, 1983–1993

	Conventional	Part-Time Inclusive	Discouraged
Canada			
Men	9.9	11.3	11.9
Women	9.9	13.7	14.7
United States			
Men	6.9	8.8	9.5
Women	6.7	9.7	10.9
Australia			
Men	8.5	10.1	10.6
Women	8.8	13.0	15.5
Japan			
Men	2.1	2.7	4.3
Women	2.8	4.3	11.8
Germany			
Men	5.2	5.5	NA
Women	7.6	8.6	NA
Sweden			
Men	4.1	5.5	6.2
Women	3.6	8.2	9.1

SOURCE: Based on Sorrentino (1995: 33, 37).

NOTE: Conventional: Persons not working but seeking and available for work as proportion of the civilian labor force (International Labor Office [ILO] standard). Part-Time Inclusive: Those seeking full-time jobs plus half those seeking part-time jobs and half those working part time for economic reasons minus half the part-time labor force. Discouraged: As Part-Time Inclusive, plus discouraged workers. NA = not available.

households. It is estimated that between 700,000 and 800,000 women left the labor force during the [1974–1975 recession], demonstrating a decisive 'discouraged worker' effect" (1993: 133).

Self-employment has been the only effective job creator in Canada for the past while. In 1996, Statistics Canada reported the public sector lost 41,900 jobs, the private sector lost 85,300 jobs, but there were 213,500 new self-employed now representing 17.8 percent of the labor force. Self-employed have accounted for three-quarters of net employment growth since 1989 and two-thirds of the growth since capital's recovery began. Nine-tenths of the growth in self-employment is concentrated in the service sector, especially business services and health and social services. Using tax return data for 1995, we know that in addition to the 2.4 million filers who are only self-employed, 1.1 million report being self-employed on top of their salary or wages. This "hidden" self-employed expands the variety of employment relationships present in postindustrial capitalism.

Sex differences in unemployment are most evident when discouraged workers are included, increasing the gap in Canada, Australia, Japan, and Sweden (table 5.7). According to Constance Sorrentino, "Japan and Sweden, the countries with the lowest unemployment rates as conventionally meas-ured, had by far the largest increases when the definition was expanded to include persons working part time for economic reasons and discouraged workers" (1995: 31).

Workers can be "discouraged" either by their assessment of labor mar-ket prospects or by domestic demands on their time. Japanese women are discouraged because of demands made by their (extended) families—child care, care of the elderly, care of overworked husbands, or care of households where husbands are transferred away.

LOW-PAID EMPLOYMENT AS DISGUISED UNEMPLOYMENT

There are quite distinct patterns in income distributions in the six countries examined here. Using the ratio of income of the highest 20 percent of house-holds to the lowest 20 percent for 1992, Japan has the lowest ratio at 4 to 3, making it the most equitable in its distribution of household income. Swe-den is not far behind (4 to 6), followed by Germany (5 to 8); then come Can-ada (7 to 1), the United States (8 to 9), and Australia (9 to 6) (OECD 1996). In what follows, the data are based on individuals rather than households, so at least part of the difference can be found in how households configure individual incomes.

In the United States, Canada, and Germany, young people and women bear the brunt of low-paid employment (table 5.8). In Japan, women are overrepresented as low paid. That is not the case in Sweden, where both women and young people benefit from solidaristic wage policies. Australian women also have relatively low rates of low-paid employment.

TABLE 5.8
Low-Paid Employment

	All	Men	Women	Under 25
Canada (1994)	23.7	16.1	34.3	57.1
United States (1994)	25.0	19.6	32.5	63.0
Australia (1995)	13.8	11.8	17.7	34.5
Japan (1994)	15.7	5.9	37.2	36.4
Germany (1994)	13.3	7.6	25.4	50.4
Sweden (1993)	5.2	3.0	8.4	18.7

SOURCE: Based on OECD (1996: 72, table 3.2).

NOTE: Data expressed as percentages. Low-paid workers are defined as full-time workers who earn less than two-thirds of median earnings for all full-time workers.

There has been considerable discussion over whether low wages are a form of "disguised unemployment." Joan Robinson defined disguised unemployment as "the adoption of inferior occupations by dismissed workers" (1937: 84). John Eatwell has extended the definition to include "employment in very low productivity sectors" (1995).[1] Using data for 1990, he finds considerable disguised unemployment for the agriculture sectors in Canada, Germany, and the United States, but most especially Japan (4.4 million workers). In the service sector (excluding finance), there is a large share of disguised unemployment, including 2.8 million workers in Canada, 5.1 million in the United States, and 6.2 million in Japan. According to Eatwell, "The scale of disguised unemployment in Japan is extraordinary, and totally transforms the traditional employment picture of the economy." His analysis "attributes the low measured rate of unemployment in North America and Japan to the presence of very high levels of disguised unemployment" (1995: 28, 31). The low pay levels in the United States are associated with an "impoverishment" strategy to unemployment, while those in Japan are associated with a "protection" strategy compared to Europe's "benefits" strategy.

AGE: THE BOOKENDS OF THE LABOR MARKET IN FLUX

Age is a key characteristic for the labor force. Young people are the most divided over good and bad jobs (and the most likely to experience no jobs).

Older workers face increased pressures to separate themselves from paid labor through buyouts and early retirement, just at the point when the highest-paid workers would earlier have been attaining their peak earnings. These are both good and bad; maybe so many young people should not be so active in the labor force (especially if the experience is a "McJob"), and maybe it is progressive for people to retire as young as possible (although more problematic for women who often accumulate less pension entitlement because of broken careers). These are part of the tensions we face in the current labor force conjuncture. Today's workforce is riddled with contradictions, such as more part-time workers and more people working longer hours alongside more unemployment.

Age appears to be a "fixed" (or ascribed) characteristic whose effect on labor markets is quite set. The same can be said of "age available for work." This depends on the meaning attributed to "work." It is, in fact, a social construct greatly influencing the contours of the labor market. Youths have long been expected to contribute to households where self-employment and home work are common, such as farming and corner stores. Now there are labor markets constructed for young people, especially in retail franchises, such as the fast-food industry.

The labor force participation of young people varies according to economic conditions. During the recent recession in Canada, for example, fewer young people (aged 15 to 24) made themselves available for work; their participation rate at the end of 1993 was 52.3 percent, a drop of over 10 percentage points from its peak in 1989 (Akyeampong 1996: 11–112). At the same time, school attendance rates for this group increased from 43 percent in 1985 to 60 percent in 1996. These young people are a kind of reserve army of labor, discouraged by the poor labor market conditions and "stored" in school longer than they would be otherwise.

Sweden has the highest ratio of youth to adult unemployment, while Germany has the lowest (table 5.9). According to Günther Schmid, "The youth labor market in Germany—as far as it is related to the apprenticeship system—is organized according to the principles of 'transitional labor markets': reduced working time with corresponding lower wages and combined with formal training in school" (1995: 432). As will become evident, German trainees receive fairly low wages, thus participating in the financing of their own education and subsidizing employers.

Japanese men in the 55-to-59 age-group are exceptional in increasing

TABLE 5.9
Youth and Adult Unemployment for Six Countries

	Adult (25+)	Youth (15–24)	Ratio (Youth:Adult)
Canada	8.5	15.9	1.9
United States	5.4	13.1	2.4
Australia	6.4	15.8	2.5
Japan	2.0	5.6	2.8
Germany	5.0	7.1	1.2
Sweden	2.7	9.7	3.6

SOURCE: Based on Sorrentino (1995: 42).

NOTE: Data are average rates, 1983 to 1993.

their employment rates over the past 16 years, while Australian men have had the greatest drop, extending the decreases into the 60-to-64 age-group, where they are matched by those in Canada and Germany (table 5.10). Older women have a contrary experience, consistently gaining in their employment rates (except for Germany). It is the Swedish women who again show themselves as the most active in paid labor, and increasingly so.

Japanese workers between 50 and 55 years of age (overwhelmingly men) who are "passed over" for promotion may be given the option to extend their employment to 63 by *tenseki*, or transfer to a subsidiary. Many of these are *tanshinfunin* employees assigned to areas where they must live without their families (who would not accept the relocation disruption, often because of children's education). This practice is common, accounting for 60 percent of transferred employees in their 40s and 83 percent of those in their 50s (Government of Japan 1993).

What age is "retirement"? Is it 50, 55, 65, 70, or whatever years old? Retirement is, in fact, a process that itself undergoes change that can often be misdiagnosed. Some leave a job because they are laid off or sick but never return to work, while others retire but later return to work. The Statistics Canada General Social Survey for 1994 found that 16 percent of the men and 9 percent of the women had returned to work after initial retirement. The younger the retiree, the more likely to return: 38 percent for those

TABLE 5.10
Employment Rate Changes for Older People

MEN

	55–59			60–64		
	1975	*1991*	*Change*	*1975*	*1991*	*Change*
Canada	83.6	69.5	−14.1	67.9	44.3	−23.6
United States	79.8	74.4	−5.4	61.6	52.0	−9.6
Australia	85.8	65.6	−20.2	66.1	43.4	−22.7
Japan	89.3	91.7	+2.4	76.8	70.6	−6.2
Germany	82.7	70.2	−12.5	55.2	31.9	−23.3
Sweden	88.9	85.0	−3.9	72.3	62.9	−9.4

WOMEN

	55–59			60–64		
	1975	*1991*	*Change*	*1975*	*1991*	*Change*
Canada	34.5	42.9	+8.4	23.4	22.5	−0.9
United States	45.2	53.5	+8.3	31.3	33.6	+2.3
Australia	30.6	33.7	+3.1	15.4	14.4	−1.0
Japan	48.1	54.5	+6.4	37.6	40.2	+2.6
Germany	37.2	35.2	−2.0	15.2	9.8	−5.4
Sweden	60.1	78.4	+18.3	37.6	53.4	+15.8

SOURCE: Based on Gower (1997: 15).

NOTE: Data expressed as percentage points.

under 55, 26 percent for those between 55 and 59, 16 percent for those between 60 and 64, 12 percent for those between 65 and 69, and only 8 percent for those over 70 years of age. Dave Gower reports for Canada that the age of retirement (comparing the period 1976–1980 with 1991–1995) went from 64.6 to 59.8 in the public sector and from 63.1 to 59.8 in the private sector but remained at 65.1 compared to 65.3 for the self-employed (1997: 12–13).

In Japan, between 50 and 55, a kind of "retirement" sets in if the person is not promoted. Rather than "lifetime employment" often associated with core workers in Japan, it may be more accurate to call them "half-lifetime" employees who begin on various exit paths from 40 years of age onward. As Yukichi Takahashi reports, "Fewer than 20 percent aged 50 or above remain with the firm until they reach the official retirement age of 60. In 1988, 40 percent of the men between the ages of 50 and 59 were required by their employer to take early retirement, with the figure rising to 37.1 percent in 1992" (1997: 61–62). They may be transferred to a branch company, given an office with a view (which he now has time to appreciate), or offered a lump sum of money to start a small business.

Germany has become famous for its use of early retirement, especially for male industrial workers. Unemployment benefits have been modified to accommodate this practice, extending their length from 12 to 32 months for older workers at 58 years of age. After 60 years of age, unemployment for one year qualifies the person for full retirement (Rudolph 1994: 85).

LEAVES: BEING EXCUSED FROM THE LABOR MARKET

Legislated leaves are those applying to all citizens in a country; many other leave provisions are labor market derived, being contained in collective agreements or employer benefits packages. Systematic evidence is available mainly on legislated leaves (table 5.11).

Leave types include long-term disability, retirement, maternity/paternity, vacation, education, unemployment, and sickness. Leaving the labor market—temporarily or permanently—for any of these six reasons does not necessarily mean a labor market "leave." To qualify for such a leave for any of these reasons, one needs to be "excused" with or without pay.

As in most other social policy areas, these six countries represent the full diversity of labor market leave practices under postindustrial capitalism. Historically, Sweden has been the paragon of universalistic, social democratic practices, whereas Germany has furnished mainly paternalistic, conservative ones. While containing certain elements of universalism and/or paternalism, the leave practices in the study's four other countries—Japan, Australia, the United States, and Canada—are primarily residualist or liberal.

This trichotomy can be observed in sickness leave, for example. According to data pertaining to 1985, the average duration (and, thus, generosity) of sickness leave per person per year was 20 days in Sweden, 12 days in

TABLE 5.11
Hours of Work, Paid Leave, and Public Holidays

	Normal Hours of Work	Annual Leave	Public Holidays
Canada	40 hours/week	2 weeks plus an additional week after 5 years	9 days federal and 5 to 9 more provincial
United States	40 hours/week	No general provisions at state or federal levels; collective agreement averages: 1 year, 1 week; 2 years, 2 weeks; 8 years, 3 weeks; 15 years, 4 weeks; 28 years, 6 weeks	10 federal with no obligation to grant paid time off; 10–13 at state level
Australia	38 hours/week	4 weeks	10 days national and up to 3 more state
Japan	40 hours/week (effective 1997)	10 days, increasing 1 day a year to a maximum of 20	14 days
Germany	40 hours/week	24 working days	9–13 days, depending on state
Sweden	40 hours/week	25 to 30 working days	12 days

SOURCE: International Labour Office Geneva (1995: 301–17 for normal hours of work, paid annual leave, and public holidays; 353–64 for special types of leave).

NOTE: Special types of leave:

Australia: *Long-service leave.* Most states provide for a right to 13 weeks of leave after 15 years of qualifying service.

Canada: *Bereavement leave.* Three days of paid leave (federal); three days of unpaid leave in several provinces.

Germany: *Leave for personal reasons.* Workers have a right under the Civil Code to be absent from work for relatively short periods of time for personal reasons, provided that the absence was not caused by a fault of the worker.

Japan: *Leave for personal reasons.* No statutory provision. Common practice: leave for marriage, birth of a child, or death of a close relative. Three months to care for elderly parents or other family members (effective April 1997).

Sweden: *Educational leave.* Available to all employees up to one year. For professional training, employees may be entitled to keep their salary entirely or partly. *Special leave.* Various leaves are available to employees, such as leave for carrying out trade union work, to nurse a sick relative, to participate in Swedish-language training for immigrants, to carry out duties in schools, and to apply for a new job.

TABLE 5.12
Statutory Provisions for Parental Leave, January 1995

	Employment Conditions	Duration of Leave	Benefits
Canada	6 months continuous	24 weeks	57% of weekly insurable earnings
United States	12 months, not necessarily continuous[a]	12 weeks	No benefits
Australia	12 months continuous	Until child is 1 year old	No benefits
Japan	None[b]	Until child is 1 year old	25% of earnings
Germany	4 weeks same employer	Until child is 3 years old	600DM per month income tested
Sweden	6 months continuous or 12 of past 24 months	Until child is 18 months old	80% for 10 months; 90% for 2 months; flat payment for last 3 months

SOURCE: Based on OECD (1995: tables 5.1 and 5.2).

[a]The United States excludes persons in military service and employees in companies with fewer than 50 workers.

[b]Japan excludes day or seasonal workers.

Germany, but only 5 days in the United States and Canada (Esping-Andersen and Kolberg 1991: 77–111; Korpi 1989).

Parental leave legislation was first adopted in Sweden in 1974, but only since the early 1990s has parental leave been adopted in Australia, Japan, and the United States (OECD 1995: 171) (table 5.12). Leave provisions in Canada are offered to employees who qualify through its Unemployment Insurance provisions. In Germany, they are through the Federal Child-Raising Allowance Act, set at a fixed rate until the child is three years old.

Since the Child Leave Law in 1992, which provides for 25 percent ben-

TABLE 5.13
Public Expenditures on Labor Market Programs in the 1990s

	1990–1991	*1993–1994*	*1995–1996*	*1997*
Active				
Canada	0.53	0.65	0.56	0.48
United States	0.24	0.24	0.20	0.17
Australia	0.26	0.75	0.73	0.66
Japan	0.11	0.09	0.11	0.10
Germany	1.03	1.58	1.33	1.25
Sweden	1.69	2.56	3.00	2.16
Passive				
Canada	1.91	2.00	1.31	1.18
United States	0.49	0.45	0.35	0.26
Australia	1.11	1.94	1.64	1.30
Japan	0.22	0.26	0.35	0.40
Germany	1.10	2.60	2.14	2.54
Sweden	0.88	3.13	2.54	2.16

SOURCE: Based on OECD (1994a, 1996, 1998).

NOTE: Data expressed as a percentage of gross domestic product.

efits for one year, some Japanese companies have adopted other benefits for workers on child care leave. One-third of the companies provide some level of wages, four-fifths cover social insurance expenses, but less than 1 percent pay full scheduled wages (Government of Japan 1993).

LABOR MARKET POLICIES

Active labor market programs provide special measures for employment services, labor market training for adults and youths, direct job creation, or special measures for the disabled. Collectively, they represent public action directed at making people employable. Maintenance programs, on the other hand, pay individuals not to work and are essentially passive in preparing people for the labor market or intentionally excluding them (tables 5.13 and 5.14).

TABLE 5.14
Public Expenditures on Labor Market Programs, 1997

	Canada	United States	Australia	Japan	Germany	Sweden
Services	0.20	0.06	0.24	0.03	0.21	0.26
Training	0.17	0.04	0.09	0.03	0.36	0.43
Youth	0.02	0.03	0.06	0.00	0.07	0.02
Subsidized	0.06	0.01	0.21	0.04	0.34	0.70
Disabled	0.03	0.03	0.06	0.00	0.28	0.67
Compensation	1.17	0.26	1.30	0.40	2.49	2.16
Retirement	0.01	0.00	0.00	0.00	0.05[a]	0.00
Total	1.65	0.43	1.97	0.50	3.79	4.25
Active total	0.48	0.17	0.66	0.10	1.25	2.09
Passive total	1.18	0.26	1.30	0.40	2.54	2.16

SOURCE: Based on OECD (1998: 211–12, table J).

NOTE: Data expressed as a percentage of gross domestic product.

[a] German expenditure on early retirement has decreased from a high of 0.59 percent in 1993.

These results clearly identify three clusters: Germany and Sweden as active; Canada and Australia as high passive, low active; and Japan and the United States as inactive with respect to labor market interventions by the state. Only one-third of the unemployed in the United States collect benefits, and in Canada the proportion is down to about one-half. This accounts for the declining rate of expenditures on passive unemployment payouts. Fewer people are entitled to receive benefits, not that there are fewer unemployed.

Rudolf Meidner reminds us that labor market policy "alone is incapable of eliminating mass unemployment." Swedish policies have been taxed to their limit in recent times. "In the deep crisis of 1993–4, active labor market measures took care of no less than 7 percent of the country's labor force" (1997: 87, 93).

There are other sets of practices that keep people outside the labor market (i.e., from seeking paid employment). These range from systems of education that keep students in school longer to practices with the disabled that marginalize them from the labor force by failing to provide needed support. These practices can also include tax policies that allow joint filing of returns versus those that require individual filing (which promotes women's labor force participation). There are also other practices, such as the availability of quality day care for young people or health care for the elderly (since it is women who stay at home to care for the ill in the absence of state facilities). Practices vary among countries.

CONCLUSION

The way in which labor is understood in particular societies reveals a good deal about the nature of those places. Ann Shola Orloff, for example, claims that "liberal states tend to respond to societal 'failures' rather than intervene to prevent problems from occurring. Thus, programs in liberal regimes avoid undercutting the market by offering only stigmatizing subsistence-level grants to those unable to participate in the market. In contrast, social-democratic and conservative regimes are pro-active and retain a larger range of welfare activities, effectively crowding out the market" (1993: 310).

The six countries concentrated on here have produced distinctive patterns of work life regimes. Each has relied on quite different characteristics of inclusion and exclusion. Sweden has used high rates of women's labor force participation, especially among older women, accompanied by very strong parental leave provisions for women in their middle years. It has become a high-unemployment country, especially for young people. Notable are its long annual leave provisions and little low-paid work. Sweden is famous for its active labor market programs, but recently its passive payments have also become high. A strong labor movement dedicated to labor market entitlements remains a key Swedish characteristic. Sweden remains a social democratic regime but is clearly liberalizing its practices in line with its joining the European Union.

Germany has low women's labor force participation and low employment for older men and women. It has strong annual leave and parental provisions. Many German youths remain in school, but those who do not receive low pay. Outside the well-known apprenticeship system, few combine school and employment. Germany has dedicated considerable resources to active labor market practices but has also had to rely recently on high passive payments (beyond its famous early retirement schemes). Its labor movement has only medium membership density but high levels of labor force coverage, still giving it considerable force within the society. Germany retains many conservative and patriarchal elements characteristic of continental European corporatist welfare states.

Japan has the largest sex gap of the countries examined, with especially high male labor force participation. Women are also prominent among the low paid. There is very little teenage labor used, and few students combine school with work. Employees work long hours with low annual leave and weak parental leave provisions. There is low official unemployment, combined with high levels of disguised unemployment. Japan has weak active labor market practices and low passive payments, combined with low levels of unionization. Japan's weak welfare state and highly patriarchal labor force practices combine with liberal market measures to make it a unique social formation.

Australia has many foreign-born workers in its labor force. There is also much teenage labor, including those who combine school and work. The high levels of unemployment are especially so for teenagers, a problem compounded by low levels of full-time educational pursuit for young people. Many Australians have become discouraged in their search for suitable work. Many workers are employed on a temporary basis and work long hours. They do, however, have fairly long annual leave provisions but weak parental leave provisions. Both their active and their passive labor market payments are medium compared to the other countries. The medium density of union membership translates into high levels of coverage because of the special "award system." As a liberal welfare state, Australia has considerably more social democratic practices than the United States.

The United States is characterized by long hours of work, high teenage labor, and high levels of low-paid work, especially for those under 25 years of age. There is a high combination of school and work. There are weak parental leave provisions and low annual leaves. All this has produced low levels of unemployment with weak active and passive labor market practices. The level of unionization is low and declining. It is the quintessential liberal welfare state.

Canada also has high levels of teenage labor and high teenage unemployment. Many students combine school and work. Like Australia, it has a high foreign-born labor force. There is a high involvement of mature women, especially in part-time work, but also a high number of discouraged workers, combined with high levels of unemployment and a good deal of low-paid work. There is low employment for older men. Canada has low annual leave provisions but medium levels of parental leave. It is at a medium level of commitment to both passive and active labor market payment. This combines with a medium level of union coverage and density.

Canada has features that resemble those of the United States, but it more closely parallels Australia in some social democratic respects. Japan is the most distinctive labor market regime, although it bears some resemblance to Germany on the side of how women and young people are treated and to the United States in terms of its weak labor market practices. Sweden remains distinctive in its leave provisions and high involvement of women in paid labor but is becoming more like North America in its treatment of young people (with the notable exception of low-paid work). None of these six countries could be said to be "the same" in their labor market regimes, even though each is subjected to similar international pressures as advanced industrial societies faced with postindustrial restructuring.

So-called labor markets are created by larger forces, including political agreements such as NAFTA, which governs many of the conditions for the sale of labor in Canada today; technological changes; the strength and skill of labor; the location of capital; state priorities; and social policies (e.g., day care and education). The response to these pressures varies greatly in terms of political will and traditions for the treatment of people by life stage and sex.

As a liberal-democratic society, Canada combines elements of both capitalist markets and political rights. In the current era, the liberal side of our society has come to dominate, some would say subordinate, the democratic side. People can fully realize themselves as members of society only when they can combine political, social, and economic rights based on reasonable assurances of education, health, housing, and income through a combination of employment and entitlement during their lives. As both the prospects for employment and entitlements diminish, we are collectively diminished as a society, even though a few privileged members may flourish.

Liberalism places individual responsibilities in market place contests, including individual responsibility for obtaining the necessary means to find a place in the "labor market." Democracy asserts entitlement for a meaningful place in contributing to society's greater good to the best of an individual's ability. Liberal democracies "contain" or have this tension (as C. B. Macpherson's brilliant writings have taught us) with Social Democrats pushing more to the "democracy" side and neoconservatives toward the "liberal" side. Other systems, such as feudalism, gave individuals a "place" in society based on their birth rank. Capitalism strove to break such bonds by creating "free wage labor," which meant free from feudal obligation but also free to find one's own place in the work world. In reality, capitalist labor markets are not "free" from collective interventions, even as basic as schools that are supported by the state (and compulsory to a certain age) to allocate labor market credentials.

We need to change, develop, and innovate around the labor market, but in a situation of confidence that jobs with decent conditions will be there in the end. This means collective rather than individual responsibility for labor market adjustments. Workplaces are themselves becoming increasingly uncomfortable as "downsizing" and fear characterizes everyday life. The specter of unemployment is on everyone's mind. What does efficiency mean in these terms, and "productive" for whom?

We must recognize that changes to the labor force and labor market should and will come about, but they can take a variety of forms. There can be either progressive or regressive part-time work situations from the points of view of both workers and employers. The notion of "flexibility," for example, can be taken both ways: as a euphemism for low-paid, available-on-demand, disposable workers or work that adapts to the variety of demands to which people are subject (family responsibilities, education, careers, and interests).

CHAPTER SIX

The Links between Paid and Unpaid Work
Australia and Sweden in the 1980s and 1990s

Mark Western and Janeen Baxter

Since the 1970s, married women's increased involvement in paid employment in most advanced capitalist countries has raised public awareness about the problems of combining paid work with domestic responsibilities. Yet this new awareness has not led to dramatic increases in men's levels of participation in domestic work, nor, as Chapter 7 in this volume demonstrates, have there been major changes in the organization of paid work to allow individuals to accommodate the competing demands of work in the family and work in the labor market. While men's involvement in housework has increased over the last four decades (Bianchi et al. 2000), women are still forced to cope with the demands of work and home by reducing the amount of time they spend on paid work, by working part-time or withdrawing from the labor force, or by reducing the amount of time spent on domestic work. Clearly, the strategies that women adopt to cope with the demands of work in the labor market and work in the family will depend on a variety of institutional and individual factors, such as the level of availability of flexible work hours and child care, personal occupational situation, and life-course stage. Research on the relationship between men's participation in domestic work and paid work on the other hand suggests very weak links between work in the two spheres. Most men tend to be in full-time employment and to do only small and unchanging amounts of unpaid work regardless of institutional arrangements, life-course stage, or socioeconomic characteristics. Pleck (1984) has consequently referred to the boundaries between work and home as "asymmetrically permeable" for men and women. While men are able to keep the boundary between work and home relatively distinct, women experience much more overlap between the spheres of work and family, with family life influencing paid work involvement and paid work impinging on family obligations.

This chapter examines these issues for Australia and Sweden in the 1980s and 1990s. We build closely on previous research by Kalleberg and Rosenfeld (1990), who examined the links between paid work and domestic work among men and women in the United States, Canada, Sweden, and Norway in the early 1980s. At the heart of Kalleberg and Rosenfeld's analysis is the recognition that work in the labor market and work in the family are reciprocally interrelated: Work in one sphere potentially influences work in the other. Empirical research must acknowledge and explicitly take account of such reciprocal interconnections. Like Kalleberg and Rosenfeld (1990), our chapter also recognizes the reciprocal links between family work and labor market work, but unlike Kalleberg and Rosenfeld (1990), we focus on Australia and Sweden. We also incorporate a temporal dimension by considering how the reciprocal relationships between work in the family and work in the labor market have changed in these two countries during the 1980s and 1990s.

THE DOMESTIC DIVISION OF LABOR: PREVIOUS RESEARCH

Previous studies of the domestic division of labor consistently show that women perform the large majority of household work (Baxter 1993; Berk 1985; Coltrane 1996; Pleck 1985; Spitze 1988; Thompson and Walker 1989). Men's participation in domestic labor typically concentrates primarily on outdoor activities that require only intermittent attention, such as taking out the garbage or lawn mowing. This limited involvement contrasts sharply with women's responsibility for daily, more time-consuming tasks, such as cooking and cleaning (Baxter 1993; Berk 1985; Pleck 1985). Moreover, there is little evidence of variations in these patterns across countries (Baxter 1997; Blau and Ferber 1990; Clement and Myles 1994; Haas 1981) or over time, despite married women's increasing involvement in paid work (Coverman and Sheley 1986).[1]

A considerable amount of research has been devoted to explaining the maintenance of these gender divisions in domestic labor patterns (for reviews, see Ferree 1990; Spitze 1988). Most studies identify three main factors that influence both the domestic division of labor (who does what) and the amount of time men and women spend on domestic work. These factors are the relative economic power of husbands and wives, the amount of time that husbands and wives spend in paid employment, and individuals' attitudes to gender roles. Economic power is argued to negatively influence domestic labor because the spouse who contributes most income to the household tends to have most household power in general terms (cf. Chapter 8 in this volume) and is thereby able to avoid menial household tasks. To quote Hobson, "The more dependent, the weaker the voice; the lower the earnings potential, the fewer exit possibilities; the fewer exit possibilities, the weaker the voice" (1990: 238). Since men typically earn more than women, the partner with the most economic power in the household is generally the husband, and hence husbands have a lower involvement in household work. Despite the intuitive appeal of the argument, however, the empirical results are varied, with some studies finding a relationship between women's relative earnings and husbands' participation in domestic labor (Baxter 1993; Ross 1987; Stafford, Backman, and Dibona 1976) and others finding no relationship (Huber and Spitze 1983).[2]

Research on the impact of paid work time on domestic labor highlights one side of the reciprocal relationship between domestic labor and work in the labor market. Very few studies find a significant relationship between men's paid work time and their time on domestic labor. Since there is little variation in both the amount of time men spend in paid work (most work full time) and the amount of domestic labor men do, the absence of a relationship between paid and unpaid work time for men is not surprising. Some studies have suggested that men's share of household labor increases when their wives are in paid work (Coverman 1985; Pleck 1985), but overall there is greater support for the view that wives' time in paid work impacts more significantly on the work that wives do in the home than on men's work in the home (Baxter 1993; Coverman 1985; Geerken and Gove 1983; Haas 1981; Pleck 1985).[3]

The final key predictor of domestic labor patterns is gender role attitudes. Most research finds that couples with egalitarian sex role attitudes have more egalitarian divisions of household labor than couples with inegalitarian or traditional attitudes toward domestic labor (Baxter 1993; Bird, Bird, and Scruggs 1984; Hardesty and Bokemeier 1989; Pleck 1985; Ross 1987). Although some studies have found no relationship (Geerken and

Gove 1983; Coverman 1985) or only a marginal impact of attitudes on domestic labor patterns (Huber and Spitze 1983), these differences depend somewhat on how gender attitudes are measured. Moreover, there is also some evidence that attitudes shape domestic labor patterns only when other factors are statistically controlled (Pleck 1985).

THE DETERMINANTS OF PAID WORK HOURS

Like domestic work, the largest determinant of time in paid work is gender. Men typically work full time in paid employment throughout their lives, while women usually work less, particularly during certain stages of the life course. Unlike domestic work, however, there has been substantial change in recent years in both men's and women's levels of participation in paid work. One of the biggest changes to employment patterns has been the entry of women into paid employment since World War II, particularly among married women and those with young children. The other noteworthy change in gender patterns in paid work has been a gradual convergence in men's and women's workforce participation rates over time. This convergence typically reflects the increase in the female labor force participation rate and, to a lesser extent, the decline in the male one.

In Australia in 1970, the labor force participation rate for females aged 15 to 64 was 36 percent; the corresponding male rate was 84 percent. In 1996, by contrast, the female rate had increased to 53 percent, while the male labor force participation rate had declined to 73 percent (Australian Bureau of Statistics 1997). In 26 years, in other words, the gender gap in labor force participation had more than halved, falling from a 48-percentagepoint difference in favor of men in 1970 to a 20-percentage-point difference in 1996.

Even more striking, however, is the increase in participation rates for women aged 25 to 34, the major childbearing years. In Australia in 1996, just under 68 percent of women aged 25 to 34 were in the labor force. In 1970, the corresponding rate was around 41 percent (De Vaus and Wolcott 1997). Much of the growth in women's employment in Australia over the last 20 years, particularly among married women, has been in part-time work. In Australia in 1993, women composed 75 percent of part-time employees (Organization for Economic Cooperation and Development [hereafter OECD] 1994). In 1995, for couple families with dependent children where both parents were employed, only 42 percent of mothers were employed full time, but nearly all fathers who were employed worked full time (De Vaus and Wolcott 1997: 85). These figures clearly demonstrate that it is women, not men, who adjust paid work hours to fit with the demands of family responsibilities, with mothers almost nine times more likely than fathers to report working part time for family reasons (Australian Bureau of Statistics 1994).

In Sweden, patterns are similar, with a sharp increase in participation rates for Swedish women since the late 1960s and the concentration of women in part-time work[4] and men in full-time work. In Sweden, however, women's labor force participation grew more markedly throughout the 1970s than it did in most other industrialized countries (Sundstrom 1993) and also started from a comparatively high base. Between 1970 and 1992, the Swedish female labor force participation rate increased from 59.3 to 79.9 percent (Sundstrom 1993: 141). This sharp increase was due to a number of factors: the separation of taxes for spouses, the rapid expansion of public child care, the introduction of paid parental leave,[5] and the rise in women's wages relative to men's (Sundstrom 1993: 139). The percentage of men employed part time in Sweden in 1993 (41.4 percent) is very similar to that of Australia in 1993 (43 percent). However, unlike Australia, the percentage of Swedish women workers employed part time has actually declined over the period from 1973 to 1993 (OECD 1994). During the 1980s, full-time work increased among all groups of Swedish women.

HYPOTHESES

Using the arguments we have just described, we can develop some hypotheses to orient the empirical analysis. Our hypotheses draw on and extend those of Kalleberg and Rosenfeld (1990). Like them, we argue that there is a zero-sum relationship between work in the home and in the paid labor market. Time spent in one domain typically implies less time available for work in the other. Consequently, the association between time in paid employment and participation in unpaid work should be negative. Moreover, as previous research implies, and as Kalleberg and Rosenfeld (1990) explicitly argue, domestic work and employment are reciprocally related. The level of participation in each sphere depends in part on the level of participation in the other. These arguments suggest the following general hypothesis:

H1: Reciprocal effects between paid and unpaid work should be negative.

This hypothesis underlies much of the empirical analysis and implies that the reciprocal interconnections between paid and unpaid work operate inversely. Increasing involvement in domestic work leads to diminished involvement in the labor market, while increased involvement in the labor market results in less involvement in domestic work.

In addition, as Kalleberg and Rosenfeld (1990) asserted, gender-specific and cross-nationally-specific factors suggest various ways that negative reciprocal relationships between paid and unpaid work will vary between women and men and between countries. Our subsequent hypotheses qualify the general hypothesis to reflect these considerations. Men in both countries continue to be employed primarily in full-time employment (OECD 1994), and previous studies have found little variation in men's involvement in housework in either country. By contrast, women in Australia and Sweden continue to have primary responsibility for housework and child care and to make up the majority of the part-time workforce. Since women have to accommodate both paid and unpaid work, while pressure exists for men to prioritize paid work, negative reciprocal effects should be larger for women than men. To the extent that negative reciprocal effects exist for men, we anticipate them only for the impact of paid work on domestic labor, as men limit their involvement in housework to accommodate the demands of paid employment (cf. Kalleberg and Rosenfeld 1990).

H2a: The negative effects of paid hours on domestic labor for women should be greater than the negative reciprocal effects for men.

H2b: The negative effects of domestic labor on paid hours for women should be greater than the negative reciprocal effects for men.

H3: Only the effect of paid work on domestic labor should be negative for men.

The first two hypotheses acknowledge that women, rather than men, are primarily responsible for managing the competing demands of family work and labor market work. Hypothesis 3 reflects the fact that there is little evidence of a reorganization of the domestic division of labor despite married women's increasing involvement in paid work.

Kalleberg and Rosenfeld (1990) argued that in countries with more flexible labor markets and more active policies enabling women to combine paid and unpaid work through part-time employment, the negative effect of family work on work in the labor market should be greater than in countries where part-time jobs are less attractive. In contrast, where part-time employment is limited or where it has comparatively high opportunity costs, women accommodate the double burden by decreasing their involvement in housework and child care. Kalleberg and Rosenfeld (1990) used North American and Scandinavian data collected in the early 1980s, when their argument implied stronger negative effects of unpaid work on paid work in Sweden and Norway than in the United States and Canada.

In the 1970s and early 1980s, family policies in Sweden and Norway principally encouraged people to combine paid and unpaid work by working part time in the paid labor market. Part-time employees in Sweden and Norway enjoyed similar benefits, income levels, and job security as full-time workers, marginal tax rates on full-time and part-time work favored part-time workers, and there were substantial opportunities for working reduced hours, with, in some cases, compensation for lost income (Kalleberg and Rosenfeld 1990; Sundstrom 1993). Swedish women drawn into the workforce in the 1970s and early 1980s also had an above-average propensity to work part time rather than full time (Sundstrom 1993).

Since the early 1980s, however, Swedish family policy has encouraged women to combine domestic responsibilities with full-time rather than part-time employment. We therefore build on Kalleberg and Rosenfeld's arguments by recognizing that social policy interventions aimed at encouraging women to combine work in the family with full-time employment will have different effects on their reciprocal relationships than initiatives that make part-time employment more attractive. Policies encouraging part-time work are associated with larger negative reciprocal effects of domestic work on paid work than policies aimed at enabling women to combine full-time paid work with domestic labor. Since the Swedish data that Kalleberg and Rosenfeld analyzed were collected (1980), publicly provided child care in Sweden expanded dramatically, parental leave benefits were extended to 15 months, and marginal tax rates of full-time workers were reduced while those of part-time workers have increased.

In Australia, on the other hand, through the 1980s and 1990s, policy initiatives have more generally been directed toward encouraging part-time work. Although there has been a major expansion of public and private child care places since the mid-1980s, paid maternity leave is generally available only to public sector employees. In 1993, only about 17 percent of the female paid labor force was entitled to paid maternity leave (National Women's Consultative Council 1993), although about 85 percent of the female workforce was entitled to paid or unpaid leave (see also Chapter 5 in this volume). In the absence of widespread paid maternity leave and in the presence of salary loadings compensating part-time and casual workers for the loss of nonwage benefits, such as maternity leave, sick leave, holiday leave, long-service leave, and superannuation, most employed Australian women and almost half of women not in the workforce indicate that they would prefer part-time rather than full-time employment (Glezer 1991).

The differential impact of Swedish and Australian family policies on shaping women's employment patterns is indicated by the fact that both the size of the part-time sector and the proportion of women in part-time employment grew in Australia through the 1970s, 1980s, and 1990s, while the size of the Swedish part-time sector remained comparatively stable through the 1980s and early 1990s (OECD 1994). In addition, as noted previously, the proportion of women employed in part-time work since the early 1980s in Sweden has actually fallen, while the proportion employed full time over the same period has grown (OECD 1993; Sundstrom 1993). The emphasis on part-time employment in Sweden in the late 1970s and early 1980s and full-time work thereafter, as well as the continuing emphasis on part-time employment in Australia as a way for women to reconcile the competing demands of paid and unpaid work, suggests two cross-national hypotheses:

H4: The impact of domestic work on paid work will not differ between Australian women in 1986 and Swedish women in 1980.

H5: In the 1990s, the negative impact of domestic work on paid work will be greater for Australian women than Swedish women.

The first of these hypotheses reflects the fact that the Swedish and Australian labor market regimes in the 1980s encouraged women to combine both paid and unpaid work by shifting to part-time employment. In the 1990s, however, the Swedish welfare state moved to encourage women back into full-time employment, while the Australian one continued to encourage women to take up part-time employment.

Moreover, since Swedish initiatives for combining paid and unpaid work have generally been more developed than Australian ones, the Swedish labor market is more flexible in enabling women to combine work and family. Consequently, Australian women are more likely to accommodate the double burden by decreasing their time spent on domestic labor since this sphere is the one over which they have greater control. This suggests the next hypothesis:

H6: The negative impact of paid work on domestic work will be greater among Australian women than Swedish women.

In addition, despite the fact that Swedish women still perform most of the domestic labor, Swedish social policy has been exceptionally strongly committed to encouraging egalitarian sex roles. Apart from changes to the taxation system, parental leave, and child care policies already referred to, the education system has consistently emphasized gender equality and equal participation of spouses in child care and housework (Haas 1981). Given the strong public endorsement of gender equality, we also expect one cross-national difference in the impact of paid work time on domestic labor for men·

H7: The negative impact of paid work time on domestic labor will be smaller for Swedish men than Australian men.

Finally, we anticipate one common cross-national trend. In both countries, married women's labor force participation has risen considerably over the decade. In part, this reflects a range of factors making it easier for women to combine paid and unpaid work. However, it has also been argued that married women's increasing labor force participation is driven partly by the decline in real male wages that has occurred throughout much of the OECD since the 1970s (Freeman 1994; Freeman and Katz 1994). In the face of falling real male wages, many married women have been forced into the labor market in order to maintain household income levels (Thurow 1996). If this argument is correct, at least some of the women drawn into the labor

market by the declining wages of their spouses are those for whom reconciling work and family responsibilities is particularly difficult. Consequently,
the net effect of their movement into paid work may be to increase the negative reciprocal relationships between paid and unpaid work. This suggests
the following hypotheses about trends in reciprocal relationships in the two
countries:

*H8: The negative impact of paid work on domestic work will be greater in
the 1990s than in the 1980s for women in both countries.*

*H9: The negative impact of unpaid work on paid work will be greater in
the 1990s than in the 1980s for women in both countries.*

DATA AND VARIABLES

Data

To investigate these arguments, we analyze survey data collected as part of
the Comparative Project on Class Structure and Class Consciousness.[6] The
Australian data were collected in 1986 and 1993, while the Swedish data
were collected in 1980 and 1995.[7] In both countries, the first sample is a nationally representative sample of currently employed persons, while the second survey is nationally representative of the adult population, regardless of
employment status. For our analyses, we confine the samples to employed
men and women between the ages of 18 and 65 who are currently married
or living in a de facto relationship. Table 6.1 describes the characteristics of
the surveys we use.

Dependent Variables

We focus on two dependent variables in this chapter: number of hours spent
in paid employment per week and the percentage of household work undertaken by the respondent. In all surveys, the number of hours in employment
is measured by the number of hours per week on the respondent's main job,
including overtime.[8]

   The domestic division of labor is based on questions about five routine
household chores: cooking meals, cleaning up after meals, doing the laundry, doing general housecleaning, and shopping for groceries. Additional
questions on domestic tasks were asked in some surveys, but these items
are the five that are common to all surveys. The questions ask about the rela-

TABLE 6.1
Year of Survey, Method of Data Collection, and Sample Size

Country	Year of Collection	Method of Collection	Sample Size after Selection Restrictions and Deletion of Missing Data
Australia	1986	Face to face and mail	733
Australia	1993	Mail	1,080
Sweden	1980	Telephone and mail	605
Sweden	1995	Mail	713

tive distribution of these household tasks between the respondent and the spouse.[9] In the Swedish survey, the questions ask respondents to indicate what percentage of each they perform. Responses to these questions were summed to create a measure of the household division of labor. A score of 0 percent indicates that the respondent does no domestic labor, a score of 50 percent indicates that domestic labor is shared equally between the respondent and the spouse, and a score of 100 percent indicates that the respondent does all the domestic labor.

The Australian questions were asked in a different way. Respondents were asked to indicate who usually performed each task. The response categories provided were "self always," "self usually," "self and partner equally," "partner usually," and "partner always." We assigned percentage scores to each response. "Self always" was coded as 100 percent, "self usually" as 75 percent, "self and partner equally" as 50 percent, "partner usually" as 25 percent, and "partner always" as 0 percent. Thus, in a household in which men report that they usually do the shopping, their contribution to this task is scored as 75 percent. Similarly, in a household in which women report that they always do the laundry, their contribution to this task is scored as 100 percent. We then combine the responses to the five items into a scale ranging from 0 to 100.[10]

Independent Variables

We include four kinds of independent variables as predictors of the domestic division of labor and time spent in paid work: measures of the respondent's location in the labor market, measures of the respondent's family and household situation, measures of individual or demographic characteristics, and a measure of attitudes to gender roles.

Labor market characteristics are measured by occupation of the respondent, position in the authority hierarchy in the organization, and whether the respondent is self-employed. The last two labor market variables tap dimensions of class relations associated with Wright's (1985) conception of class structure. Occupation is included as a set of dummy variables measuring upper-white-collar, lower-white-collar, upper-blue-collar, and lower-blue-collar jobs. The last category is the reference category. Self-employment is a dummy variable coded 1 for the self-employed and 0 otherwise. Position in the authority hierarchy is a continuous variable based on a question that asks respondents whether they are nonmanagers (1), supervisors (2), lower managers (3), middle managers (4), or top/upper managers (5).

Family and household situation is assessed in terms of levels of economic dependency, whether there is a nonworking spouse, and whether there are children living at home. Economic dependency is measured by a question that asks respondents to indicate how much their spouse contributed to their joint income in the previous year. The variable ranges from 0 to 100 percent. Children living at home is included as a dummy variable coded 1 if children are living at home. We also include a dummy variable for spouse's employment, coded 1 if the spouse is not working.

Personal characteristics include gender, age, and education. Gender is included as a dummy variable coded 1 for men. Age is measured in years. We also include age squared since we expect that the effect of age on paid work hours will be curvilinear. Education is measured by years of schooling.

To measure gender role attitudes, we construct an additive index based on responses to three Likert items:

> a. If both husband and wife work, they should share equally in the housework and child care.
> b. It is better for the family if the husband is the principal breadwinner outside the home and the wife has primary responsibility for the home and children.
> c. Ideally, there should be as many women as men in important positions in government and business.

Scores on the items were summed to construct a scale ranging from 3 through 12. A high score reflects more liberal attitudes to gender roles.[11]

METHOD OF ANALYSIS

We investigate our hypotheses by fitting nonrecursive regression models for the two equations incorporating reciprocal relationships between time spent on paid work and the proportion of housework undertaken by the respondent. These models allow time spent on paid work and the amount of household work to reciprocally influence each other. They also allow us to include other independent variables as statistical controls. The exogenous variables common to the equations for each dependent variable are age and age squared, position in the managerial hierarchy, a dummy variable for having a nonworking spouse, and the gender attitudes scale. The equation predicting the respondent's proportion of housework also includes education, the variable for spouse's economic power, the dummy variable for children at home, and a missing data dummy variable for the economic power item. The equation predicting time in the paid labor market includes the occupation dummy variables and the dummy variable for self-employment. Each equation also includes the other dependent variable as a predictor.

With two countries, two sexes, and two time points, we have eight different groups or subpopulations to analyze. The two equations (one each for domestic labor and time in paid employment) are estimated simultaneously across these eight subpopulations with a covariance structure (i.e., "LISREL type") model estimated using maximum likelihood. To keep the analysis straightforward, we do not allow for measurement error in either the sex role attitudes scale or the scale measuring the respondent's percentage of housework. Since there undoubtedly is measurement error in both these variables, at least some regression coefficients are attenuated toward zero.[12] Before fitting the model, we also screened the data for potentially influential observations. On the basis of this data screening, we omitted 12 observations from the eight subsamples. Following selection restrictions for age, cohabitation status, and current employment and listwise deletion of missing data (excluding the economic power variable), this leaves a sample size of 3,131.

RESULTS

The Domestic Division of Labor

Figure 6.1 presents box plots describing the domestic division of labor for Swedish and Australian women and men in the 1980s and 1990s. The center boxes describe the middle 50 percent of the distribution (the inter-quartile range), and the lines at the end of each box extend to a maximum of 1.5 interquartile ranges. More extreme observations are shown with stars. The star within the box indicates the mean.

Figure 6.1 makes it obvious that responsibility for household tasks is divided sharply by gender but not by country or time. Distributions for the four groups of women are virtually identical, as are those for the four male subsamples. However, there is no evidence of either a Swedish or an Austra-lian pattern of involvement in housework or of patterns characteristic of the 1980s or 1990s. Figure 6.1 confirms that women clearly do more housework than men, with women on average (mean and median) reporting that they do about three-quarters of work in the household. Average figures for men, on the other hand, vary from about 20 percent (Australian men in 1986) to about 28 percent (Australian and Swedish men in the 1990s). These figures are very close to those found in previous studies (e.g., Haas 1981; Kalleberg and Rosenfeld 1990). There is also a very weak trend for Swedish and Aus-tralian men to do more housework in the 1990s than the 1980s, but the fe-male distributions remain virtually unchanged. The other striking finding from figure 6.1 is that the distributions for women and men in both countries are essentially disjoint. Three-quarters of Australian and Swedish women in the 1980s and 1990s do at least 60 percent of the housework, while three-quarters of Swedish and Australian men do less than 35 or 40 percent of it. On these figures, there is no evidence that differences in gender ideology or in social policy in these liberal and social democratic welfare states matter for reshaping the way in which women and men organize household work. The domestic division of labor seems largely intractable to institutional in-tervention aimed at equalizing the degree of involvement of women and men.

Hours Worked

Figure 6.2 describes the distributions of hours employed for women and men in each country in the 1980s and 1990s. As expected, men report more time in employment per week than women do. Australian men, on average, were employed about 45 or 46 hours a week in both the 1980s and the 1990s, while Australian women spent about 36 hours per week in paid employment in 1986 and 30 hours a week in 1993. This fall in average hours among women undoubtedly reflects the growth in part-time employment among

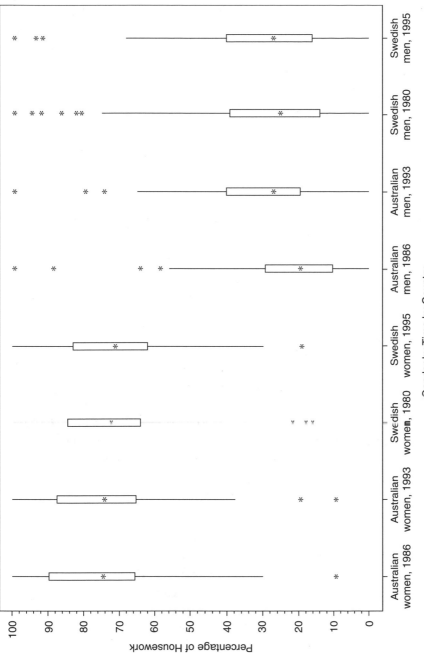

Figure 6.1. Percentage of Housework: Australia and Sweden

women over this period. By comparison, Swedish men were employed on average about 43 hours a week in 1980 and 46 hours a week in 1995, while the mean time in employment for Swedish women increased from about 31 to about 37 hours per week.

The box plots also show that part-time employment was comparatively common among women in both countries in the 1980s but that it declined in Sweden and grew in Australia in the 1990s. In Australia and Sweden in the 1980s, 50 percent of women worked less than 32 hours a week in the labor market, while in 1995, median weekly employment for Swedish women was around 40 hours and for Australian women about 30 hours. At least half of men, on the other hand, were employed for more than 40 hours a week in both countries over the 1980s and 1990s, and the employment distributions are much more highly compressed than they are for women. The distribution of hours worked is particularly compressed among Swedish men in 1980, which is consistent with the uniformity of wages and working conditions of the Swedish labor market under the Social Democrats.

RECIPROCAL RELATIONS BETWEEN HOURS WORKED AND THE DOMESTIC DIVISION OF LABOR

Table 6.2 examines how paid and unpaid work go together by presenting simple correlations between hours employed and involvement in housework for Australian and Swedish men and women in the 1980s and 1990s. As expected, given the zero-sum relationship between work in the family and work in the labor market, all correlations are significantly negative. Increased involvement in one institutional sphere is associated with decreased involvement in the other. With the exception of Australia in 1993, the correlations are also larger for women than men, providing tentative evidence that it is more difficult for women to accommodate the competing demands of paid and unpaid work than it is for men. This pattern of statistical association is identical to that found by Kalleberg and Rosenfeld (1990).

Table 6.3 presents regression estimates of reciprocal effects between time in paid employment and domestic labor. These estimates are derived from a nonrecursive regression model incorporating these variables and the exogenous controls simultaneously fitted to the eight subsamples. In the interest of brevity, we do not present results for the control variables, although we discuss them briefly. The goodness-of-fit statistics at the bottom of table 6.3

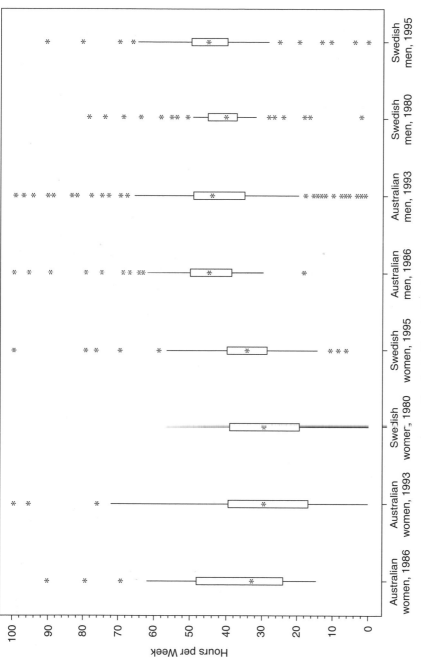

Figure 6.2. Time Spent in Paid Employment: Australia and Sweden

TABLE 6.2

Correlations between Hours Employed and Responsibility
for Housework by Sex, Time, and Country

CORRELATION	AUSTRALIA 1986		SWEDEN 1980		AUSTRALIA 1993		SWEDEN 1995	
	Women	*Men*	*Women*	*Men*	*Women*	*Men*	*Women*	*Men*
Hours employed with percentage household tasks	−0.23	−0.13	−0.44	−0.27	−0.20	−0.22	−0.24	−0.16

$p < 0.001$.

show that these variables and hypothesized relationships between them are plausible ones for the data. Individual goodness-of-fit statistics for each sub-sample (not presented) confirm that the model fits extremely well in each group, although it fits slightly less well among Australian women in 1993 and Swedish men in 1995 than in other subsamples.

Table 6.3 provides fairly strong support for the general hypothesis (H1) that reciprocal effects between both types of work are negative. Eleven of the 16 regression coefficients are negative, and nine of the 10 statistically significant coefficients are negative. The only significant positive coefficient is for the effect of domestic labor on paid work among Swedish men in 1995, and it is only marginally statistically significant at 0.05.

The patterning of significant coefficients also provides some support for subsidiary hypotheses, particularly those pertaining to gender differences. The only significant negative effects for men are those for the impact of paid work on domestic labor. This strongly supports hypothesis 3. The reciprocal estimates between paid and unpaid work for Swedish and Australian men in the 1980s and 1990s show that men who spend longer hours in paid employment do less household work than men who spend less time in the labor market. Men in both countries thus accommodate incompatibilities between work in the family and work in the labor market by doing less work in the family.

Women, on the other hand, reconcile their commitments to paid and unpaid work by spending less time in the labor market. The only statistically significant negative coefficients for women indicate that increased time on

TABLE 6.3
Reciprocal Effects of Paid and Unpaid Work by Time, Sex, and Country

EFFECT	AUSTRALIA 1986		SWEDEN 1980		AUSTRALIA 1993		SWEDEN 1995	
	Women	*Men*	*Women*	*Men*	*Women*	*Men*	*Women*	*Men*
Paid work → domestic labor	−0.15	−0.29*	−0.34	−0.97**	−0.32	−0.48**	1.51	−0.80**
Domestic labor → paid work	−1.16**	0.02	−0.70**	−0.23	−2.13**	−0.25*	−1.29**	0.62*

NOTE: Chi-square = 62.76, df = 48, p = 0.075. Goodness-of-fit index = 0.99. RMSEA = 0.0099, p for test of close fit = 1.00.

*$p < 0.05$, **$p < 0.001$.

domestic labor is associated with diminished time in employment. This pattern holds in both countries and at both time points. The results in table 6.3 thus suggest that work in the family and work in the labor market still comprise two distinct and largely gendered realms. Women participate in the labor market but limit their participation to accommodate the prior demands of work in the family, while men participate in housework but scale down their involvement in response to the time demands of labor market work.

Table 6.4 presents summary results for all the hypotheses based on the regression coefficients in table 6.3. The hypotheses entail assertions about sex, country, or time differences in reciprocal coefficients. These differences were tested statistically, and the results are shown in table 6.4.[13] Where the regression coefficients clearly contradict a particular hypothesis, for example, by implying a positive reciprocal effect between paid and unpaid work rather than a negative one (this is shown in table 6.4) and no statistical tests are presented.

The sex-specific hypotheses H2a and H2b stated that negative reciprocal effects between domestic labor and paid work should be greater for women than men. Table 6.3 estimates show that in each subsample, time on paid work diminishes time available for domestic work more for men than women, thereby contradicting H2a without requiring any statistical tests of differences in coefficients. However, the estimates for the impact of domestic labor on paid work are ordered as expected, with time in paid em-

TABLE 6.4
Results for Hypotheses about Reciprocal Relationships between Time in Paid Employment and Domestic Labor

Hypothesis	Chi-Square	df	p	Decision
H1: Reciprocal effects between paid and unpaid work are negative				Generally supported
H2a: Paid work → domestic labor larger for women than men				Rejected by point estimates
H2b: Domestic labor → paid work larger for women than men	45.70	4	0.0001	Supported
Australia 1986: women − men	8.94	1	0.0028	Supported
Australia 1993: women − men	11.15	1	0.008	Supported
Sweden 1980: women − men	7.02	1	0.0080	Supported
Sweden 1995: women − men	18.58	1	0.0001	Supported
H3: Only paid work → domestic labor negative for men				Supported
H4: Domestic labor → paid employment 1980s: Australian women − Swedish women	1.29	1	0.2566	Supported
H5: Domestic labor → paid employment 1990s: Australian women − Swedish women	1.68	1	0.1951	Rejected
H6: Paid work → domestic labor: Australian women − Swedish women				Rejected by point estimates
H7: Paid work → domestic labor: Australian men − Swedish men				Rejected by point estimates
H8: Paid work → domestic labor: women time 2 − women time 1				Rejected by point estimates
H9: Domestic labor → paid work: women time 2 − women time 1	4.77	1	0.0919	Rejected
Domestic labor → paid work: Australian women 1993 − Australian women 1986	2.11	1	0.1460	Rejected
Domestic labor → paid work: Swedish women 1995 − Swedish women 1980	2.66	1	0.1028	Rejected

ployment declining more as a result of housework for women than men. Table 6.4 reports several statistical tests of this hypothesis (H2b). The first hypothesis test uses four degrees of freedom and examines whether at least one gender difference in the impact of domestic work on labor market work exists in Australia and Sweden in the 1980s and 1990s. This multivariate hypothesis test is highly statistically significant ($p < .0001$), implying that in at least one county in the 1980s or 1990s, the impact of family work on labor market work was greater for women than for men. The next four lines then test this gender difference in Sweden and Australia at each time point. Each of these is also highly statistically significant. We thus have unambiguous evidence that in Australia and Sweden in the 1980s and 1990s, responsibility for domestic labor negatively affected time in the labor market more strongly for women than men.

Hypothesis 3, that reciprocal effects for men will only take the form of diminished participation in housework in response to increased time in the labor market, has already been discussed. It is strongly supported in both countries in the 1980s and 1990s.

The remaining hypotheses pertain to cross-national or over-time differences in reciprocal linkages for women and men. Because social policy in both Sweden and Australia in the 1980s encouraged women to combine work in the home and work in the labor market by shifting to part-time employment, we anticipated no cross-national difference in 1980s in the impact of domestic labor on paid employment among women (H4). This hypothesis is supported. By the 1990s, however, in response to changes in social policy, more Swedish women were combining domestic work with full-time employment, while Australian women continued to accommodate work in the family by working part time in the labor market. This suggested that cross-national differences in the impact of housework on time in employment would be apparent in the 1990s for women (H5). Although table 6.3 shows that the relevant gap between Swedish and Australian women has widened in the 1990s in a manner consistent with the hypothesis, the difference is not statistically significant, as table 6.4 shows. We therefore cannot reliably conclude that women's responsibility for domestic work affects their involvement in paid employment more strongly in Australia in the 1990s than in Sweden.

Hypotheses 6 and 7 asserted larger negative effects of paid work on domestic labor among Australian than Swedish women and among Australian than Swedish men, respectively. Each hypothesis is contradicted by the re-gression coefficients in table 6.3. Among all groups of women except Aus-tralians in 1986, coefficients for the impact of paid work on household work are positive (but not significant). Among men in the 1980s and 1990s, the Australian coefficient indicates a weaker negative effect of paid work on do-mestic labor than the Swedish coefficient does. Neither the more developed social policy initiatives in Sweden nor the stronger ideological support for egalitarian sex roles are associated with cross-national differences of the kind we expected.

Finally, hypotheses 8 and 9 predicted stronger reciprocal effects between paid and unpaid work among Swedish and Australian women in the 1990s than the 1980s, as the female workforce became increasingly heterogeneous. Hypothesis 8 is again contradicted by the point estimates, but the pattern of coefficients in table 6.3 for the impact of domestic labor on paid work is as expected with women in the 1990s who find it more difficult to reconcile work at home and in the labor market than women in the 1980s. The two-degrees-of-freedom test is not significant, and the trend among Austra-lian women is clearly insignificant. However, the over-time difference is only just insignificant among Swedish women (on a one-tailed test), and given the comparatively small size of the Swedish sample, there is little statistical power to detect a difference of this kind. An optimistic interpretation of this result might therefore be that there is weak evidence that domestic responsi-bilities in Sweden influenced women's paid employment more strongly in the 1990s than they did in the 1980s.

RESULTS FOR CONTROL VARIABLES

We have not presented the regression coefficients for the control variables, but in this section we provide a brief summary of the main findings. In terms of the domestic division of labor, there is general support for the impact of feminist attitudes and economic power on the organization of work in the home. As other studies have found, women with more feminist views do less housework than women with traditional gender attitudes, while among men this pattern is reversed. Among both women and men, greater economic power is associated with individuals doing a smaller percentage of house-work than their counterparts with less economic power in the household. These results hold generally true in Australia and Sweden in both time points. In addition, having children in the home results in a greater share of housework for wives compared to their husbands, while for husbands, having children in the home results in a reduced share of housework. Finally, education is a consistent predictor of men's share of housework, with more educated men doing more work in the home. There is virtually no evidence that labor market characteristics, such as occupation, have an impact on the distribution of labor in the home.

In contrast, for paid work hours the key control variables are whether the respondent is self-employed and whether they occupy a managerial position. In particular, the results clearly show that the self-employed and managers work longer hours than employees and nonmanagers, respectively. This result is consistent for both men and women in Australia and Sweden at both points in time. In general, individual and household characteristics do not impact on time spent in paid work.

CONCLUSIONS

Our analyses provide clear evidence that women in Sweden and Australia are still primarily responsible for domestic labor. In aggregate terms, Swedish and Australian women report responsibility for approximately 70 percent of household tasks. There is little evidence of change over time or of variations across countries. This suggests that variations in institutional arrangements at a macro level, for example, the greater availability of child care or access to parental leave under the social democratic welfare state, have little impact on domestic labor arrangements between husbands and wives. Moreover, there is no evidence that men are assuming increasing amounts of domestic work in recent years, despite the postindustrial reorganization of paid work that sees married women's involvement in this sphere increasing dramatically.

In relation to paid work time, we find that Swedish and Australian men spend more time in paid employment than women in these two countries. In both countries and at both time points, men spend about the same amount of time per week in paid employment, about 43 to 46 hours. For women, however, we see a divergence in hours in the 1990s, with Swedish women increasing their average hours from 31 to 37 per week and Australian women decreasing their hours from 36 to 30 per week.

It is clear that the reciprocal links between paid and unpaid work are gendered, or, as Pleck (1984) suggests, "asymmetrically permeable." That is, increases in paid work time lead to a decrease in the proportion of housework done by men, but the same pattern does not hold for women. On the other hand, increases in the proportion of domestic work done by women lead to a decrease in the amount of time spent in paid work, but the same pattern does not hold for men. This indicates that prevailing gender relations encourage men and women to accommodate the competing demands of paid and unpaid work in different ways: Men cope by reducing their involvement in domestic work, while women cope by reducing their involvement in paid work. This pattern is consistent in both Sweden and Australia, suggesting that institutional variations in welfare state regime have little impact on the links between public and private work. The consistency of these findings suggests that work in the family and work in the labor market still constitute two largely gendered realms. Women assume responsibility for household work and adjust their participation in the labor market to accommodate it, while men prioritize activity in the labor market and fit their domestic work around it.

For the most part, we did not find significant cross-national differences in the links between paid and unpaid work of the kind we expected. Moreover, those cross-national differences that did exist were not the same as that found by Kalleberg and Rosenfeld (1990), who found larger negative effects of domestic work on paid work in Scandinavia compared to North America. At both time points, we find a larger negative impact of domestic work on paid work for Australian women than Swedish women. It may be that Sweden and Australia are more similar than Sweden and North America. Alternatively, given the very strong emphasis on part-time work as a way for women to combine work and family responsibilities within the Australian labor market and the very strong preferences of Australian women for part-time employment, it may be that Australia is distinctive in the degree to which women reduce paid work hours to accommodate domestic responsibilities. Overall, our results highlight the mutual interconnections between labor market and family work, but they also reinforce Pleck's (1984) account of asymmetrical permeability. In these two postindustrial societies, the boundaries between work and home are clearly permeable for women and men, but in different directions that reflect traditional gendered responsibilities for work in the home and work in the labor market.

CHAPTER SEVEN

Employment Flexibility in the United States

Changing and Maintaining Gender, Class, and Ethnic Work Relationships

Rachel A. Rosenfeld

"Flexibility" is a current catchphrase, discussed in at least two contexts. On the one hand, some of this discussion is from the perspective of what helps workers. As the number of two-earner and single-parent families has risen, some employers have developed flexible employment arrangements as part of an agenda to help parents (especially mothers) balance work at home and on the job. Flextime, job sharing, home work, reduced hours, family leaves, and greater employee discretion have been debated and used as ways to make the workplace more "family friendly."

On the other hand, researchers and policymakers have discussed flexibility as part of changing job structures and work contracts that accompany rapid technological innovation, quickly shifting product demand, and heightened global competition. Flexibility, supposedly, enables employers to deploy labor in the most efficient, cost-effective way. Some strategies involve giving core, long-term, especially skilled workers greater autonomy and scope on their jobs, while others focus on reducing the proportion of workers in regular, stable, full-time jobs. Part-time, contract, and on-call work, for example, are among the ways to get this flexibility, as is using workers in the informal economy.[1]

This chapter brings together these two discussions, provides empirical evidence on the extent of family-friendly and employer-benefiting flexibility, and tries to trace out the implications of recent trends for different groups of women and men in the United States, with some reference to other advanced industrialized countries. As the previous brief descriptions illustrate, there are many dimensions to "flexibility"—schedules, hours, leaves, job security, location, and autonomy. The sorts of arrangements described in the family-friendly and employers'-flexibility literature overlap a great deal. Which workers benefit and which lose from different kinds of policies and employment relationships?

Wright (Chapter 3 in this volume) discusses various conceptualizations of the relationship between gender and class that guide the analysis of social and economic inequality. At the least, gender (cross-cutting race and ethnicity) may sort people into different job settings and work arrangements. Women's domestic responsibilities may be the impetus to implement family-friendly policies to recruit, retain, and enhance productivity of women workers. These responsibilities may also be the rationalization for women's overrepresentation in part-time and short-term jobs because of women's presumed lower commitment to paid work (see Baxter and Western, Chapter 6 in this volume). Further, gender may affect class when jobs with lower rewards and stability are organized around a female labor force. Gender may also *interact* with class (as well as race/ethnicity): Those with more authority and skills are better able to benefit from flexibility of various kinds, but those with less power in the labor market generally, such as women, may be affected by flexibility differently from those with more power in ways that vary across class.

U.S. DISTINCTIVENESS

The United States is in many ways distinctive among advanced industrialized democracies, an extreme of the "liberal" welfare state regime (Esping-Andersen 1990). At the same time, other nations see the United States as possibly foreshadowing their futures.

The United States has a relatively high rate of female labor force participation, including among mothers of young children, although not as high as in the Scandinavian countries (or under state socialism) (Blau, Ferber, and Winkler 1998; Clement, Chapter 5 in this volume). In 1999, 61 and 58 percent of black and white women 20 and older were employed or unemployed, compared with 75 percent of white men (U.S. Department of Labor 1999). Statistics from a few years earlier show that 53 percent of all mothers of children under one year old were in the labor force, as were 61 percent of mothers with children two years old. Both parents were employed in 64 percent of married couples with children under 18. Sixty-two percent of mothers of children under 18 in families maintained by women held jobs (U.S. Department of Labor 1998a).[2] However, the United States has one of the lowest levels of federal support for people who are both workers and family caregivers, with considerable variation among employers (Gornick, Meyers, and Ross 1998). For example, in the late 1980s, employed women in Sweden had a year of parental leave, with almost full pay and with job protection, as well as the right to part-time work until children were eight years of age. For German women, maternity leave was 14 weeks at full pay, with more paid child care leave available afterward. Yet in the United States, it was not until 1993 that there was a federally mandated Family and Medical Leave Act (FMLA). Even this is extremely limited: It requires establishments with 50 or more employees to grant up to 12 weeks of unpaid leave, with a job-return guarantee, to full-time, long-tenure men and women who have or adopt a child or face a family emergency, with some critical employees exempted[3] (see also Clement, Chapter 5 in this volume). Such lack of support for families fits the description of liberal welfare states as having an individualistic ideology.

Compared with other countries at the same level of development, U.S. workers have lower collective power and perhaps less job protection. In 1994, for example, only 13 percent of the workforce belonged to unions, and only 5 percent of workers were part of an employee participation scheme (Kerbo 2000: 243; Rosenberg 1989). Absence of centralized bargaining among labor, the state, and employers is a characteristic of the liberal regime. During the early 1980s, some European policymakers began to argue that the "flexibility" of the U.S. labor market—in contrast with Europe's more regulated job contracts—was behind its stronger economic recovery and job growth (Rosenberg 1989; see also Peck 1996: chap. 8). Others see moves in Europe in the last part of the twentieth century toward American "neoliberalism," with its supposedly increasing government promotion of competition, expanding contingent workforce, and shrinking welfare safety net (Brodsky 1994; Gottfried 1997; Peck 1996).

The United States, then, is less family friendly in general, and its employers have more "flexibility" than many other advanced industrialized countries. Because of this, the uneven impact of the different kinds of workplace flexibility may be more evident than in other countries.

FLEXIBILITY FOR WHOM?

Some commentators view flexible jobs as simply responses to workers' wishes or lack of interest in standard jobs, so that they have largely positive consequences for employees' lives. On the other hand, some argue that they benefit mainly employers, depending on and reinforcing existing labor market inequalities, deepening class, ethnic, and gender divisions. Wickham (1997: 136) organizes his analysis of part-time work across Europe by cross-classifying employer and employee perspectives, as adapted in table 7.1. Those who examine employment arrangements to see how they help workers take care of home and job responsibilities often emphasize the first view, of flexibility's positive consequences for workers. Social scientists who start from flexibility as employers' response to changing economic structure, technological possibilities, and global competition tend to focus on the negative and unequal impact on jobholders. Researchers who study a particular type of work arrangements, such as part-time work (Negrey 1993; Tilly 1996; Wickham 1997) or telecommuting (Tomaskovic-Devey and Risman 1993), are most likely to point out its pros and cons for employees.

Ideally, I would generate trends for the distribution across categories of flexible arrangements, along with any changes in the distribution of types of workers within categories. This, of course, is not possible given the current state of our concepts and data. My assessment will be much more impressionistic, despite inclusion of various statistics.

FAMILY-FRIENDLY JOBS IN THE UNITED STATES

Increasing proportions of American workers, both men and women, need work arrangements that help them balance their job and family lives. In addition, more families need to care for not just children but also elderly parents and other relatives as the population of the "old old" grows. Glass and Estes (1997) cite studies suggesting that large numbers of employees would like their employers to be more family responsive: "The National Study of the Changing Workforce, utilizing a nationally representative sample of 2958 employees [of whom 87 percent claimed to have daily family responsibilities], revealed that close to one fourth of employees without flexible schedules or the ability to work at home would change jobs to gain these benefits. Additionally, 47 percent of those lacking leave time to tend to family illness

TABLE 7.1
Employer and Employee Perspectives on Workplace Flexibility

	Employer −	*Employer +*
Employees +	Tight labor market, flexibility as incentive, for retention	Both sides want, voluntary flexibility
Employees −	Both sides uninterested, "traditional" employees, regular jobs, flexibility only if imposed from outside firm	Unemployment, involuntary flexibility

SOURCE: Adapted from Wickham (1997: 136).

said they would sacrifice pay or benefits to gain leave for sick family members" (Glass and Estes 1997: 293). Jacobs and Gerson (1998) show that about 50 percent of respondents to this survey would like to work fewer than their actual hours, with an average difference of five hours between actual and ideal work weeks. The patterns of gaps between actual and ideal hours are similar for women and men. Using the 1977 Quality of Employment Survey, Glass and Camarigg (1992) found that having a more flexible and less pressured job, as well as working fewer hours, reduced employees' sense of work-family role conflict. A number of researchers optimistically argue that in response to workers' needs (as well as, perhaps, tight labor markets for skilled and productive workers), increasing numbers of firms will institute policies that make work life easier to balance with family roles (Haas and Hwang 1995: 30).

Types and Trends of Family-Friendly Flexibility

Flexibility here means employees' being able to choose to work other than a regular work schedule in the usual place in order to better balance family and job responsibilities. While my focus is on integrating family and paid work, workers might want to take advantage of this flexibility for other reasons as well (e.g., to do community work, continue education, or engage in hobbies; see Negrey 1993). Glass and Estes (1997) group "family responsive" benefits and working conditions into three categories: (1) reduction in hours, including the ability to work part time, phase back slowly into full-time employment, avoid overtime, and take leave at the time of childbearing; (2) flexibility in timing or location of paid employment, leaving hours employed the same, such as home work, flextime, a compressed workweek, and regular shifts; and (3) workplace social support. This last category encompasses child care assistance as well as supervisor and co-worker support and cooperation in dealing with family responsibilities and worker discretion in taking time off for family emergencies or illness.

Overview of Benefits across Establishments   Table 7.2 gives an overview of the extent of some of these family-friendly benefits across U.S. workplaces. In 1994–1996, after the FMLA was implemented, many medium and large private establishments offered paid leaves (sick leave and personal leave) and disability insurance that could be used for childbirth. In addition, a fairly large proportion gave unpaid parental leaves. Almost all state and local governments offered paid and unpaid leaves. Smaller private workplaces (with fewer than 100 employees) were less likely to have these benefits. The FMLA clearly increased the availability of unpaid family leave in all three employer categories. In 1992, for example, only 18 percent of small private establishments (which could be part of large firms) and 59 percent of state and local governments had unpaid maternity leave (U.S. Bureau of the Census 1995b, 1996).

Much lower proportions, especially in the smaller locations, gave paid parental leave or social support, such as child care or elder care. At the same time, other sorts of flexibility for family care actually decrease with size: In 1987, 62 percent of workplaces with fewer than 50 employees had some alternative work schedule or possibility of home work, compared with 58 percent of midsize establishments and 59 percent of places with more than 249 employees (U.S. Bureau of the Census 1990b: 414). Within each private establishment category, white-collar employees were generally more likely to be covered by a given benefit type than blue-collar and service workers (U.S. Bureau of the Census 1998: 440).[4]

Part-Time Work   Part-time work is the type of "flexible" employment on which there is the most data, for the United States and across other countries. In 1999, about 17 percent of the U.S. labor force worked fewer than 35 hours a week. Over 80 percent of this part-time work was "voluntary," where "voluntary" is defined as giving a noneconomic reason for reduced hours. Further, over two-thirds of these voluntary part-timers were women.

TABLE 7.2
U.S. Establishments and Family-Friendly Benefits,
1988 and 1994–1996

Benefit	State and Local Government (1994)	Medium and Large Private Establishments (1995, unless noted otherwise)	Small Private Establishments (< 100 Employees) (1996, unless noted otherwise)	Medium and Large Private Establishments (1988)[a]
Paid sick leave	94	58	50	69
Paid personal leave	38	22	14	24
Paid family leave	4	2	2	—
Paid maternity leave	—	—	—	2
Paid paternity leave	—	—	—	1
Unpaid family leave	93	84	47 (1994)	—
Unpaid maternity leave[b]	—	—	—	33
Unpaid paternity leave[b]	—	—	—	16
Short-term disability insurance	—	53	29	—
Child care	9	8	3	4
Elder care	13	31 (1993)	33 (1994)	—
Medical insurance	87	77	64	90
No. of employees (1,000s)	13,443[c]	45,347[d]	54,987[d]	

SOURCES: U.S. Bureau of the Census (1990b: table 679; 1996: tables 505, 508, 671, and 838; 1998: tables 866, 703, and 704).

NOTE: Data expressed as percentages. Coverage for full-time employees for benefits for which employer pays part or all of the expenses, except for unpaid leaves.

[a] First-year parental leaves were listed.

[b] Before the 1993 Family and Medical Leave Act went into effect.

[c] Full-time state and local government employees, 1993.

[d] All nongovernment employees, except railroad workers, 1995.

Despite variation in the proportion of reduced-hours workers across countries (see Clement, Chapter 5 in this volume), this pattern of mainly voluntary and overwhelmingly female part-time employment holds across advanced industrialized societies (Delsen 1998; Hakim 1997).[5]

Nearly two-thirds of U.S. women aged 25 to 54 usually working part time (for any reason) were raising children (Nardone 1995), but those mothers who were married were the ones most likely to have a regular part-time job (Kalleberg et al. 1997: table 33A). Again, it is true in other countries, as well, that wives and mothers are the most likely to be part time, although the exact family patterns associated with part-time work vary (Delsen 1998; Hakim 1997). Surveys of U.S. firms in the late 1970s and late 1980s showed almost 90 percent said that housewives were among the people they employed at reduced hours (Tilly 1996: 15–17). While regular part-time employment can make it easier to combine child rearing and other caregiving with paid work, in the United States it usually does not provide benefits such as paid vacations, paid leaves, health insurance, or retirement contributions, as I show later in this chapter. This may be part of the reason why the proportion of part-timers among employed women is lower in the United States than in many comparable countries (e.g., 25 percent in the United States compared with 66 percent in the Netherlands, 44 percent in the United Kingdom, 44 percent in Sweden, and 33 percent in Germany in 1994 [Blossfeld and Hakim 1997; see also O'Reilly and Fagan 1998; Rosenfeld and Birkelund 1995]). Further, this employment may be voluntary only in the sense that other options are limited. In addition, irregular part-time hours can be worse than full-time employment for combining paid work with other activities (Negrey 1993).

Scheduling   Among those normally working daytime hours full time, more had flexible schedules in 1991, giving them the ability to decide when to start and end the day, than six years earlier (15.1 percent compared with 12.3 percent in 1985). Men, whites, the unmarried, and professionals and managers were the groups with the largest proportions in this category (U.S. Bureau of the Census 1995b: 410). Other research has found that flextime is more common than other scheduling options, such as compressed work weeks, job sharing, and home work (Glass and Estes 1997: 299). Put another way, married women, racial/ethnic minorities, and blue-collar workers are not especially likely to be able to set their time on the job when they work during the regular workweek.

Home Workers The proportion of home-based workers has increased in the last two decades, in part because of advances in information technology but also because of the growth in women workers and two-earner families. In 1997, 18 percent of nonfarm workers did at least some of the work on their main job at home (U.S. Department of Labor 1998b), but most of these people had work sites away from home where they did most of their work. Only about 3 percent of all wage and salary workers, for example, were paid for the time they put in at home (up from 1.9 percent in 1991). Almost 90 percent of these workers were in white-collar occupations. The self-employed are overrepresented among those doing at least some work at home, and 20 percent of these had a home-based business.

Women were slightly more likely than men to do at least some of their job at home (18.3 percent compared with 17.3 percent in May 1997) (U.S. Department of Labor 1998b). So were white, non-Hispanics; published data, however, do not cross classify gender and race/ethnicity. The rate of any home work (24 percent) and of paid home work (6 percent) was especially high for married women with young children. Women, especially, were more likely to be part time when they were home workers as compared with office, factory, or store workers, although they were also more likely to work more than 40 hours per week. Among both the self-employed and wage and salary workers, those working at home made less per hour and per year than those working away from home. This gap was larger, however, for the women (Edwards and Field-Hendrey 1996).

The proportion of the population who are home workers is small, and there is a great deal of diversity within this group (see also Tomaskovic-Devey and Risman 1993). Women, in particular, report that it is hard to make others (family and nonfamily) recognize the boundaries between the job and home when the location does not differ. At least some employment or self-employment at home, however, seems to have the potential to provide flexibility for balancing women's paid work and home responsibilities, especially when they have a husband's income.

Who Benefits and How?

The situation with respect to family-friendly policies would seem to go into the upper-left-hand category of table 7.1: The employees are interested in and gain from flexibility, and the employer needs to provide this to retain and motivate employees because of tight markets for skilled and productive, especially female labor, high costs of replacing workers, and competition and comparison with other companies (Glass and Estes 1997; Glass and Fujimoto 1995; Negrey 1993; Tilly 1996). If workers organize in their demands for such benefits, then this could also influence employers. Government regulation is another factor. In some cases, an employer's need for a flexible workforce might match employees' desire for reduced hours or home work, the category in the upper-right-hand side of table 7.1. This possibility will be discussed later.

Overall, there seems to be a slight increase in potentially family-friendly employee benefits. While national figures do not provide direct evidence as to how well the need for them is being met, they suggest that sizable parts of the labor force do not have access to policies, benefits, and schedules that would make it easier to have a balanced life. Those who are the most vulnerable—working in smaller firms, belonging to ethnic/racial minorities, and holding lower-level occupations—are usually the least likely to be covered. It is not clear that women as a group have less support, given their overrepresentation in white-collar work (Rosenfeld 1996). Glass and Camarigg (1992), however, found that employed men without dependent children had the highest score on a measure of job ease and flexibility and employed mothers with the dependent children the lowest. Women as a group had especially large disadvantages with respect to job ease and flexibility in professional/technical and blue-collar occupations.

Glass and Fujimoto (1995) give more direct evidence on the match between workers' family responsibilities and employers' offerings of flexibility and support. They report on the policies of employers of Indiana and Michigan women who had been employed at least 20 hours a week during the first trimester of pregnancy. Substantial proportions of these women had access to reduced hours and leaves. Fewer had employers who allowed flexible schedules and location. A fair number had social support and discretion—other than direct child care support—at work (see table 7.3).

The evidence for arguments about why employers offer family-friendly benefits is mixed (Glass and Estes 1997). There is more research showing that these policies do reduce turnover and increase worker productivity (Glass and Estes 1997). Raabe (1996) points to Germany for support of this. In Germany, negotiated labor legislation resulted in a regular work year that in 1995 was only 80 percent as long as that in the United States (Kerbo 2000: 510). Yet productivity does not seem to have declined but rather increased.[6]

TABLE 7.3
Family-Friendly Policies and Support among
Employers of Pregnant Women

Benefit, Policy, or Characteristic	Mean
Parental/maternity leave (1 = yes, 0 = no)	.62
Disability leave	.55
Vacation leave	.83
Sick leave	.67
Leave of absence	.51
Child care money, voucher	.08
Child care information/referral	.11
Possibility of part-time/phased-in work	.60
Possibility of work at home	.23
Possibility of using sick leave to care for others	.66
Job flexibility (0–5)	2.40
Supervisor support (1–4, very positive to very negative)	1.92

SOURCE: Glass and Fujimoto (1995: appendix).

NOTE: Data are from 324 women employed at least 20 hours per week in the first trimester of pregnancy. Respondents were recruited from prenatal hospital records in St. Joseph County, Indiana, and were surveyed in 1991–1992.

A number of analysts, though, have emphasized that what matters most in actual access to flexibility is whether middle managers and supervisors, who must implement such policies, believe that they are worth it (Haas and Hwang 1995; Negrey 1993; Raabe 1996). Even when an employee has a right to take advantage of a nonstandard work arrangement, she may be able to negotiate the actual schedule only if she is in a strong position in her workplace, as Negrey's (1993) interviews with Michigan job sharers show. In memos on the Expanded Family and Medical Leave Act for federal employees, President Clinton and other officials recognized the importance of supervisors in implementing family-friendly policies: "Supervisors are urged to accommodate employees' needs as mission requirements permit, even when it is not possible for employees to anticipate or schedule [up to 24 hours of unpaid] leave in advance for the purposes stated . . . above [children's school activities, children's medical visits, and elderly relative care]. In addition, supervisors are asked to schedule paid time off . . . for these family activities when such leave is available to employees" (Facteau 1997).

Further, despite formal rights to family-friendly benefits, those who take them may have their career commitment questioned and lose advancement opportunities. Such attitudes may draw on and reinforce ideology about the gendered division of labor, with women assumed to put less emphasis on paid work and men more committed to the breadwinner role. Women may find it easier than men to get parental leave because of this (Hochschild 1997; Negrey 1993) but may find themselves on the "Mommy track" as a result. This is true even in family-friendly Sweden (Haas and Hwang 1995; Rosenfeld et al. 1998).

In a controversial book, Arlie Hochschild (1997) reports on a three-year study of a large, multinational, profitable company ("Amerco" [Corning, Inc.]) that introduced family-friendly policies in 1985 with strong support from upper management. She found, though, that despite their feelings of pressure from trying to combine family and job, parents were not taking advantage of the possibility to reduce hours or do some work from home. Fathers did not take parental leaves. On the other hand, a quarter of all workers and a third of employed parents used flextime—but put in increasingly long hours, beyond the usual 40-hour week. She argues that this is because work is an escape from the mess and stress at home—for women and men.

Hochschild describes a company that has a strong, managed company culture that engages the loyalty of its employees. The family-friendly policies were part of this culture. At the same time, it is a company where new employees get a handbook listing "unwritten" norms, which include an emphasis on long hours as an indicator of commitment, an attitude reflected as well in Hochschild's interviews with a senior manager. She documents the difficulties employees had in getting paternal leave and time off for family care. Moreover, in the last chapter, she reports that in 1995 the company basically dismantled its "Work-Life Balance" program, began downsizing, and started emphasizing the need to meet global competition in its company culture as part of a "reengineering process" called "Amerco Competes."[7]

Family-Friendly Flexibility: Conclusions

Family-friendly policies can be seen as benefiting many workers, at perhaps a cost to the employer. In the United States, there is enormous variation across workplaces in degree of family-friendly conditions. Large corporations—perhaps because of greater bureaucratization, more extensive coverage by government and union regulations, and higher motivation and ability to retain skilled workers—are generally more likely than small ones to have formal family policies. Smaller firms may be more willing to make informal arrangements to accommodate their workers' families, though they may not be required to give as many benefits. Generally, workers in higher-level positions have more flexibility than those in lower-level ones. Even in firms where employees have formal coverage, however, they may have to fight for their entitlements or suffer career consequences for taking advantage of them. This could happen whether the employee fits or fails to fit gender stereotypes by doing so because taking time for family is seen as indicating lack of commitment to the job. Women and minority men in higher ranks may be especially cautious about violating stereotypic male bread-winner behavior. Workers in the lower-blue-collar and service jobs may not be able to afford to take unpaid leaves or reduced hours, even when these are available. Those most in need of help in managing their lives at home and on the job—especially lower-skilled ethnic/racial minority and poor women—are probably the least likely to have any access to family-friendly flexibility, let alone be able to negotiate for it. Finally, in the United States, where there is only weak federal support for parents, employees may lose their unmandated benefits when the competitive pressures increase, regardless of increasing need and rhetoric.

FLEXIBLE FIRMS AND CONTINGENT WORKERS

In contrast with the family-friendly-workplace literature, that on employment flexibility and contingent work begins with the needs of the employer. Much of the discussion starts from a relatively short-term perspective, seeing employers' demand for a more flexible workforce as a result of increasing global competition, rapidly changing product demand, and continuing technological innovation over the last several decades. One image is that of the "flexible firm" (Atkinson 1987). To remain profitable and to control their labor forces, large firms in the United States will maintain a core of highly skilled workers filling essential positions. Increasingly, however, firms will have relationships with a periphery of workers, often off-site or even in other countries, with weaker ties to the organization. Within the firm these are part-time, on-call, or temporary workers, and outside the firm they are subcontractors and suppliers of labor, parts, and services. Not only employees but also owners of companies dependent on the large firms will be in an insecure situation (see the discussion in Peck 1996: 56–65). As Tam (1997) emphasizes, however, increases in workers with nonstandard work arrangements are also part of long-term increases in the service sector (which includes service, trade, communications, and transportation industries). This sector is larger in the United States than in all other OECD (Organization for Economic Cooperation and Development) countries except Canada (almost 73 percent of total employment in 1992 [OECD 1994: 6]).

Definitions

The literature on employment flexibility uses a wide range of definitions for workers and work arrangements studied. This is one reason it is difficult to make comparisons across countries and time. The other problem, discussed in the following, is a lack of data that fit these definitions.

Classification of Flexibility   Rosenberg (1989: 9) describes four types of flexibility that employers can seek: wage, numerical (employment), functional, and working time:

> *Wage* flexibility refers to the extent to which wage levels or differentials can be adjusted to prevailing labor market conditions. With increasing wage flexibility at the microlevel, wages become more enterprise and worker specific. Questions of intrafirm, interfirm, and interindustry parity are relegated to the background. At the macrolevel, wages more quickly adjust to trends in unemployment, productivity, and terms of trade. Various institutional factors, or rigidities, such as rules and regulations concerning minimum wages or automatic wage-indexing provisions, are eliminated or decline in importance.
>
> *Increasing numerical flexibility* means expanding the freedom of employers to vary the amount of hours of work and the size of the work force in response to cyclical or structural variations in demand and/or technological change. As restrictions, or rigidities, on dismissals, fixed-term contracts, temporary work, and part-time work are weakened, numerical flexibility is enhanced.
>
> *Functional flexibility* concerns the ability of a firm to effectively utilize its relatively permanent full-time work force by varying the work performed to the changing requirements of production. This type of flexibility is related to the mobility of workers within the enterprise. Such mobility is enhanced if workers are able to perform a variety of tasks and contractually established work rules are not out of step with the changing requirements of production.

Working time flexibility concerns the adaptability of work schedules and the organization of working time. It covers a variety of elements including laws and collective agreements fixing hours of work and duration of paid vacation and paid leave, overtime, work outside of authorized hours such as weekend work, and entry into or retirement from the labor force. This form of flexibility is often related to reduction and restructuring of working time.

One might add to this last category *work location flexibility*. This would include telecommuting and other home work to enhance productivity, increase control, and lower overhead, as well as the spatial division of labor-intensive from capital-intensive work (Peck 1996). In general, the periphery workers contribute to numerical flexibility and sometimes to wage, working time, and location flexibility. Most recent research focuses on numerical flexibility.

This description implies that the degree of flexibility attainable depends on government regulation, employers' preferences, and collective bargaining agreements. As discussed, U.S. postindustrial, globally competitive society is likely to be more "flexible" than most other advanced industrialized societies because of its relative lack of "rigidities" (Esping-Andersen 1993b; Myles and Turegun 1994; Peck 1996). Much of this type of flexibility would fit into the lower-right-hand category of table 7.1, where employees are disadvantaged. In some cases, there may be a match between employer and employee scheduling needs, given existing options (in the upper-right-hand category). One could argue that "functional" flexibility works to the benefit of the employee as well, broadening and perhaps upgrading skills. Smith and Gottfried (1998) use the terms "restrictive" and "enabling" flexibility to emphasize the effects of employer-instigated flexibility for different types of workers. "Functional" flexibility is not a major theme in this chapter, although I will return to it briefly later.

Periphery Work Arrangements   Pfeffer and Baron (1988) talk about employers "externalizing," so that workers have only a weak connection to the organization in terms of physical location, administrative control, or duration of employment. Various categorizations of periphery work arrangements highlight different combinations of these dimensions. The defining characteristic of *contingent jobs* is expected employment duration. In 1989, the U.S. Bureau of Labor Statistics defined contingent work as "any job in which an individual does not have an explicit or implicit contract for long-term employment" (Polivka 1996a: 4). Administrative control is important for the definition of *alternative work arrangements*. Those in alternative work arrangements are "individuals whose employment is arranged through an employment intermediary such as a temporary help firm, or individuals whose place, time, and quantity of work are potentially unpredictable," including independent contractors, on-call workers, workers paid by temporary help agencies, and workers whose services are provided by contract firms (Polivka 1996a: 7). *Nonstandard work arrangements* are other than regular full-time, on-site jobs, including a wide range of situations, such as self-employment, "regular" part-time, home-based, shift, and informal sector jobs. These often have weaker administrative, physical, and/or tenure connections to the employing or contracting firm. These three broad categories—contingent, alternative, and nonstandard—overlap (Kalleberg, Reskin, and Hudson 2000; Polivka 1996a; Rosenfeld, Kalleberg, and Hudson 1997).

Trends and Characteristics

Until recently, it was difficult to even approach a precise count of periphery workers in the United States and elsewhere. Often, part-time employment is used as a proxy. The February 1995, 1997, and 1999 U.S. Current Population Survey (CPS) supplements on contingent and alternative work arrangements were designed to provide a more detailed description of nonstandard work.[8] Houseman (1999) used the 1997 data to develop a description of flexible wage-and-salary workers (table 7.4). She showed that aside from regular part-timers (14.3 percent), just under 6 percent of employees were (numerically) "flexible," with another 11.8 percent self-employed. There was relatively little change from 1995 (Ken Hudson, personal communication; Kalleberg et al. 1997).

By these counts, the proportion of U.S. workers in "new" flexible arrangements at any particular time is relatively small. "Flexible" workers may be undercounted because of the effort at precision. For example, here temporary workers are defined as employees of temporary help agencies. Those in more informal situations may not respond to the survey in such a way that they would be considered to be in an "alternative" work arrangement (Smith and Gottfried 1998). Further, the number of workers who will ever have such jobs is much larger. In addition, a large number of employers use these arrangements (table 7.5). Establishments in service industries are

TABLE 7.4

U.S. Incidence of Low Wages, Health Insurance, and Pension Rights
by Type of Employment Arrangement, 1997

Worker Type	% of Work Force	% with Hourly Wage $4.25– $5.15	% Eligible to Participate in Employer Pension Plan	% with Health Insurance from Any Source	% Eligible to Receive Health Insurance from Employer
Agency temporaries	1.0	9.3	9.5	48.1	23.8
On-call or day laborers	1.6	13.9	25.9	68.5	29.6
Contract company workers	.6	5.5	46.3	83.1	68.8
Independent contractors	6.7	4.3	NA	74.6	NA
Other direct-hire temporaries	2.6	17.9	23.3	74.1	35.9
Other self-employed	5.1	6.0	NA	82.3	NA
Regular employees	82.4 (17.4% of which are part time)	7.0	60.7	85.9	75.0

SOURCE: Houseman (1999: tables 1, 5, and 6).

NOTE: NA = not available. Data calculated from the February 1997 Current Population Survey. Workers reporting earnings of less than $4.25 per hour, the federal minimum wage just before February 1997, were excluded from the tabulations on hourly earnings.

more likely than those in manufacturing to use short-term hires, part-time workers, and on-call workers but less likely to use temporary or contract workers (Houseman 1997).

There is evidence that the number of "flexible" jobs has been growing. The rate of U.S. part-time employment has gone up since the late 1950s (see the cross-national comparisons in Blossfeld and Hakim 1997; O'Reilly and Fagan 1998). Starting in the 1970s, increases in part-time employment have

TABLE 7.5
Percentage of Establishments
Using Flexible Staffing
Arrangements

Type of Staffing Arrangement	%
Agency temporaries	46.0
Short-term hires	38.2
Part-time workers	71.6
On-call workers	27.3
Contract workers	43.5

SOURCE: Houseman (1997: table 3).

NOTE: Data are from a 1996 survey of private-sector establishments with at least five employees in the continental United States (*N* = 550).

been the result largely of involuntary part-time work (Tilly 1996). Growth in services and trade is behind some of the rise in part-time work over this period, but there were also changes within industries, as is true in other countries as well (Smith, Fagan, and Rubery 1998; Tilly 1996). From 1990 to 1995, temporary employment agencies, along with full-time employment firms, were the top generators of new jobs (Aley 1995). In 1993, Manpower, Inc., was the largest U.S. private-sector employer (Smith and Gottfried 1998). Temporary work is growing in other advanced industrialized countries as well (see Clement, Chapter 5 in this volume). Manpower, for example, is a multinational company with 1,900 offices in 36 countries (Smith and Gottfried 1998).

Clement (Chapter 5 in this volume) combines part-time, temporary, and self-employment into a "nonregular" category. Nonregular forms of employment have increased in each country he studied, although the relative contribution of the components vary. Work time (scheduling) flexibility seems to have gone up as well. In the United States, fewer workers who were usually full time had a regular daytime schedule in 1991 as compared with 1985 (81.8 versus 84.1 percent) (U.S. Bureau of the Census 1995b: 410). There were similar increases in other OECD countries for this period, especially in manufacturing (OECD 1998: table 5.6). Women, whites, married people, and managers and professionals were most likely to have a fixed day shift. In Europe, Saturday work has increased in services (OECD 1998).

Who Benefits, Who Loses, and How?

In the United States, those other than regular full-time employees often have less job security, fewer promotion opportunities, and lower pay and benefits than other workers, as table 7.4 illustrates (see also Kalleberg et al. 1997; Kalleberg et al. 2000). Those outside the "regular" workforce may not be eligible for unemployment insurance when their jobs end. The American expectation tends to be that a person in a job without health insurance will be covered by the policy of someone else in the family. In the absence of a national health system, however, a substantial minority of workers even in dual-earner families lack any health insurance, especially when they hold other than regular full-time jobs (Kalleberg et al. 1997). The declines in medical insurance coverage and paid leaves seen in table 7.2 may reflect an increasing number of "nonregular" workers. Elsewhere, workers in nonregular jobs usually also have lower benefits and other compensation. However, labor regulation coverage, hours and earnings cutoffs for receiving social welfare benefits, and rules about benefit proportionality vary considerably across countries (O'Reilly and Fagan 1998; Smith and Gottfried 1998).

Not surprisingly, women, members of ethnic/racial minorities, the young, and the less educated are more likely than other workers to be in short-term and nonstandard jobs (Cohany 1996; Kalleberg et al. 1997; Polivka 1996c). At the same time, there is considerable variation within these categories. Independent contractors are disproportionately male and white. They are older and more likely to be college educated than those in traditional work arrangements (Cohany 1996). Further, contract employees and independent contractors earn more than conventional workers, although they are also more likely to be at the very low and very high ends of the earnings distribution (Hipple and Stewart 1996; Kalleberg et al. 1997).

Those working informally or off the books would not be guaranteed benefits. These are disproportionately minority racial/ethnic group women who lack skills to find other types of work, especially if they are immigrants whose English is poor (Peck 1996), or who can get only low-skilled jobs. Private domestic workers are an example. They generally have no explicit work contract, get benefits only if the employer decides to offer them (even though, depending on total hours worked, they may have the legal right to social security contributions from the employer), and must negotiate any time off (Dill 1988; Glenn 1992). Many welfare mothers (who are disproportionately black) find that it is impossible to live on the transfer payments they receive and fill in the gaps with unreported jobs (Schein 1995).[9]

Employers use nonstandard and contingent work arrangements to cut costs, cover fluctuations in demand, and increase control. In a number of European establishment surveys, management said that they used part-time workers to meet their, rather than the workers', needs (OECD 1998: 160). In the establishment survey on which Houseman (1997, 1999) reports, employers were much more likely to say that they used flexible workers because of staff level needs than because of costs. Consistent with this, Polivka (1996c) finds some relationship between an industry's variation in employment levels and use of contingent workers. However, costs of wages and benefits are usually lower or at least no higher for temporary, short-term, part-time, and on-call workers.

Employer-initiated flexibility may have a different character from that responding to employee needs. When introducing part-time work, for example, European managers preferred short hours (under 20 hours a week), variable schedules, and manual and low-skilled workers. When part-time work was initiated for the benefit of workers, it tended to involve longer and fixed hours (OECD 1998: 160). Part-time work in Sweden, in part supported by the ideology of allowing people to combine parenthood and employment, has longer hours, more job security, and at least proportional pay and benefits, in contrast with the United Kingdom and the United States (Smith and Gottfried 1998). Where expansion of part-time jobs has been in part to create jobs, especially for men, as in the Netherlands, benefits and compensation may be more like those of full-time, regular jobs (Delsen 1998).

In the United States, employers seem to segment their workforce into those with regular, full-time employment who receive benefits and those who are "flexible" and receive few if any benefits. Likewise, Tilly (1996) finds for the United States that where more jobs are part of secondary labor markets (with low security, low pay, few benefits, and little advancement opportunity) to begin with, employers tend to use more part-time employees. He emphasizes that it is not simply the nature of the technology and the labor process that constrains employers to use secondary part-time workers but that employers actively choose how to structure jobs. While Polivka

(1996c) shows that there is little relationship between industrywide union-ization and use of contingent workers, in general contingent workers are less likely than noncontingent workers to be covered by a union contract. Pfeffer and Baron (1988) argue that the use of "externalized" work arrangements may be a way to avoid unionization: Fewer workers within the organization are "at risk" of being unionized, dispersion of the workforce makes it more difficult to organize, and the existence of alternative sources of labor provides a threat for those currently employed.

Why do workers take contingent and alternative work arrangement jobs? Reasons vary across type of nonstandard work, gender, and family status. In the 1995 CPS, a large majority of those who were self-employed or independent contractors said that their job arrangement reflected their own preferences. Much temporary or on-call work was for economic reasons (such as not being able to find a full-time job). Women overall were more likely than men to say that they needed the work schedule flexibility, had child care problems, or had other family obligations. At the same time, among women in two-earner families with children, a majority of those in temporary work were doing it for involuntary, economic reasons. Among employees with nonstandard work arrangements, controlling for workers' characteristics, most had a preference for standard employment. Controlling for type of job, men had a stronger preference for regular jobs than women, as did minority group members. Married women with children and those under 25 and over 54 were less likely to want a regular job (Kalleberg et al. 1997; see also Polivka 1996b). Even among married women with children, however, 41 percent in single-earner families and 16 percent in dual-earner families wanted a full-time rather than part-time job. This was even more true for black and Hispanic women (Kalleberg et al. 1997). Likewise, in Europe, significant proportions of women employed part time would like longer hours, including full-time jobs (Smith et al. 1998; see also Jacobs and Gerson 1998).

As Peck (1996) emphasizes, there is a dynamic relationship between the location of workers with lower power in the labor market and "flexible" jobs. Employer flexibility not only creates periphery workers but also depends on them and their real and stereotypic characteristics (Smith and Gottfried 1998; Tilly 1996). A case study of microelectronic manufacturing in the Silicon Valley of California illustrates how labor markets are structured around ethnic and gender stereotypes, which are often accepted by the workers themselves. A very large proportion of production workers there, especially assembly workers, are Latin American and Asian immigrant women. They and their employers see them as secondary and temporary workers. They therefore get lower-level, lower-pay, and less-secure jobs, with poorer working conditions than their male compatriots. Many of the women, however, even when they are married, are the major wage earners, although they do not necessarily feel that is a good situation. Further, they may stay in these "temporary" low-wage jobs for many years, unable to save up for school, a family business, or full-time homemaking (Hossfeld 1990). The jobs may be involuntarily temporary if the need for these workers disappears with automation or increased outsourcing.

At the same time, employers and managers ignored gender differences in family roles leading to special needs. "When the first quality circle was introduced in one production unit at this plant, the workers, all of whom were women, were told to suggest ways to improve the quality of work. The most frequently mentioned concern . . . was lack of decent child-care facilities. The company replied that child care was not a quality of work-related issue but a 'special women's concern' that was none of the company's business" (Hossfeld 1990: 168).[10]

Labor market regulations may build in expectations that contingent and alternative jobs have a certain kind of labor force. Smith and Gottfried (1998) point out that Japanese law confines temporary contracts to female-typed administrative and clerical occupations. In this country, nearly all temporary workers are women. In Germany, in contrast, male industrial workers are more likely than women to be employed by companies such as Manpower, Inc., perhaps because legally such workers must be hired on a full-time basis.

When there is a shortage of "flexible" labor, employers may restructure jobs (e.g., from part time to full time), but they may also simply move— to the suburbs where there are mothers willing to work part time (Tilly 1996); back into the home in urban areas where immigrant, especially undocumented, women have restricted job options (Peck 1996); or overseas (Ward 1990).

In the terms of the "flexible firm," the blue-collar jobs that women and minority men are most likely to hold—unskilled manual work—may be exactly those that become contingent (Smith and Gottfried 1998). Routine clerical work can be done by temporary workers. The large proportion of women in these occupations may make it easier to justify using short-term employees. Those at higher levels—men and women—are also affected. Women have been entering lower-level and middle management in increasing numbers (Jacobs 1992; McGuire and Reskin 1993). When restructuring eliminates jobs at these ranks, women and minority men, as newer entrants, suffer disproportionately. Professionals and technicians may be increasingly used on a contingent basis. As the statistics on independent contractors suggest, even for those who prefer regular employment, this can provide satisfying and remunerative employment, perhaps moving to the category of mutually beneficial, flexibility. The independent contractors, however, were disproportionately male and white. It is not clear whether women professionals will be more or less likely to become part of the periphery or what kind of alter-native work arrangement they would have when there. To the extent that women have the managerial and other skills that firms want to retain, they may be able to negotiate for job flexibility, as in the first cell in table 7.1 (see the discussion in Smith and Gottfried 1998; see also Negrey 1993; Tilly 1996).

The same sorts of technologies and demands that make it possible to create periphery jobs in white-collar as well as blue-collar occupations can make it possible to outsource offshore or eliminate the need for a particular job entirely. At least some clerical work has been upgraded with computerization as other jobs are eliminated; increasing amounts of both clerical tasks and computer programming and engineering work are leaving the country. Even higher-level majority men's jobs are potentially insecure. Further, while some argue that functional flexibility empowers workers, in some cases it is an excuse to expect more from fewer permanent employees, who sometimes must work with undertrained temporary workers. Rather than empowerment, functional flexibility can lead to heightened stress, especially in the context of downsizing (Deborah Kohls, personal communication).

Employment Flexibility: Conclusions

While it is somewhat difficult to get a handle on trends in employer-initiated flexibility, available statistics show it increasing in the United States and elsewhere. In general, these jobs provide lower pay and benefits to workers, although some nonstandard work arrangements, such as independent contractor, may lead to higher-than-average pay. Even here, there is greater job insecurity than in a regular job. While some workers prefer these arrangements, many do not. Many workers cannot afford part-time, temporary, or irregularly scheduled jobs but have little choice about the kind of work they have. Periphery work arrangements may have different consequences for different types of workers as well as being structured around those seen as less committed to or having less power in labor markets, such as white middle-class women, immigrants, and racial/ethnic minorities. Even within gender or race, however, the impact of periphery work arrangements varies by class and position in the occupational hierarchy.

FLEXIBILITY FOR WHOM, AGAIN

In this chapter, I have brought together two literatures: that on family-friendly workplaces and that on employer-instituted flexibility. The conclusion for the United States is that there is both an insufficient degree of job flexibility for people trying to balance their work and family lives and too much employment flexibility to allow some groups of workers an acceptable standard of living. Even when there appears to be a balance between worker and employer needs, the lack of federal regulation guaranteeing family-friendly and other benefits can leave the employee vulnerable to changes in employers' policies in the face of pressures to be more competitive. Further, the access to and impact of flexibility is uneven across gender, class, and race/ethnicity.

In the United States, at least some people have to choose between a regular full-time job and no job or between a full-time job and no or low benefits. Tilly (1996: 164) estimates that in 1985 about 10 percent of those employed full time would have liked to work fewer hours, even for less money. Women, especially in white-collar occupations, were more likely than men to be involuntarily full time. Further, more dual-earner couples means more families with long workweeks (Jacobs and Gerson 1998). For at least some of these women—and men—inflexible jobs make it more difficult to take care of families. There has been some progress in the United States in provision of at least unpaid parental leave. Those in larger firms and working for the government have more family benefits, while those in smaller firms and with more labor market power may be able to negotiate some flexibility to help balance job and other activities. Despite the expansion of single-parent and dual-earner families and of the elderly population, the United States is still far from being a family-friendly country. Reforms being pushed by Democrats are likely to be undone by Republicans.

Employers are also looking for flexibility. Currently, relatively few workers are in contingent jobs and alternative work arrangements, although a fairly large proportion of employers use them. While the impact of restructuring depends on a person's race, ethnicity, citizenship status, gender, education, and occupation, it seems that a large part of "flexibility" in the labor market as a whole is structured by race/ethnicity and gender in the United States and in the global division of labor. The search for flexibility is likely to increase race/ethnicity, gender, and class divisions. At least some in the upper-middle and middle class who cannot afford to take "flexible" jobs attain flexibility in their lives by buying services from lower-class, especially racial/ethnic minority men and women, whether in the formal or the informal labor market. If increasing numbers of parents take family leaves, then this would provide additional impetus for the creation of short-contract work (e.g., as has occurred in Sweden).

Some argue that there can be a match between the flexibility desired by employers and employees—that these needs can converge in the upper-left-hand category of table 7.1. In some cases, this is true. In the United States, most part-time employment, for example, is voluntary. A third of contingent and on-call workers, over a quarter of temporary help agency employees, and over 80 percent of independent contractors prefer these arrangements (Negrey 1993; Polivka 1996b; Tilly 1996). Glass and Estes (1997: 308) conclude that "this win-win scenario assumes that the timing of workers' family needs will coincide with employers' needs to trim costs; moreover it assumes that employers can cut costs and still meet caregivers' needs for adequate income." Further, those in the prime of their work life may pay a penalty for deviating from a "regular" career. In addition, as Negrey (1993) emphasizes, even those who would like flexibility find that unpredictable, irregular, low-paid work makes it harder rather than easier to participate in home and community activities. The issue is one of who really gets to choose hours and schedules.

Many of the industries predicted to grow the fastest in the early years of the twenty-first century are in the service sector and especially likely to demand part-time and other alternative arrangements (OECD 1998; U.S. Bureau of the Census 1995b: 417). The jobs projected to grow the fastest include many high-tech and high-skilled jobs, such as systems analysts and physical therapists. For some of these jobs, long hours may be a problem (Jacobs and Gerson 1998). However, the largest number of jobs may come from lower-level service-providing jobs, such as retail sales, janitorial, and food counter work, that are not easily computerized or sent abroad but are easily included in a periphery/secondary labor market based on less advantaged workers (Edmondson 1996).

Cross-national research demonstrates that the nature of flexible work is not predetermined by demographic and economic needs. Government regulations, tax and social welfare policies, union strength and coverage, and national priorities and values all affect why, how, and for whom flexibility is created. These factors help determine the consequences for different gender, class, citizenship, and other groups in a society. Creating flexibility that benefits—or at least does not harm—families and workers without increasing inequalities depends on learning more about these larger lessons.

CHAPTER EIGHT

Gender and Access to Money
What Do Trends in Earnings and Household Poverty Tell Us?

Paula England

INTRODUCTION

What is the relationship between gender and class? Has this changed in recent decades? Our answer to this depends in good part on what we mean by class and whether we think of individuals or households as having a class location. In this chapter, I examine the extent to which a person's sex, through various gendered processes, affects personal earnings and affects whether the individual lives in a household that is in poverty. Either of these speaks to the relationship between gender and class to the extent that we think that access to money and its fruits is part of what we mean by "class" or results from class position. The first indicator, individual earnings, is relevant if we think that class should be measured at the individual level. The second indicator, poverty, is a household income measure (one that is also dichotomous and size adjusted). It can be argued to be the best measure available to tap an individual's access to a certain minimum level of goods and services. For each of these indicators of class (or results of class position), this chapter will examine whether class is gendered and whether the "gendering of class" has increased or decreased over time. If the two indicators do not trend in the same direction, what does this mean? My argument will not be that one indicator is the "true" indicator while the other is inferior but rather that they tell us different things about the outcomes of the overall systems of production (including reproduction) and distribution. For those who prefer not to think of either personal earnings or household poverty as having anything to do with "class," my project in this chapter is better described as examining trends in whether personal earnings and household poverty show gender

131

inequality and discussing what this means about women's relative access to those things in life that one can buy with money. My observations were formulated largely from study of the United States; however, I also include some comparative discussion of patterns in other affluent nations.

If access to money is our focus, what is the argument for using an individual versus a household measure? The argument for using a household measure is that households (at least families) generally pool and share income, so that an individual's access to the goods and services money can buy on the market is better indexed at the household level.[1] This view is supported, for example, by the observation that the wives of rich men seem to consume a lot even if they do not hold a job. The formal assumption is that all members of a household share the same standard of living. To assume this may be too extreme. Perhaps there is sharing but not perfect sharing. In particular, what if who brings the money into a household affects the relative power of the spouses, including but not limited to power in decisions regarding what to spend money on? If this is true, household income is a misleading indicator that understates male advantage. In data on poor nations, there is evidence that relative earnings affect the amount of food and medical care girls and women get relative to boys and men and how much of family income is devoted to children (more of both when women's relative share is higher). Thus, for these nations, access to even the most necessary goods and services is affected by power within the family and by the fact that all members of a household do not have a common standard of living. I am not aware of evidence for industrialized nations showing effects of relative earnings on access to basic material necessities. However, there is evidence of effects of relative earnings on decision-making power on a number of issues, including how money and time are spent (including who does how much household work and who has more leisure). Such issues presumably affect individuals' utilities and thus are relevant to "standard of living" in a broad sense. This argues for the relevance of women's earnings relative to men's as an indicator of access to those utilities that flow from money.

The discussion I will pursue fits into two of the five categories suggested by Erik Wright (Chapter 2 in this volume) as fruitful modes of conceptualizing relations between gender and class. One of his categories is examining gender as a sorting mechanism into class locations. If we consider groups of jobs to be class locations, then the discussion of the sex segregation of jobs and its role in the sex gap in pay is an instance of this category. Here we are interested in sex discrimination in access to jobs or to the qualifications that lead to them, socialization that affects job aspirations, or aspects of household division of labor by sex that affect women's ability to hold certain jobs. To the extent that pay is itself seen as an indicator of "class," the discussion of sex differences in pay that are not generated by segregation of men and women into different jobs but by pay differences within or between jobs that are linked to credentials, productivity, or direct pay discrimination, is also an instance of this category. However, a difference between Wright's perspective and mine is in what dimensions of job positions are seen as relevant. Wright sees class as positional, and, while his conceptualization of class has changed over the years, in one way or another it is generally linked to the extent to which positions involve ownership of property, authority, autonomy, or expertise. While authority is a very gendered dimension of jobs (with many more men than women in jobs with authority over others), the most important dimensions of gender segregation do not relate to property, autonomy, or amount of expertise. A critical gendered dimension involves whether jobs involve performing a face-to-face service (with women heavily represented in such jobs) or clerical work. Thus, one needs to broaden Wright's conceptualization of the dimensions of jobs relevant to class or see amount earned itself as a dimension of class in order to see much of this analysis as speaking to class. Some readers may prefer a tighter concept of class, together with recognizing that many of the relevant gendered dimensions of inequality are not captured by class.

The second of Wright's categories exemplified in this chapter is what he calls "gender as mediated linkage to class location." Women are linked to the occupation and earnings-based class locations of their husbands to the extent that status and earnings are shared by all family members. Men's consumption is also affected by the class location, broadly defined, of their wives, insofar as class affects earnings. I will emphasize that women's poverty is affected not only by their own earnings but also by whether they have access to a share of men's earnings through marriage or cohabitation. Here again, however, to see this discussion as relevant to class, one needs a broader (looser) conception of class than characterizes Wright's work.

I begin by reviewing trends in the sex gap in personal (not household) earnings and some of the things that underlie it. The direction of change is toward a convergence between men's and women's employment, occupations, and earnings. We would expect this equalizing trend to disproportionately increase the income of households containing women and thus, if there were no countervailing trends, to decrease the sex gap in poverty rates. I then examine whether women are more likely than men to live in households in poverty in the post–World War II period in the United States. The answer is clearly yes. However, the trend in the ratio of women's to men's poverty rates is nonmonotonic. Poverty was feminizing between 1950 and 1980, a trend captured in the phrase "the feminization of poverty." However, the feminization of poverty has ceased and even reversed in some groups since 1980, particularly nonelderly whites, although women are still more likely to be in poverty than men. How is it possible for women to have lost ground to men in freedom from (household) poverty during some of the time that their personal earnings relative to men's were going up? It is possible because of trends in household structure that led fewer women to live in households with men and thus that led fewer women (and children) to have a secure claim on a share of men's earnings. These trends include later marriage, increased nonmarital childbearing, and increased divorce. It is an empirical question whether the gain in women's own earnings or the loss in access to a share of men's earnings will have a larger effect on women's poverty rates relative to men's; apparently, the latter loss dominated in the first part of the postwar period, whereas the gain from women's increasing relative earnings has dominated more recently.

In a final portion of the chapter, I consider a macro-level model of the causal linkages between some of the variables related to women's relative statuses. I argue that women's increased employment and earnings should raise women's power within marriages, making marriage more satisfactory for women. However, employment and their own earnings also make it more feasible for women to leave unhappy marriages or avoid getting married. While women's roles have changed dramatically, there is much more resistance to changing men's roles in the family to include more traditionally female responsibilities of child care, household work, and emotional work (see Western and Baxter, Chapter 6 in this volume). It is this asymmetry of gender role change that makes women living apart from men—rather than enduring in egalitarian marriages—the predominant response to women's increased earning power relative to men.

THE ENDURING BUT DECLINING SEX GAP
IN PERSONAL EARNINGS

If we measure income at an individual rather than a household level and look only at earned income, women's progress relative to men is unmistakable. Personal earnings are obtained through employment. Thus, trends in employment are relevant to women's access to earnings. In the United States, the proportion of women over 16 years of age in the labor force[2] has increased steadily in the postwar period, increasing from 33 percent in 1950 to 59 percent in 1995 (Blau, Ferber, and Winkler 1998: 80). If we look only at women 15 to 64 in age, half were in the labor force in 1972, up to 69 percent by 1992 (Blau et al. 1998: 336). Thus, more women than ever before have their own earnings, so fewer are entirely reliant on men or the state, the other two major options, for money. If we look at women's trends relative to those of men's, our sense of a declining gender gap is increased because men's labor force participation has decreased: Between 1960 and 1990, the proportion of women who were not employed even for one week in the previous year dropped from 57 to 38 percent, but the corresponding figures for men increased—from 14 to 21 percent (Spain and Bianchi 1996: 84).

Most affluent nations have seen large increases in women's employment in the last few decades and have higher female employment rates than poorer southern nations, although they have seen increases as well (Blau et al. 1998; Clement, Chapter 5 in this volume). The nations with the highest rates of female employment are the Nordic countries (Sweden, Norway, and Denmark). The United States is below most of the Nordic nations but substantially above Austria, Germany, France, Italy, Ireland, Switzerland, and the Netherlands in its female employment rates (Blau et al. 1998).

One might wonder whether figures showing average hours worked per year would show a different story—if, as more women become employed, there would be a higher proportion of those employed working part time. If this were true, simple increases in the percentage of women employed would give an exaggerated impression of the increase in women's involvement in employment. In the United States, this is not true; the proportion of employed women who work part time has been relatively stable since 1970, at between 20 and 25 percent (Kalleberg 1995). Of all women with any employment experience, the proportion of those aged 25 to 54 who were employed both full time and all year increased from 46 percent in 1968 to 57 percent in 1986 (Taeuber 1991: table B1-22).[3] Indeed, the United States is exceptional in how few employed women work part time; most of the nations that have higher female employment rates than the United States also have a higher proportion of employed women working part time (Gornick 1999: fig. 1; Rosenfeld and Birkelund 1995).

One major factor affecting women's earnings relative to men's is less continuous experience (England 1992: 28–35; Wellington 1994).[4] Men and women are converging in experience levels in the United States (England 1992: chap. 1; Wellington 1993). Since most affluent nations have had rising female employment rates, we would expect this to be leading to more continuous experience in successive cohorts.

Another important factor in the sex gap in pay is segregation of jobs by sex (England 1992; Petersen and Morgan 1995). Segregation has been declining in the United States. Studies exploring this generally use the index of dissimilarity, which, roughly speaking, tells us what percentage of men or women would have to change occupations to achieve integration, defined as a state where the percentage female (male) in each occupation is the same as the percentage women (men) constitute of all workers. Segregation changed little between 1950 and 1970 but has declined substantially since. The index declined from 68 to 53 between 1970 and 1990 (Gross 1986: table 2; Spain and Bianchi 1996: 94).[5] These figures are computed on detailed census categories that divide occupations into several hundred categories. A problem in comparing nations in their segregation is that to find comparable occupational categories, they have to be very broad, which masks segregation (e.g., combining doctors, nurses, pilots, and accountants in "professional"). Studies using very broad categories have found the United States to be lower than many nations in degree of segregation. Indeed, Sweden, which has one of the lowest sex gaps in pay, has relatively high segregation that has not been declining (Blau et al. 1998: 34–35).

Trends in the United States in the sex gap in annual earnings for full-time year-round workers are shown in table 8.1. Here white women made little progress relative to white men between 1955 and 1980, but since 1980 the women's median as a percentage of men's went from 59 to 71 percent. Black women have made more continuous progress relative to black men, from 55 percent of black men's median in 1955 to 85 percent in 1995.[6]

However, it is important to note that women's relative progress in av-

TABLE 8.1
Women's Median Annual Earnings as a Percentage
of Men's by Race, 1955–1995

Year	White Women/ White Men	Black Women/ Black Men[a]
1955	65.3	55.1
1960	60.6	62.2
1965	57.9	62.5
1970	58.6	70.3
1975	58.5	74.8
1980	59.3	78.7
1985	64.1	81.2
1990	69.4	85.4
1995	71.0	85.0

SOURCES: Figart et al. (1989: 25–33); U.S. Bureau of the Census (1990a); unpublished tabulations from the March 1996 Current Population Survey.

NOTE: Data are for full-time, year-round workers.

[a]Data for 1955 through 1970 are for all nonwhites; data for blacks are unavailable for these years.

erage earnings has been as much because of declines in men's real earnings than because of increases in their own. Between 1979 and 1995, if we pool racial groups together, the median annual earnings of men employed full time year-round fell in real terms, from $30,629 to $27,011 in constant 1990 dollars. The comparable figures for women are from $18,274 to $19,294 (although their highest point was $19,972 in 1992). Thus, if we take this entire period from 1979 to 1995, 72 percent of the increase in the ratio of women's to men's median earnings came from declines in men's pay rather than increases in women's. If men's wages had stayed at their 1979 real level but women's had moved as they did, the ratio of women's to men's median would have moved from about 60 to 63 percent rather than from 60 to 71 percent (Institute for Women's Policy Research 1997).

Overall, the convergence in men and women's earnings is explained by declines in men's average earnings caused by restructuring of the economy that has brought men's wages down more than women's, women's increas-

ingly continuous employment experience (Wellington 1993), and the deseg-
regation of occupations, the latter probably encouraged both by declining
hiring discrimination and by changes in women's occupational aspirations.

How does the United States compare to other nations in the sex gap in
pay? In the 1990s, it was similar to West Germany, in the middle of the pack
of affluent nations, with Sweden, Australia, Norway, Finland, Denmark, and
France having higher ratios of women's to men's earnings and the United
Kingdom, Canada, and Switzerland having slightly lower ratios, while Japan
had a much lower ratio (Waldfogel 1998: 140). A look at trends in the sex
gap in pay shows no uniformity in what decades had most convergence
across affluent nations, although most have seen some convergence since the
late 1960s (Waldfogel 1998: 139). While cross-national differences in continuity of experience and segregation probably affect differences in the pay
gap, research has not clearly established this. However, one factor that has
been shown to affect the sex gap in pay is the overall level of pay inequality
in the labor market; other things being equal, this increases the sex gap in
pay (Blau and Kahn 1996, 1997). This factor makes the convergence in men
and women's pay in the 1980s in the United States all the more surprising
since the United States has more overall inequality in its wage structures than
most industrial nations, and its inequality grew more rapidly than other nations' since 1980 (Blau and Kahn 1997).

To note the decrease in the sex gap in pay in the United States is not to
say that gender has disappeared as a factor influencing an individual's work
experiences or earnings. Women are still more likely to spend time out of the
labor force for child rearing than men, occupations are still quite segregated,
and women still earn less than men. The point is that all these inequalities
have decreased. Other aspects of gender inequality in paid work may not
have decreased—for example, the sort of discrimination at issue in "comparable worth" in which the sex composition of jobs affects the pay offered,
the extent to which nurturant work pays less than other work requiring no
more training, or the extent to which organizational rules invented with
male workers in mind have an adverse impact on women (Acker 1990; England 1992). Nonetheless, on the "bottom line" indicator of earnings, wom-
en's progress relative to men is unmistakable. More women have earnings
than previously, and, among men and women who have earnings, women's
relative earnings have increased.

Thus, if we were to use individual earnings as an index of class, we would conclude that class is becoming degendered. Both purchasing power between households of single individuals and power differentials between spouses are affected by personal earnings. This is an argument for using individual earnings. On the other hand, to the extent that people who live together generally share income, especially when they are part of the same family, household income, adjusted for household size, is a more appropriate indicator of access to goods and services. Because of this, I turn to a comparison of the overall incomes of the households in which women and men live.

THE SEX GAP IN HOUSEHOLD POVERTY

How is an individual's sex related to household income? To examine this, let us use a measure of household income that is dichotomized at the official U.S. government's "poverty line." The poverty line was originally devised by estimating what a minimally adequate food budget would cost, adjusting this by family size[7] and multiplying by 3 (since data for the 1950s showed poor families spending about a third of their income on food). The poverty lines (for families of various sizes) are adjusted each year by the consumer price index. Thus, it is an absolute, not a relative, measure of poverty. "Poverty," thus measured, applies to households consisting of either families (defined as people related by blood, marriage, or adoption who share a household) or unrelated individuals living alone.[8] It tells us whether the income of the household, before taxes, from all sources (earnings of any household member from employment or self-employment and nonearned income, such as dividends, government transfer payments, or alimony or child support payments) was above or below the poverty line for that year.

Table 8.2 draws on recent work on the United States by Sara McLanahan and her colleagues (McLanahan and Kelly 1999; McLanahan, Sorensen, and Watson 1989). It shows that a higher percentage of U.S. women than men lived in households in poverty in every year shown from 1950 to 1996. This is true for both blacks and whites and in every age-group, with the exception of whites between the ages of 18 and 24 in 1950 and 1960. Thus, household poverty is gendered.

What drives the higher poverty rate of women than men? To understand this, it is important to remember that this table takes individuals as the units of analysis and reports on the percentages of individual women and men in

TABLE 8.2

Ratio of Female to Male Poverty Rates for
U.S. Whites and Blacks by Age, 1950–1996

	1950 Census	1960 Census	1970 Census	1970 CPS	1980 CPS	1996 CPS
Whites						
Total	1.10	1.23	1.46	1.53	1.56	1.52
Young	0.83	0.99	1.00	1.33	1.48	1.47
Middle aged	1.16	1.24	1.51	1.50	4.43	1.33
Elderly	1.13	1.24	1.45	1.49	1.64	2.33
Blacks						
Total	1.17	1.19	1.37	1.47	1.69	1.71
Young	1.05	1.11	1.11	1.49	1.78	1.65
Middle aged	1.15	1.25	1.56	1.59	1.72	1.68
Elderly	1.05	1.05	1.14	1.16	1.44	2.09

SOURCES: Census figures from McLanahan, Sorensen, and Watson (1989); CPS figures from McLanahan and Kelly (1999).

NOTE: The age classifications differ by source. The census figures use 18–24 for young, 25–64 for middle aged, and 65 + for elderly. The Current Population Survey (CPS) figures use 18–30 for young, 31–64 for middle aged, and 65 + for elderly. The only notable effect is the difference for the young age-groups, where the ratio of women's to men's poverty is lower if only 18–24-year-olds are included.

poverty in various years, but the assessment of whether the individual is in poverty is based not on the individual's income alone but on whether the total income of the person's household puts it in poverty.[9] In husband-wife families (whether or not they include children), either both the husband and the wife are in poverty or both are not. This means that if all adults were married, there could not be any sex gap in poverty, given how the term is defined in U.S. government statistics. The other major types of households are those containing a man living alone or with children and those containing a woman living alone or with children. Let us refer to these three types of households as couple, male headed, and female headed, respectively. Given that there is no sex gap in poverty by definition within couple households, the sex gap in poverty arises from female-headed households being poorer than male-headed households, and any given disparity between the poverty rates of these two groups of noncouple households will affect the overall sex gap in poverty more the higher the proportion of all adults that live in noncouple households.

Why are female-headed households more impoverished than male-headed households? This is true for two main reasons. First, women earn less than men, so the earnings of those heading female-headed households are generally less than the earnings of the men heading male-headed households. Thus, since, except for the elderly, earnings are the major source of income for most households, the sex gap in pay contributes to the sex gap in poverty.

A second factor contributing to the sex gap in poverty is sex differences in who lives with children. Since poverty lines are adjusted for household size, the presence of children in a household raises the income necessary for the household to escape poverty, and thus, other things being equal, adults who live with children are more likely to be poor. Single women are much more likely to live with children than single men since women usually have custody of the children in cases of divorce or nonmarital births. Unless this tendency of a higher proportion of adult women than men to live with children is entirely offset by transfers of income from either the nonresident fathers, the government, or someone else, it will increase women's poverty relative to men's. Clearly, such transfers do not fully offset women's responsibility for children. In 1991 in the United States, only 57 percent of divorced mothers received any child support from the children's fathers, and among those receiving support, the average amount received during the year was only $3,623. Separated and never-married mothers were even less likely to receive child support (34 and 20 percent, respectively) and, among those receiving support, received even less per year ($2,735 and $1,534, respectively; figures are from Scoon-Rogers and Lester 1995, as cited in Spain and Bianchi 1996).

Is the gender gap in household poverty unique to the United States? A recent analysis for eight industrialized nations in the 1980s shows that all nations but Sweden have higher poverty among women than men, but the United States has the largest sex gap in poverty (Casper, McLanahan, and Garfinkel 1994).[10] In descending order of the size of their ratio of women's to men's poverty, the United States, Australia, West Germany, Canada, and the United Kingdom all had a sizable gender gap. In Italy and the Netherlands, women's poverty rate was 1.02 times men's, virtually equal. Sweden is the only nation in which a lower proportion of women than men were in poverty; the women's poverty rate was 90 percent of men's. Casper et al. (1994) attribute the low sex gap in poverty in Italy to high marriage and low divorce rates, the low sex gap in the Netherlands to a relatively generous state-provided safety net that brings most single mothers' households above poverty, and women's favorable poverty position in Sweden to high female employment, a relatively small sex gap in pay, and a sturdy safety net. It is also interesting to note that, in general, nations with higher poverty rates have a higher gender disparity in poverty. The United States has both a high poverty rate and the largest gender disparity. The high disparity by gender in the United States results in part from its less generous social welfare programs and a higher ratio of mothers living apart from men (England et al. 1998).

THE FEMINIZATION OF POVERTY: THE MODERN PARADOX

We have seen that women have higher poverty rates than men in the United States and a number of other nations, but what is the trend in the gender gap in poverty in the United States? Has there been a feminization of poverty, as claimed by Diana Pearce (1978), who coined the phrase? If what we mean by the "feminization of poverty" is a "relative feminization"—that is, the extent to which women's poverty rates as a ratio of men's[11] have gone up—table 8.2 (drawing from McLanahan et al. 1989 and McLanahan and Kelly 1999) answers the question. Focusing on the row pertaining to all ages (18 and over) combined, we can see that for whites the ratio of women's to men's poverty rate went up markedly—over 30 percentage points—between 1950 and 1970 but went up only a few points from 1970 to 1980 and declined about the same few points between 1980 and 1996. Thus, it has been fairly constant since 1970. However, if we break things out by age, we see that the dramatic increase in women's rates relative to men's has continued among the elderly, but the ratio of women's to men's poverty was stable among young adults after 1980 and has declined among those aged 30 to 64 since 1970.

Blacks in the United States showed a continued and dramatic increase in women's poverty rates relative to men's among the elderly. The younger age-groups showed increases in women's relative poverty until 1980, but poverty has "defeminized" a bit since then. When we look at all ages combined, there is a dramatic increase in the ratio of women's to men's poverty rates until 1980 but little increase in the ratio after 1980 (two points). More of the increase in the feminization of poverty for blacks occurred between 1970 and 1980, whereas for whites the increase was almost over by 1970.

This trend in relative poverty [12] gives a very different picture of women's progress relative to men than the figures on women's employment and earnings discussed previously. One might have thought that the great increase in women's employment and earnings would have reduced women's poverty relative to men's among the nonelderly during the whole period. (We would not expect this among the elderly because employment is not the major source of earnings for either men or women in this group.) Had there been no countervailing force, this would have been true. What is the countervailing force that increased women's poverty relative to men's from 1950 to 1980?

The countervailing factor is the increase in the proportion of women living independently from men and the increasing portion of these who have children. As discussed previously, given the low rates and levels of child support payment and levels of government cash subsidy to welfare recipients that seldom bring them above the poverty line, female-headed households containing children are very vulnerable to poverty. Several forces had led to an increased proportion of all women living in such households, and this has detached an increasing proportion of women and children from men's earnings

Americans have been marrying at later ages since 1960. After a slight decrease in age at marriage during the 1950s, average age at first marriage has increased steadily (Spain and Bianchi 1996: 27). This may not reduce the proportion who never marry. However, it means that women are spending more years of their life living independently of men. This trend is especially pronounced for African Americans (Raley 1996).

The proportion of women living without men in their households is also affected by the divorce rate. In the United States, divorce increased fairly continuously from 1860 to 1940, spiked dramatically during World War II, then came down to its prewar level and was fairly stable during the 1950s. It increased dramatically during the 1960s and 1970s and has declined slightly since 1980 (Cherlin 1996: 353). Even if further increases do not occur (and this is debatable), it has leveled off at a very high level that implies that half or more of all new marriages will end in divorce (Martin and Bumpass 1989).

In addition, since the 1970s, divorced women have waited longer to remarry, which also contributes to a higher proportion of women living independently of men (Spain and Bianchi 1996: 34–35).

Another trend affecting women's relative poverty is nonmarital childbearing. While overall fertility has fallen dramatically since the peak of the baby boom in 1956 (though it rose slightly since 1980) (England and Farkas 1986: 13; Spain and Bianchi 1996), the proportion of births that are to unmarried women has increased continuously since the 1950s. It was under 5 percent in 1950 and is over 30 percent today (Moore 1995).

Both divorce and nonmarital births increase the proportion of single women who are supporting children, and this will, other things being equal, increase women's poverty rates relative to men's since the poverty line is adjusted for household size.

All these trends—later marriage, increased divorce, and an increasing percentage of births to unmarried women—mean that more women, and especially more women with children, are living independently of men. The small amounts that such households get in state transfer payments and in transfers from men outside the household means that many of them are surviving largely on women's earnings. While women's employment and earnings have grown, apparently before 1980 this increase was not great enough to offset the increasing detachment of women (and children) from men's earnings. This is why women's poverty rates increased relative to men's. However, in the United States since 1980, although poverty has gone up for men and women, women's continued gains in employment and earnings and/or men's losses (either being an improvement for women relative to men) have apparently been large enough to offset the continuing increases in the proportion of women living independently of men, and it is these gains that have brought the ratio of women's poverty to men's downward again among the nonelderly over 30. This explanation is consistent with the finding in table 8.2 that the ratio of women's to men's poverty decreased since 1980 among those aged 30 to 64. We would not expect women's recent gains in employment and earnings, which were concentrated among younger cohorts of women, to affect the poverty of women relative to men among the elderly for many more decades since most of the elderly are not employed and live on Social Security and pensions, the amounts of which were determined by employment records stretching back many decades.

Thus, to summarize the trends for the United States, poverty feminized from 1950 to 1980, but this trend was over among the nonelderly by 1980. Women's poverty as a ratio of men's went up between 1950 and 1980 despite women's increased employment. This is because more women were living in households without men and thus losing access to a share of men's earnings. Since 1980, among those in the 30-to-64 age-group, trends toward women living independently from men without access to their earnings have continued. But increases in women's earnings and decreases in men's earnings apparently were at least offsetting among blacks and substantially more than offsetting among whites.

A few caveats to the discussion are needed. Table 8.2 shows sex ratios of poverty rates, not the underlying rates themselves. However, if those are examined, we see that the feminization of poverty does not necessarily mean that women's absolute poverty is increasing (McLanahan et al. 1989; McLanahan and Kelly 1999). Indeed, the basic pattern is that poverty came down for most all groups between 1950 and 1980, but because it came down faster for men than women, women's poverty relative to men's increased. Since 1980, poverty has gone up for all groups, but because it has gone up faster for men than women except among the elderly, women's relative poverty has decreased in nonelderly age-groups. However, we should remember that in virtually every race/age/year combination, women have higher poverty than men. Overall, in 1996, white women had poverty rates 52 percent higher than white men's, and black women had rates 71 percent higher than black men's (table 8.2).

To return to the terminology of gender and class with which I began, if our interest is on freedom from the deprivation of poverty and we can think of household poverty as one crude measure of class, then class is gendered and became increasingly so from 1950 to 1980 but decreasingly so since 1980. Most of the increase in the "gendering of class," the "feminization of poverty" that occurred through 1980 was, at least in a proximate sense, because of changes in whether men and women live together and pool income.

A MACRO-LEVEL MODEL AND INTERPRETATION

Let us step back from the details discussed so far to consider what theoretical assertions we might make about the causal relationship between the major factors considered. Figure 8.1 presents my view of the causal linkages. In principle, it is a model that could explain variation over time within a society or variation between societies (or smaller units).

The model starts with women's relative earnings. I am thinking here of a concept that would best be measured as annual earnings of the individual, where those who are not employed have earnings of zero. Thus, the issue is not just relative wage rates but how much the individual earns, letting that amount be impacted by employment versus nonemployment, hours per week and weeks per year of employment, and the wage rate. Earnings would then be aggregated in some measure of central tendency, and a ratio or difference between women's and men's would be computed. As discussed previously, such a measure would show increases for women's relative earnings in the United States fairly continuously since at least 1950 even though wage rates have converged only since 1980. The model asserts that women's relative earnings affect women's power relative to men in their marriages. As mentioned in the introduction, I think most of the available evidence suggests this, although further research is clearly needed. (For conceptual discussions of effects of spouses' relative resources, including earnings, on material or other manifestations of marital power, see Behrman 1992; Blumberg 1991; Bourguignon and Chiappori 1992; Browning et al. 1994; England and Kilbourne 1990; Hobcraft 1997; Thomas 1990).

Why would we think that who earns more of the family income would affect power within the family? One relevant set of ideas comes from what sociologists call exchange theory and what economists call a "bargaining" perspective, which is in turn essentially a version of game theory. The basic idea is that what one can successfully bargain for with a spouse is increased the more one's alternatives outside this relationship increase relative to the gains from staying in the relationship and the less one's partner's alternatives outside this relationship increase relative to the partner's gains from the relationship. Thus, contrary to how exchange theory is sometimes portrayed, the notion is not simply that bargaining power is proportional to contributions. If that were true, the conclusion that men have more power by virtue of bringing in money would by no means follow, despite the fact that it is often portrayed as being self-evident. If the issue is relative contributions, who is to say that men are contributing more to the family by bringing in earnings than a woman who is a homemaker is contributing by providing care for children and other household work? From the vantage point of this per-

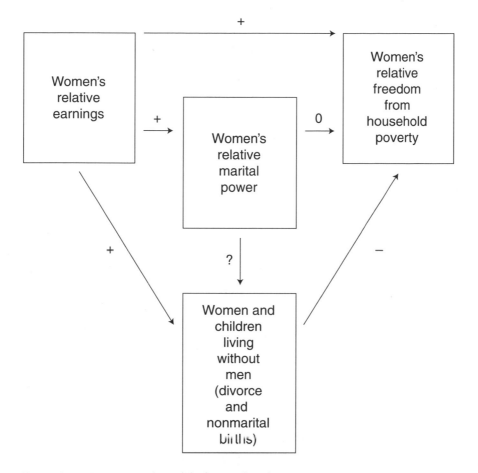

Figure 8.1.   Macro-Level Model of Causal Linkages

spective, the salient way in which earnings differ from homemaking is that earning power is portable if one leaves the marriage. Thus, if there is a divorce, a wife loses access to a husband's earnings and a husband to the wife's earnings (except to whatever extent alimony or child support is enforced); thus, earnings give either spouse power vis-à-vis the other. This suggests that men's higher earnings have been a source of greater marital power. The provision of child rearing is not analogous since women generally continue to take care of the children in the case of divorce. Thus, to the extent that women's contributions to the marriage are to provide things that they would not take away from their husbands in the case of a divorce (child-rearing services) whereas men's role is to provide things that they will largely withdraw if the marriage ends (earnings), women have less power than men.[13] Thus, women's lesser employment and earnings relative to their husbands in marriage give women less credible "external threat points" than men, in the language of game theory, but they have more favorable threat points the higher their own earnings are. At the abstract level, the idea is that the more one could threaten to withdraw from the partner if one left a relationship and the worse their options outside the relationship, the more one can exercise power within a relationship[14] (for a more extended theoretical discussion, see England and Kilbourne 1990).

This approach differs from Gary Becker's (1991) approach to the family, which assumes a single family utility function and altruism of the family head (for critiques of Becker, see England and Budig 1998; England and Farkas 1986: chaps. 3, 4; Folbre 1994). However, one need not assume complete selfishness of marital partners to think that the bargaining approach has some merit. I believe that there is a mix of altruism and selfishness in most all social relations. To the extent that some degree of selfishness vis-à-vis spouses is present, the bargaining perspective should have some explanatory power.

The bargaining perspective has some empirical support in findings suggesting that employment and/or women's earnings relative to their husbands' affect who gets their way when there is conflict on various issues (Bahr 1974; Blumstein and Schwartz 1983; Duncan and Duncan 1978: 205; McDonald 1980). If we assume that most people would prefer to have more leisure and do less housework, then findings on the division of housework in the United States also provide indirect support for the bargaining model: A spouse having higher earnings is predictive of doing less housework (Brines 1994; Presser 1994).[15]

If relative earnings affect marital power, this may affect how satisfying marriages are to the partners on a large number of dimensions that partners implicitly or explicitly negotiate, things as diverse as how money is to be spent, who will do what household chores, the couple's sex life, when and if they will have children, how children are reared, the timing of children, where the family will live, and so on. If this is true and if an individual's relative power affects how much they can negotiate for what they want within the marriage, we would expect marriages to be more satisfying to women when their earnings are higher.

Marital power should not have any effects on household poverty, so figure 8.1 shows a 0 on the arrow from marital power to freedom from household level poverty. Figure 8.1 also shows a positive, direct effect from women's relative earnings to their relative freedom from household poverty. As discussed previously, if household structure is held constant, this is almost definitional. It will be true as long as any increases in women's relative earnings apply to those who head households and thus bring female-headed households out of poverty at higher rates than other households. However, as discussed previously, during the period between 1950 and 1980, when women's employment and earnings were increasing, women's relative freedom from poverty was not always improving. This is because the effect of women's relative earnings on their poverty, operating indirectly through effects on the proportion of women living apart from men, works in opposition to the direct effect, as shown in figure 8.1.

The lower section of figure 8.1 says that women's earnings relative to men's lead to more women and children living in households without men, and this decreases women's relative freedom from (household) poverty. Let us examine the first path in the link. Why would women's increased earnings increase women's tendency to live independently of men? One way is through increasing divorce.

Is there evidence that the increase in women's employment and earnings has increased divorce? There is no question about the fact that women's increased employment and increasing divorce have moved upward together over the last century (Greenstein 1990: 659). What is more difficult to assess is whether the increased employment and earnings of women have had a causal effect on divorce through making it possible for women to live independently of men. Many commentators argue for a causal relationship (Cherlin 1981; England and Farkas 1986: chaps. 1, 3) and some time-series (Michael 1988; Ruggles 1997a, 1997b) micro-level analyses (Greenstein 1995; South and Spitze 1986) find effects of either women's employment or earnings on divorce, although the evidence is mixed (Greenstein 1990; Hoffman and Duncan 1995; Tzeng and Mare 1995).

However, divorce is not the only force increasing the number of female-headed households. The movement to a later age at marriage (and some possibly not marrying at all) combined with an increase in the proportion of births that are out of marriage are also important. We might expect that women's increased employment and earnings would also make it more possible for women to choose to forgo marriage, even if they want children. (The evidence, however, on this is weak since there is some evidence that employment encourages rather than discourages first marriage for women [reviewed in Oppenheimer 1997: 471].)

There are at least two theoretical perspectives that can generate a prediction that women's employment increases divorce. From the point of view of the neoclassical "new home economics," Becker (1991) sees increasing divorce to be explained by declining gains from marriage because there is less specialization by sex when both women and men are employed. Specialization, in his view, makes families more efficient in their combined efforts to procure income from the market and to engage in household production (his term for household work and child rearing).

There is another way to look at the same empirical relationships that I find more compelling because it pays more attention to the patriarchal nature of marriage. In any feminist account and in the game theory–informed view mentioned previously, men have had disproportionate power in marriages because of their earning power. This has led many aspects of the relationships to be unsatisfying to women. In this view, what has held marriages together, in part, is women's dependence on men for money. When women's earnings lessen this dependence, women are more free to leave bad marriages or to forgo marriage in the first place.[16] Notice that, on this view, marriages are not made less happy by women's employment (at least not for women). Indeed, employment should increase their satisfactoriness to women. Rather, what changes is whether women can leave unhappy marriage partners without experiencing the worst levels of destitution for themselves and their children. Of course, if women are freer to divorce, they are also freer to delay or avoid marriage and to have children outside marriage.

It would be consistent with the way I am telling the story to find that it is women's decisions prompting a majority of divorces rather than an increase in men deserting women. Of course, sometimes it is not clear that it was one person who wanted the breakup while another wanted the union preserved; and we definitely cannot rely on data indicating who filed for the divorce since that may not correspond with who really initiated the decision. However, surveys in the United States that have asked people whether one party wanted the divorce find that a majority are prompted by women (Kelly 1986: 309; Kitson 1992; Spanier and Thompson 1984; Wallerstein and Kelly 1980). This is true for England as well (Hobcraft 1997). Swedish data show the same (Svedin 1994). I thus suspect that this may be true in all affluent, industrial nations.

This is not to say that women's employment is the only factor affecting the century-long increase in divorce. Increased emphasis on individualism in the culture may also be a factor (Cherlin 1981, 1996; England and Farkas 1986), perhaps prompted in part by advertising and consumerism; and, of course, any trend tends eventually to become self-reinforcing by producing values consistent with it. If enough people divorce or have nonmarital births, it becomes less stigmatized, and this may prompt further increases.

When more women and children live independently of men, especially in a context of low earnings for women, low state enforcement of child support, a below-poverty state-supported cash payment system for lone mothers, and a lack of universally provided health and child care services by the state, this increases women's poverty relative to men's. In figure 8.1, the negative effect of women living apart from men on women's relative freedom from poverty, net of women's earnings, results from more single women than men living with children (recall that the poverty threshold is adjusted for household size). Consistent with this, changes in family structure were behind the increases in the ratio of women's to men's poverty in the United States between 1950 and 1980, and national differences in family structure explain the relative ratio of women's to men's poverty across nations (England et al. 1998).

There is, to be sure, something a bit paradoxical about arguing that women's earnings lead to divorce because it allows more women to leave men without destitution and then to further say that one result of this is women's increased poverty relative to men's. Yet I think that this is what has occurred. While female-headed families with children have always fared badly, more women can support families, and more adequately than previously, even if some fall below the poverty line, at least for a period.

One interesting way to think about the effect of women's relative earnings on both marital power and living independently of men is to use the terms coined by Albert Hirschman (1970). In a classic formulation, he argued that people in a situation that they do not like have three possible responses: exit, voice, or loyalty. According to the model here, women's increased power through increased earnings can be used as "voice" to bargain to make marriages better but can also be used to "exit" unhappy marriages. Presumably, women's increased employment has had both effects, although we do not have trend data on marital power. In earlier decades, women's economic dependence and resulting limited marital power meant that even those deeply dissatisfied with their marriages generally chose "loyalty" (staying married) because their only option was destitution. Men's greater power allowed them to respond to dissatisfaction through either exit or a bargaining "voice" in which their greater power usually brought them concessions. The low divorce rate of the earlier period suggests that men generally chose "voice." If women's power has increased because of their increased employment and earnings, they can choose either to leave unsatisfactory marriages (exit) or to utilize their new power by bargaining harder for what they want in marriage. That the two options of voice and exit go hand and hand is implied by the view that resources one would withdraw from a partner if one decided to end the relationship also lead to power within it.[17]

While we lack trend data on marital power, are there some more indirect indicators that would suggest whether women are successfully bargaining for more satisfactory marriages? One thing that might make us doubt the increase in women's successful utilization of their new power is the fact that as women have increased their employment dramatically, men have increased the time they spend in domestic work much less, and, as a result, women, especially employed mothers, generally enjoy less leisure than men (see literature reviewed in England and Kilbourne 1990). One presumes that employed women would like to use their bargaining power to bring about a more equal sharing of domestic work. There is also evidence that women would like to change the degree to which men provide emotional empathy. Both of these things would require a significant change in men's roles. However, there is much greater resistance, psychologically, culturally, and structurally, to changing men's roles than to changing women's roles. Men grow up and live in a culture that denigrates "feminine" males more than "masculine" females. In addition, employers are more willing to incorporate female workers into male jobs than to redefine "male" jobs that were constructed assuming that men did no domestic work and had wives to do it for them. Thus, women may use exit because of the resistance they encounter when they try to use voice in ways that significantly require changes in men's roles. One result of women using exit rather than voice is to protect men's roles from having to change. As a result, there is a profound asymmetry in gender role change. This is particularly true since women continue to do all the child-rearing work in divorced households and households with nonmarital births. Women have taken on traditionally male responsibilities much more than men have taken on traditionally female responsibilities. Thus, the question of why exit is used more often than effective voice may reduce to the question of why men's roles are so much harder to change than women's. It may be the resistance that women find to changing men's roles to include more traditionally female activities that leads them to often opt for exit over voice. This is consistent with the evidence that it is disproportionately women who initiate marital breakups. However, the result of the "exit" (or "never enter") decisions, in the aggregate, is to increase women's relative exposure to household poverty, and, given low child support enforcement, this increasingly disconnects children from men's incomes as well.

Thus, a modern paradox is this: Women have gained access to money through increased employment, which improves their marital power, but their ability to use this power to get men to share in traditionally female responsibilities is limited. Thus, many instead use their economic independence to form separate households, often with children. In doing so, they continue to take responsibility for child rearing, but they lose a realistic claim to a share of men's earnings for themselves and their children. Whether, in net, what has been lost or what has been gained is greater is difficult to answer. I suspect, however, that if male resistance to taking on more traditionally female responsibilities were to lessen, the empowerment provided by women's employment and earnings would be more likely to translate into an increased voice within marriages than currently and less likely to lead to divorce and the retreat from marriage.

CHAPTER NINE

Women and Union Democracy—Welcome as Members but Not as Leaders?

A Study of the Scandinavian Confederations
of Labor

Gunn Elisabeth Birkelund and Siv Øverås

INTRODUCTION[1]

The debate on class and gender has developed through several stages, as argued in Chapter 1 of this volume. Some elements of these stages are reflected in the theme of this chapter, which is about women and the Scandinavian confederations of labor: the LOS in Norway, Sweden, and Denmark and SAK in Finland.

As Wright notes in Chapter 2 of this volume, gender relations and class relations may be interconnected in various ways and might reciprocally affect each other. Gender relations might have an overall impact on the structuring of the labor market and class relations. The male-breadwinner family and the notion of the "family wage" limited married women's supply of labor, and male domination within the labor markets was also reflected within labor unions (Hirdman 1998). At the same time, changing gender relations may lead to changing class relations. In the 1970s and 1980s, new jobs within the welfare state emerged, and women's employment rates and their proportion in the labor force rapidly increased (Hernes 1984). Thus, changing gender relations implied changes in the gender composition of the national confederations of labor in Scandinavia: The Scandinavian working class[2] and associated labor unions have been "feminized." In Norway and Sweden in 1995, women made up almost 50 percent of all union members.

Gender may also be a sorting mechanism into class locations and occupations (Wright 1997: 245; Wright, Chapter 2 in this volume). The Scandinavian labor markets are highly sex segregated: Men dominate in industrial working-class jobs and the associated unions, whereas women dominate in service-sector jobs, often within the public sector, and their associated unions. Most of the unions within the confederations are either female or male dominated. The power balance within the confederations between the unions is a complex issue that often arises in discussions about women's access to vital decision-making areas and leading positions.

Class relations might also have an impact on gender relations: "The physical demands of many blue collar, industrial working class jobs put a premium on toughness, which in turn may help to reinforce a macho gender culture among working class men" (Wright 1997: 244; see also Wright, Chapter 2 in this volume). The labor unions of industrial workers have been associated with a masculine working-class culture, and the national confederations of labor unions are often referred to as male bastions.

To what extent has the entry of women into the unions entailed a concomitant share of union power? Two explanations have dominated the debate on women and union democracy: a feminist argument emphasizing men's reluctance to give up power and a structural argument emphasizing the power balance between the unions within the confederations (Skjeie 1989).

The feminist argument addresses the thorny issue of male resistance based on a macho culture within the most powerful unions. The structural argument addresses the fact that increased influence for women and the female-dominated unions may undermine the influence of the traditionally male-dominated unions, both with regard to the overall policy of the national confederations, perhaps leading to a more service-oriented outlook and also with regard to the power structure within the national confederations (e.g., some unions with declining membership enrollments may have to give up positions). We will return to these arguments.

SCANDINAVIAN LABOR UNIONS

In his recent book *Class Counts*, Wright (1997) argues that "the relationship between class structure and class formation at the macro-level of analysis and between class location and class consciousness at the micro-level of analysis are at the core of class analysis" (1997: 449). Situated between these two levels of analysis, we find class-based organizations, such as trade unions, that organize and mediate the collective interests of the working class.[3] As argued by Korpi (1983), working-class mobilization and the manifestation of conflicts of interests in the political arena of Western societies might be conceived of as a democratic class struggle (see also Therborn 1983). Despite their emphasis on the undemocratic internal character of most unions, Lipset, Trow, and Coleman (1956) argue that the labor movement has played a vital role in shaping modern societies, in "fostering institutions of political democracy in the larger society and in fostering the ideology of equalitarianism" (411).

The history of Scandinavian labor unions goes back about 100 years, and today these institutions, as well as their leaders, are a vital part of the political power distribution within Scandinavian societies. A brief look at the statistics reveals that Scandinavian societies are characterized by powerful national confederations of labor. In 1995, 85 percent of the Swedish workforce was unionized, 78 percent of the Finnish, 75 percent of the Danish, and 56 percent of the Norwegian (Stokke 1998).[4] Thus, Scandinavia has the highest level of unionization in the Western world.

Labor unions represent workers' power, and unions may thus be a threat to business capital. The corporate political system in the Scandinavian countries emphasizes the powerful position of the national confederations of labor. In each country, the national confederation participates in the annual centralized wage bargaining process. The confederations usually advocate a macro perspective in negotiations, often by emphasizing the importance of full employment within the society. They have therefore been willing to accept that there is a trade-off between wage increase and unemployment (Dølvik and Steen 1997; Høgsnes 1996). Thus, together with the National Confederations of Employers, the confederations of labor play an important role as "responsible institutions" by regulating strikes and work conflicts (see also Elster 1989). Thus, cooptation seems to be the price for political acceptance, power, and influence. These two faces of unions are well known (Burawoy 1979; Korsnes 1981), and the Scandinavian confederations of labor are no exception.

The national confederations also have strong political links to the Social Democratic parties, which have been in power for most of the postwar period.[5] The powerful position of the confederations of labor within the corporate system of centralized wage bargaining and collective agreements is also a part of "the Scandinavian model of welfare":

> A high degree of unionization and a centralized organization of the unions on the one hand, and a tradition of comprehensive agreements based on consensus with the employers on the other hand have provided a stable basis for eco-

nomic efficiency as well as for the continued development of welfare policies. (Karvonen 1995: 133)

The Scandinavian confederations of labor are not only oriented toward economic gains. They also initiate negotiations about issues that, at least in a short-term perspective, are noneconomic issues, such as work time, work environments, increased vocational training over the life course, and so on. This distinguishes the Scandinavian unions from the more instrumental orientation of American trade unionism, for example. This is an important point to bear in mind for non-Scandinavian readers.

THE FEMINIZATION OF THE SCANDINAVIAN CONFEDERATIONS OF LABOR

Women had to fight for the right to organize, and in the 1920s and 1930s, Scandinavian male working-class organizations wanted to exclude married women from paid work in order to maintain a family wage.[6] More recently, the modernization process of the Scandinavian societies has implied two interconnected features: the growth of postindustrial employment, particularly within the public sector, and the growth of women's employment.[7] Changing gender relations implied greater supply of female labor power, and larger demand for service workers implied more job openings for women. The result of this ongoing process has been a declining male-dominated industrial-based working class and a growing female-dominated working class within the service sector. While the national confederations of labor could prosper without women when men dominated the workforce, today inclusion of female workers is vital for the future strength of the confederations.

The changing gender composition within the national confederations of labor might imply changing values and norms, although this may not necessarily be the case. Rather, it seems fair to say that the confederations are ambivalent on gender issues. While equal opportunity policy has been successfully implemented within political parties, such as the Social Democratic parties, the national confederations of labor have not been willing to adopt such a strategy in order to improve women's access to vital decision-making arenas. In addition, conservative attitudes against women and feminism continue to exist within the male working class.

Today, the national confederations of labor organize a very high, but in relative terms decreasing, number of workers. Over the last decade, unions outside the confederations have expanded faster. International Labor Organization (ILO) figures show that throughout the world, trade unions have difficulties adapting to changes in the world economy. Globalization, new technology, and unemployment constitute challenges that the traditional unions seem unable to handle. In particular, the ILO argues that unions ought to attract the new groups of workers that enter the labor markets, such as women and youth.

While women's unionization earlier was a matter of much controversy (Clayhills 1972; Cliff 1987), in Scandinavia today this battle is more or less over: Nearly half the Scandinavian labor force is female, and nearly half of all union members in Scandinavia are women.[8] Table 9.1 shows that during the last two decades, the national confederations of labor in Scandinavia have undergone a dramatically rapid process of "feminization."

From 1970 to 1991, 81 percent of the total growth of union members in Denmark were women (union membership rose by almost 550,000 from 1970 to 1991, and roughly 440,000 were women). In Finland, 65 percent of the growth was due to women (284,000 new female union members); in Norway 96 percent (182,000) of the growth was due to women, and in Sweden no less than 98 percent (487,000) of union growth was due to women (Karvonen 1995: 139). Thus, in 1995, women made up 44 percent of the Norwegian and 46 percent of the Swedish labor organizations (Øverås and Nergaard 1997).[9] Inside the confederations, this development has brought about an uneven pattern of change. Some unions have experienced a dramatic growth, while others display stagnation or declining membership.[10]

However, women do not unanimously choose unions within the national confederations of labor. Since the end of the 1970s, the national confederations have been challenged by new unions outside the confederations.[11] There are a number of national trade unions that stand outside the confederations, representing other groups of employees, such as academics, white-collar workers, and professionals. However, there are also—and this is perhaps more dangerous to the national confederations of labor—unions that compete with unions inside the confederations over the same workers, in particular within the public sector, where the level of unionization is high. These unions outside the confederations are to some degree centralized unions (less in Denmark, more in Sweden), they are neutral in party political terms, and many of them have a female-friendly image. These unions have successfully recruited more women than unions within the confederations have done, re-

TABLE 9.1
Percentage of Female Members in Unions Belonging to the National
Confederations of Labor in Scandinavia, Selected Years

Years	Denmark	Finland	Norway	Sweden
1970–1971	28	32	23	30
1982	43	43	33	42
1990–1991	48	45	41	45
1998	48	46	45	46

SOURCES: 1970–1991: Karvonen (1995). 1998: Information provided directly from the central offices of LO Denmark, LO Sweden, SAK Finland, and LO Norway.

NOTE: For Denmark, Finland, and Norway, 1970; for Sweden, 1971; for Sweden and Norway, 1990; for Denmark and Finland, 1991.

sulting in a stagnation and even decline (in relative terms) in enrollment for the national confederations of labor (Stokke 1998).[12] Figures not shown here reveal that for these unions it is the influx of women that account for union growth in Scandinavia (Karvonen 1995). The result of this process is that, in Norway today, a majority of unionized women are organized outside the national confederation of labor, whereas approximately 60 percent of all unionized men are organized within the national confederation.

Leading Positions

All the national confederations have basically a three-layered decision-making structure; the Congress, the General Assembly, and the Executive Board.[13] The Congress meets every two, three, or four years. All unions are represented through their top leaders as well as their elected Congress candidates. The number of Congress delegates is determined by the number of union members. The Congress has the highest decision-making authority, and, in addition to a wide range of policy issues, the Congress elects the General Assembly and the Executive Board, which have the power to make important policy decisions in between the congresses.

The increasing female membership within various unions has, however, not resulted in a corresponding increase in women union leaders and women's representation in vital decision-making bodies. However, as table 9.2 shows, women's representation has improved substantially over the

TABLE 9.2

Women's Representation in Decision-Making Bodies of the Finnish,
Norwegian, and Swedish Confederations of Labor, Selected Years

		Board	Assembly	Congress
Finland	1974	4	15	23
	1986	15	30	33
	1993	22	41	37
Norway	1969	0	NA	6
	1981	7	13	18
	1985	20	16	26
	1989	20	17	31
	1993	20	25	36
	1997	20	32	40
Sweden	1972	0	2	13
	1988	7	19	27
	1992	13	25	26
	1996	27	27	39

NOTE: Data expressed as percentages. NA = not available.

SOURCES: Finland and Sweden: Karvonen (1995); Norway: Øverås and Nergaard (1997).

last decades, and "the ratio of growth of women's representation is well abreast of the increase of the share of women among the members" (Karvonen 1995: 144).

Nevertheless, it is still the case that women's representation lags behind their numeric share of members. Many unions within the confederations have an internal structure that is fairly similar to that of the confederations. A study of unions within the Norwegian national confederation showed a skewed gender distribution; even within female-dominated unions, men dominated at the higher levels within the union hierarchy (Øverås and Nergaard 1997: 69).[14]

Why do women participate less than men in the most important of the unions' decision-making arenas? Is it because they are squeezed out by men, the predominant feminist argument? Or is the lack of women at these three levels of decision making related to the power balance between the unions within the confederations, pointing toward structural barriers?

STRUCTURAL ARGUMENTS

The unequal representation of women within vital decision-making arenas might be caused by the internal structure within the national confederations of labor. This is the explanation that official representatives of the Norwegian confederation gave us when we interviewed them. Because of the sex segregation of the labor market, women and men are usually found in different unions, and the growth of members in female-dominated unions has changed the internal balance between the unions within the confederations: Unions organizing public employees have outnumbered the traditional male blue-collar unions. The unions that represent the public sector also tend to be female dominated. The influx of women has therefore created new centers of gravity within the labor movement, with the possibility for a new power balance between the male- and the female-dominated unions within the confederations.

The Assembly consists of a selection of union leaders. Increased representation of female-dominated unions will therefore happen only at the expense of another union's seat—certainly a matter of much controversy. In addition, since most union presidents are men, even in female-dominated unions, this implies that the Assembly is male dominated. The present president of the Norwegian Confederation of Labor has pointed to the autonomy of the unions as a major reason for the low female representation within the organization's vital decision-making bodies: "This is not in my hands; the unions must elect women, then the Congress, the Assembly and the Executive Board will reflect this" (Yngve Hågensen, president of the Norwegian Confederation of Labor). The Norwegian Confederation of Labor adopted a pamphlet of equal opportunity at the 1997 Congress, yet the suggestion of applying positive discrimination in favor of women—which has successfully improved the gender balance within the Social Democratic Party—was not accepted. This brings us to attitudes to women within the unions.

FEMINIST ARGUMENTS

Cultural Ambivalence

The then top leader of the Swedish Confederation of Labor perhaps had a bad day when, in 1992, he sneered, "Fucking crowd of c———s" [15] ("Fittstim") to characterize the Social Democratic women's association, implying a certain tiredness of feminist arguments about equal representation and—perhaps even worse—feminist policy. "Fittstim" has later been associated with men's reluctance to give up power, and the statement can also be seen as a token of male chauvinist attitudes toward women in general and of equal opportunity policy in particular.[16] It is, however, rarely the case that attitudes like these are publicly announced. In Scandinavia in the 1990s, this is certainly not "politically correct," yet there is reason to believe that attitudes like these still exist backstage.

Based on strategic considerations, however, the leaders of unions in Scandinavia are aware of the need for more women at the top. As pointed to previously, unions compete in a member market, and women in visible positions would be an important feature of recruitment (see also Bradley 1999). A survey conducted in 1996 among male and female union leaders and delegates to the Congress of the Norwegian Confederation of Labor showed that about two-thirds of both men and women wanted more women in top positions within the confederation (Øverås and Nergaard 1997). Whereas there was no gender difference with regard to this question, more women than men favored positive discrimination (quotas). This could, of course, be an indication of cultural ambivalence. Although men seem to approve of more women as union leaders and in top positions within the confederation, they lack the willingness to act accordingly.

The Homemaker Presumption

In order to be a union activist, one has to be willing to undertake a lot of work in addition to the job and family life. Øverås and Nergaard (1997) also found that a clear majority of local Norwegian union activists were not willing to be reelected or to run as candidates for a higher position within their union at the regional or national level or at the confederated level. With a few exceptions, all confederated unions have their main offices in the capital. This implies that for many union leaders, they must be willing to and have the opportunity to live away from home during the period of election. For many women with family responsibilities, this is not an option. "When women take leading positions within the unions, they have to adapt to the 'male' requirements. This includes overtime work, evening meetings, courses that run a full week at hotels in remote places, etc." (LO Sverige 1995).

However, also at local and regional levels, union activism might be difficult to combine with work and family life. Elisabeth Brolin of the Swedish Union of Municipal Workers hopes that a new generation might bring about a change in attitudes: "In the Union we have a way of working which makes it difficult to combine trade union work with family obligations. We have inherited an old attitude which demands that we give our soul to the Union. I don't believe that neither young girls nor young men are ready to do that."

Based on a study of gender and trade unionism in Great Britain, Sinclair argues that "clearly, the culture of trade unions, which has been characterized by the 'mystique of a kind of male brotherhood,' helps explain women's position as outsiders" (Sinclair 1996: 250). Sinclair also points to women's family responsibilities as an explanation of women's reluctance to get involved in unionist activities, arguing that there is a need to examine the impact of the union's policies and practices as a whole on the propensity to participate in union activities.[17]

WOMEN AND UNION DEMOCRACY

"The important struggle goes between labor and capital, not between women and men" (*Folkbladet/Ostgoten* [Swedish newspaper], August 5, 1992). Union democracy within a confederation involves complex processes of election and policymaking at the local, regional, and national levels within each union and also at the confederated level. Despite structural and attitudinal resistance, changes have in fact occurred (as seen in this chapter's tables). Women's situation within the labor market is now regarded as an important area of policy for the confederations, both in order to secure women better wages and working conditions and in order to recruit more female members by representing their interests as wage earners. In Norway, for example, the national confederation has implemented a "solidarity alternative." This implies that at central wage negotiations, the lowest paid get a larger relative wage increase than the best-paid workers. It seems fair to say that this policy has been women friendly since most low-paid occupations are female dominated. However, at the local level, the negotiations usually favor men in male-dominant "high productive" occupations and industries. Thus, the end result has usually sustained the differences between the low- and the better-paid occupations. The national confederations of labor have also adopted a policy of trading work time for money in order to facilitate early retirement and shift-share work, also favoring men.

The position of the Scandinavian national confederations of labor can still be characterized as strong. As documented here, the Scandinavian unions have undergone a dramatic "feminization" in the past two to three decades as a reflection of the structural changes within the labor markets, with a steady growth of the service sector (both public and private) at the same time as the industrial sector has decreased. This development is well known within most Western, advanced capitalist societies. Inside the confederations, this growth has brought about an uneven pattern of change; some unions (representing service workers and other public employees) have experienced a dramatic growth, while others (traditional blue-collar unions) display stagnation. This development has a bearing on the labor organizations, yet the consequences for the confederation of labor and their strategies and policies are still difficult to predict.

It seems that in order to maintain their strong position within the Scandinavian societies, the confederations of labor need to develop a policy that manages a delicate balance between the interests of the traditional male-dominated industrial working class and the interests of the newer and often female-dominated occupational groups within the service sector. The male-dominated unions are still powerful (the old aristocracy of the workers) compared to the "new service working class" unions, and there is still recruitment potential within the male industrial occupations. If the confederations of labor adopt a female-friendly policy to recruit more women in service occupations (often within the public sector), the confederations run the risk of being disregarded by male industrial workers. The dilemma is not solely about gender. It also has a bearing on the division between the public and the private sector. Some commentators and researchers have argued that one outcome of this dilemma might be that the confederations dissolve.

Just as male-dominated unions in export-oriented sectors may grow impatient with "bearing the burdens of public sector workers," women may grow tired of supplying the confederations with their membership growth while having their claims for representation voted down by the traditionally (male-) dominant unions. In such a situation, a fundamental realignment in the labor market along the private/public sector distinction is not out of the question (Karvonen 1995: 151).

Female workers represent challenges to union democracy. Their interests relate to their class as well as to their gender, and many women would prefer to be regarded as fellow workers rather than female workers. Yet the Scandinavian working class is divided by gender and sector, and these cleavages have a bearing on the future of the main interest organizations of the working class.

Chapter One. Introduction

1. Postindustrial theory clearly refers to more than just a set of characteristics of advanced societies. As Esping-Andersen and Kolberg (1991) and Esping-Andersen (1993) highlight, theories of postindustrial social change typically imply optimistic or pessimistic scenarios about current and future stratification processes in those societies. It is not necessary to engage these arguments here. We simply use the term "postindustrial" to denote the key features of these societies that matter for the reconfiguration of class and gender relations.

2. Wright's (1985: chap. 3; 1997: chap. 1) account is more complex than this and is embedded within an explanatory framework that links class locations to exploitation and production relations. These issues are dealt with in more detail by Wright in chapter 2 in this volume.

Chapter Two. Foundations of Class Analysis

This chapter was originally presented at the panel of the "Foundations of Class Analysis" at the annual meeting of the American Sociological Association, Chicago, August 1999.

1. This may not seem to be the standard definition of feudalism as a class structure. Typically, feudalism is defined as a class system within which extraeconomic coercion is used to force serfs to perform labor for lords, either in the form of direct labor dues or in the form of rents. Here I am treating "direct economic coercion" as an expression of a property right of the lord in the labor power of the serf. This is reflected in the fact that the serf is not free to leave the land of the lord. This is equivalent to the claim that the flight of a serf from the land is a form of theft—stealing labor power partially owned by the lord. For a discussion of this conceptualization of feudalism, see Wright (1985: chap. 3).

2. Class structures are thus complex for two reasons: The rights and powers within given forms of class relations can be redistributed in various ways, and a given class structure may combine a variety of different kinds of class relations.

3. For a more extensive discussion of these three principles, see Wright (1997: 9–19).

4. While Weberians generally do not talk about exploitation, domination is an important theme within Weberian sociology. It is not, however, generally linked so directly with the problem of rights and powers over economic resources and thus is less closely tied to the problem of class as such. Weberian discussions of domination are thus typically found in general discussions of forms of authority and power rather than the specific issue of class.

5. It is important to note that one need not accept the normative implications of the concept of "exploitation" to recognize the problem of the "extraction of labor effort." This is one of the central themes in discussions of principal/agent problems in transaction-costs approaches to organization. For a discussion of class and exploitation specifically in terms of principal/agent issues, see Bowles and Gintis (1990).

Chapter Three. A Conceptual Menu for Studying the Interconnections of Class and Gender

This chapter draws heavily from two previously published works: "Explanation and Emancipation in Marxism and Feminism," chapter 10 in *Interrogating Inequality* (London: Verso Press, 1993), and "Conceptualizing the Interaction of Class and Gender," chapter 9 in *Class Counts* (Cambridge: Cambridge University Press, 1997).

1. It may be controversial to characterize feminism as an emancipatory tradition directed against gender oppression rather than simply against the oppression of women. Certainly until recently, feminists did not explicitly embed their understanding of the oppression of women in a theory of gender relations and thus characterized the struggle as strictly against the oppression of women as such. Many contemporary feminists, however, understand the ramifications of male domination within gender relations more broadly than simply men dominating and oppressing women. In any case, throughout this discussion of feminism, I will refer to the domination and oppression of women within gender relations. This does not imply that women are the only categories of people oppressed by existing forms of gender relations. Male homosexuals, for example, are also oppressed under existing gender relations, and while it is a more complex (and contentious) argument, I think that many heterosexual men can also be viewed as oppressed within gender relations. There is no need to work through these issues in the present context.

2. The idea that in a multicausal system one factor is "more important" than another is fraught with ambiguities and is very difficult to pin down. For an extended discussion of the problem of causal primacy, see Wright, Levine, and Sober (1992).

3. For a discussion of the slide from historical materialism toward sociological materialism, see Wright et al. (1992: chap. 5).

4. This would strictly be true only if it were the case that all women were

slaves, which does not seem to be the case in the historical examples cited by
Gerda Lerner (1986). The dystopia portrayed by Margaret Atwood (1987) in
A Handmaid's Tale comes closer to a society within which class and gender are
fused into a single relation.

5. There has been a lively debate over the explanation of the family wage (see,
e.g., Barrett 1984; Hartmann 1979; Humphries 1977; Lewis 1985). In contrast to
Brenner and Ramas's argument that the family wage was in the interests of both
male and female workers, many feminists have argued that the family wage should
be viewed primarily as a victory of men over women, reflecting the strategic interests of men in keeping women in their place. Insofar as it was the gender interests
of men that formed the basis for the struggle over the family wage, this would be
another instance of the way in which gender relations shape the class structure. In
any case, once the family wage is in place as a specific feature of class relations, it
becomes an important material condition constraining transformations of gender
relations.

6. It may also be possible to conceptualize the complementary causal relation:
class as a sorting mechanism of people into "gender locations." At first glance, this
might seem like a bizarre claim since we tend to think of gender categories as dichotomous, polarized, and isomorphic with sexual categories—male and female.
This image reflects the tendency for most people (including most sociologists) to
conflate gender categories with sex categories despite the formal acknowledgment
that gender is a social, not biological, category. Once we break from the biological specification of gender relations, however, it is clear that men and women can
occupy many different sorts of gender locations, and class may influence where
people end up in such relations.

7. Detailed descriptions of each of these studies can be found in Wright (1997).

Chapter Four. The Gendered Restructuring of the Middle Classes

1. See, for example, the domestic labor debate.

2. The most often cited example was clerical work, which occupies a crucial
position on the boundary between "working" and "middle" classes in most class
schemes. However, whereas for men clerical work was often a stepping-stone to a
managerial career (see Lockwood 1995), for women, it was more usually a dead-
end occupation (see Crompton and Jones 1984). It may be suggested that recent
changes in the structure of employment have reduced the salience of these issues.
"Clerical" was in any case a catchall label for a wide range of lower-level "white
collar" occupations. In Britain, the category is in decline (Rubery and Fagan 1994),
but this is probably also a consequence of the relabeling of occupations as a result
of technical and organizational change. The category of "management" is particularly suspect here.

3. The term "advanced service economy" is being used in preference to other
more contentious descriptive concepts including "postindustrial," "post-Fordist,"
and so on. Industry is still important in an advanced service economy and hence

not "post," but services dominate employment. The "Fordist" appellation immediately raises the question of whether "Fordism" itself was ever a reality.

4. It is of some interest that the work of Esping-Andersen and his colleagues, particularly *Changing Classes* (1993), has not been given significant attention in recent debates on "class analysis."

5. Industrialization took place at different periods in different countries, a fact that has had important consequences for the development of class relations (see Ingham 1974; Therborn 1983). Women's employment in agriculture and family enterprises remained significant for much longer in some countries than others, and thus the "male breadwinner" label may not always be appropriate. Indeed, it has been suggested that in some countries (e.g., Finland), the label may never have been useful (see Pfau-Effinger 1993, 1999).

6. A central question examined in Esping-Andersen's recent work is whether a new "service proletariat" is in the process of developing. Esping-Andersen argues that in general, high levels of fluidity among low-level service workers mitigates against the development of a "postindustrial proletariat" but also notes that the extreme fluidity and flux of the occupational order renders any attempt at generalization highly unstable (1993a: 240). He also argues that another element of cross-national continuity is that in the postindustrial or advanced service economies, an individual's educational credentials and social skills will become of increasing importance in negotiating the labor market. Esping-Andersen's work has been the subject of extensive feminist debate and criticism, which has been concerned mainly with his analysis of "decommodification" and welfare states (Lewis 1992; O'Connor 1993). Much of this criticism stems from his failure to incorporate caring (i.e., unpaid) work into his analysis of the impact of state welfare on employment. However, although these debates have generated many new insights, in this I will be concerned mainly with women's paid work, although, as will become apparent, it is not possible to explore the impact of these changes in isolation from domestic work and vice versa.

7. Besides the very obvious example of the fate of women under Islamic fundamentalism, in ex–state socialist Eastern Europe, explicit patterns of gender segregation are emerging in rapidly expanding employment sectors, such as finance.

8. The countries were Britain, France, Norway, Russia, and the Czech Republic. This research was funded by the ESRC (R000235617) and is described in Crompton (1999, chap. 1).

9. These differences are statistically significant (see Crompton and Harris 1999). On the domestic responsibilities of women in managerial positions, see also Wajcman (1996).

10. The point may be made that this generalization is valid only for the West, as part-time work was/is virtually unknown in Eastern Europe. However, our interviews suggest that considerable latitude was given to the mothers of small children—taking time off when they were sick and leaving early to collect them from school. Indeed, it was suggested that "marketization" of health care was going to

make the combination of work and child care more difficult, as these practices were likely to disappear.

11. For example, there is now much more of an emphasis on the selling of financial services in the West. Changes in the East have been even greater with the coming of marketization.

12. It may be noted that this analysis incorporates a binary conceptualization of gender, in which "masculinity" is characterized as an absence or lack of the "feminine."

Chapter Five. Who Works?

Thanks to Adnan Turegun for research assistance on leaves.

1. John Eatwell's operational definition of disguised unemployment is "the number of jobs which would need to be lost if a sector is to attain a level of value productivity per head equal to 80 percent of the level of productivity in manufacturing" (1995: 28).

Chapter Six. The Links between Paid and Unpaid Work

1. Gershuny and Robinson (1988) have argued that women's time on housework in the United Kingdom and the United States has declined since the 1960s, while men's time on housework has risen slightly. See also Gershuny, Godwin, and Jones (1994) and Bianchi et al. (2000). Nevertheless, it seems clear that there have been no dramatic changes in recent years in the distribution of labor between husbands and wives in the home.

2. Part of the reason for the wide variation in findings relating to the domestic division of labor is undoubtedly due to differences in measurement. For example, some studies examine the relative distribution of housework tasks between husbands and wives, while others focus on time spent on housework.

3. Women's time in paid work then may lead to more proportionately egalitarian divisions of household labor, not because men do more but because women do less at home.

4. In Sweden, women in part-time work are typically employed for 20 to 34 hours, whereas in Australia in 1994 the average number of hours worked by women in part-time work was 16.1.

5. Haas (1992) has shown that the level of father's participation in parental leave has been comparatively low compared to mothers. Only 3 percent of fathers took parental leave in 1974, the first year it was available, compared to virtually all mothers. In 1977, only 10 percent of fathers took leave, and by 1979 the figure had risen to 23 percent. It has remained at around 22 to 24 percent. In addition, when fathers do take leave, they tend to do so for a much smaller period of time than mothers. In 1974, the average leave time taken by fathers was one month out of a possible six months. By 1978, this had increased to about two months but according to Haas has not increased much since (1992: 60–63).

6. This project, initially begun by Professor Erik Olin Wright in the United States, involved comparable surveys in approximately 15 countries (see Wright 1985, 1997). A number of countries, including Australia, Sweden, and the United States, conducted two surveys, the first in the early 1980s and the second in the early 1990s. Unfortunately, the second U.S. survey did not include questions on the domestic division of labor and so has not been included in the current analyses.

7. Throughout this chapter we will refer to the 1980 Swedish survey and the 1986 Australian survey as indexing the 1980s and the 1993 and 1995 surveys as indexing the 1990s.

8. The 1995 Swedish survey is somewhat ambiguous. It is not clear whether the question is meant to include time spent on the main job alone or time spent on all jobs. The question asks, "Approximately how many hours a week do you usually work all in all, including any overtime, regular work and extra work? Please state the number of hours."

9. An alternative means of examining the domestic division of labor is to measure the amount of time spent on domestic labor. The Australian survey included questions on how much time respondents spent on particular household tasks in an average week, but this was not included in the Swedish questionnaires.

10. Respondents with valid data on at least three items were assigned mean scores for specific items.

11. Cases with at least one valid response were assigned mean scores on individual items. Unfortunately, the 1995 Swedish survey included only the second attitude item. In this case, we have confined the scale to this item only.

12. This model specification is very similar to that used by Kalleberg and Rosenfeld (1990). Like them, we argue that occupation should only indirectly influence personal responsibility for housework through its impact on time spent in paid work. Unlike them, we include a variable to capture the longer hours associated with self-employment. Also unlike Kalleberg and Rosenfeld, we do not control for union membership at all, and we allow for direct effects of gender attitudes on time in paid employment. There is no reason to expect union membership to predict domestic work, and studies of the determinants of union membership frequently see it as an outcome rather than a cause of time spent on paid work (e.g., Gottfried 1992; Western 1996). We also thought that gender attitudes would matter directly for time in paid work, particularly among women, since it seemed likely that women with egalitarian attitudes would be more likely to prioritize labor market work than women with traditional attitudes.

13. These tests are univariate and multivariate Wald tests based on the covariance matrix of the parameter estimates.

Chapter Seven. Employment Flexibility in the United States

I thank Arne Kalleberg for his useful comments, Ken Hudson for unpublished Current Population Survey data, and Stephanie Moller for her research assistance.

1. Portes and Sassen-Koob (1987: 31) define the informal sector as "all work

situations characterized by the absence of (1) a clear separation between capital and labor; (2) a contractual relationship between both; and (3) a labor force that is paid wages and whose conditions of work and pay are legally regulated . . . the informal sector is structurally heterogenous and comprises such activities as direct subsistence, small-scale production and trade, and subcontracting to semiclandestine enterprises and homeworkers."

2. The pattern of labor force participation by age and family status varies by race and ethnicity (see, e.g., England 1992).

3. The need for maternity leave was not completely ignored in the United States. The 1978 federal Pregnancy Discrimination Act prohibited discrimination against workers on the basis of pregnancy. It also required employers who offered medical disability programs to provide these benefits for pregnancy and child birth on the same basis as for other medical conditions. Further, by the time the FMLA was passed, about half the states had adopted some form of maternity or parental leave legislation (Blau et al. 1998).

4. The pattern is somewhat different in state and local governments, where the "blue-collar and service" category includes police and firefighters, who often have very good benefits. As Glass and Estes (1997) point out, there is considerable variation among companies in the nature of these benefits, for example, in length of leaves and extent of child care support. Further, the degree of coverage within workplaces varies. They cite Capowski (1996) as quoting one consultant: "When companies say, 'Oh we have flextime, we have telecommuting,' what they mean is, 'We have an individual working here who does this.' They don't mean they have an integrated system" (Glass and Estes 1997: 300).

5. As Delsen (1998), Hakim (1997), Rosenfeld and Birkelund (1995), Clement (Chapter 5 in this volume), and others discuss, the definition and measurement of part-time work varies considerably across countries, so that comparisons such as these are only approximate. There is considerable variation in the nature of part-time work as well. I discuss this briefly in a later section.

6. Extensive support in West Germany for mothers to remain at home with young children, however, seems to increase labor market gender inequality (Trappe and Rosenfeld 2000), as well as encourage women to leave paid work, especially full-time jobs, when they become parents.

7. Jacobs and Gerson (1998) examine the "time bind" with nationally representative data and do not find a flight from family to work: Over 80 percent of those putting in more than 50 hours a week would like to work less. A 1997 follow-up on "Amerco" found that Corning, Inc., was still trying to implement "work-life balance" policies, including efforts to make supervisors more sensitive to family issues and options (Hammonds 1997). At the same time, the intense work atmosphere continued to make it difficult for employees, especially women, to do it all. Women's attrition rate had fallen and was low compared with other companies but was much higher than men's (8 percent compared with 3 percent).

8. The October 1996 *Monthly Labor Review* was devoted to a discussion

of results from this survey. I cite many of the articles from this issue. However, the number of contingent workers may have been underestimated in the statistics reported there because of a problem with skip sequences (Ken Hudson, personal communication).

9. Ironically, the work requirements of the 1996 federal welfare reform, implemented in July 1997, may increase poor women's access to child care and other benefits (Glass and Estes 1997).

10. Hossfeld (1990) points out that workers may consciously use gender and ethnic stereotypes to resist managerial control. She gives the example of a Haitian woman whose supervisor kidded her about voodoo. The woman was able to move to the day shift when she insisted evil spirits were out at night. While this was a victory of resistance, it still reinforced the stereotypes.

Chapter Eight. Gender and Access to Money

1. Goldthorpe (1983) argues for a household measure of class in studies using occupation as the indicator. He argues for using husband's occupation. His focus seems to be what is most appropriate for studies of how intergenerationally permeable the occupational structure is or how class affects consciousness (for debate on this, see Roberts 1993). My concern here is with what is a useful indicator of overall access to goods, services, and any other nonpecuniary utilities that flow from money.

2. The labor force refers to those who are employed plus those who are unemployed but looking for paid work. By this definition, homemakers, the retired, and full-time students are considered out of the labor force as long as they are not looking for paid work.

3. While the increase is less dramatic in England, a similar trend prevails. All parties to a recent debate in British sociology over women's employment seemed to agree that the percent of British women employed full time has been fairly stable in the postwar period, with any increase in the total percentage of women employed offset by the increase in the proportion of employed women working part time, so that women's "full-time equivalents" have not increased (Bruegel 1996; Ginn et al. 1996; Hakim 1995, 1996). But Joshi (1996), who has a firmer grip on the relevant numbers, provides evidence that this is simply not true—that there has been over-time and across-cohort increase in women's participation. Nonetheless, many more women work part time in most of Europe than in the United States (Rosenfeld and Birkelund 1995).

4. In the United States, the sex gap in pay has never been caused by women's lower educational attainment. In fact, among those in the labor force, black women have had slightly more education than black men since at least 1950, and this was true for whites until sometime in the 1960s, when men caught up (England 1992: 28). The occupations in which women are concentrated also require about the same amount of education, on average, as those in which men are concentrated. It is more accurate to say that typically "female" and "male" occupations require dif-

ferent kinds of skill than to characterize them as requiring different amounts of skill (England 1992).

5. Since the number of census-detailed occupational categories has increased with nearly every decennial census, these index values are not perfectly comparable over time. However, pieces that have explored various solutions to this methodological problem agree on the basic conclusion that segregation changed little in this century until 1970 but has declined substantially since (England 1981; Jacobs 1989).

6. All figures in this note are from calculations combining all racial groups. For a discussion of trends in the sex gap in pay that examines how changes in ratio of women's to men's median earnings have been driven by changes in different portions of each gender's distribution, see Bernhardt, Morris, and Handcock (1995) and Cotter et al. (1997).

7. It is also adjusted for age of family members and whether the family lives on a farm.

8. Unrelated individuals who cohabit, whether "roommates" or "couples," are assigned a poverty score as if each lived alone. This formulation probably makes sense for roommates, who often do not pool income. However, cohabiting couples probably pool income less than married couples but more than roommates. Thus, the poverty of cohabiting individuals is probably overstated in U.S. government statistics.

9. As mentioned in note 8, the one exception to this is unrelated individuals who cohabit. Their poverty is assessed as if they lived alone on their individual income.

10. For international comparisons, it is difficult to use an absolute rather than relative definition of poverty (as U.S. government statistics do) because this requires us to equate currencies by their buying power rather than by more readily available official exchange rates. To avoid this problem, Casper et al. (1994) used a relative definition of poverty for their international comparisons. Using data from the Luxembourg Income Study (LIS), they consider an individual as poor if she or he lives in a household whose disposable income (after taxes and government cash transfers) is less than 50 percent of the median disposable income for all households in that country. For the United States, the change to the relative definition of poverty from the absolute definition used by the government increased the ratio of women's to men's poverty rate from 1.39 to 1.41 for 1985. Casper et al. adjusted income for differences in family size by using an equivalence scale developed for the LIS data that is comparable to the one used to define the official poverty lines in Canada, Sweden, and the United States. Overall, the computation of the gender poverty ratios in table 8.2 (from McLanahan and Kelly 1999) in this chapter differ from those in Casper et al. (1994) in three ways (other than being from different data sets): McLanahan and Kelly use an absolute and Casper et al. (1994) a relative definition of poverty; the former use before-tax income, the latter after-tax income, and the former treat cohabiting couples as two households, whereas the latter treat them as one. They have in common that similar equivalence scales are used to ad-

just income for household size in each and that in-kind benefits provided by the government or an employer (e.g., health insurance or Medicare) are excluded from income in each.

11. Pearce (1978) suggested looking at the proportion of adults in poverty who are women. In a population with a fixed sex ratio of about 50 to 50 in every age-group, that ratio would move together with the measure I suggest—a ratio of women's to men's poverty rates—and both capture the concept of how poor women are not in absolute terms but relative to men. However, given that the sex ratio of the population in a particular age-group can change (e.g., women's mortality has declined faster than men's, making them a higher proportion of the elderly), this would move the proportion of the poor who are women, so this measure would then be misleading as a measure of women's poverty relative to men's. In contrast, changes in the ratio of women's to men's poverty rates are not affected by changes in the sex ratio in the population (they are, in effect, adjusted out). Thus, I believe that such ratios are a better measure to capture what I think Pearce's underlying concept was—women's freedom from poverty relative to men's (McLanahan et al. 1989).

12. For comparison, let us examine the trends in the ratio of the average household income of women to that of men. Spain and Bianchi (1996: 143) provide these figures for per capita income. The ratio of the average per capita income of the households in which women lived to those in which men lived was .96 in 1960, .93 in 1970, and .91 in both 1980 and 1990. The absolute deviation from parity of these numbers is smaller than for poverty, suggesting that the gender disparity in being in the bottom tail of the household income distribution is greater than the average gender disparity in household income. However, these numbers, like the poverty rate ratios, show a deterioration in women's relative position up to 1980 but little change afterward. (Note that in the case of the female-to-male poverty ratio, a number over 1 indicates women's disadvantage, whereas with the female-to-male household income ratio, a number under 1 indicates female disadvantage.)

13. Of course, while women do not generally withdraw the services of child rearing on divorce, men do lose access to wives' services to the husband himself, and, where the wife has custody of children, the children themselves are withdrawn (with visitation allowed). These should be a basis of some power for women. However, the fact that men typically do not do the primary child rearing probably means that they are less attached to the children and less habituated to spending time with them and even care less about the children. All these reduce the suffering that withdrawal of the children from living with the man brings, which reduces the extent to which the implicit threat of withdrawing the children can give women power.

14. Actually, neither game theorists nor economists typically use the word "power" to describe what flows from being the source of a resource for someone who has limited alternative sources. However, they do typically claim that these factors affect the outcome of bargaining such that one gets more of what one wants in interaction with any party when one provides them with more resources and their alternative sources are limited. By a loose commonsense definition of power, get-

ting one's way as a result of good alternatives to the marriage (or as a result of one's partner's bad alternatives) can be seen to occur through the intervening mechanism of power.

15. Although Brines's (1994) findings are largely supportive of the view that spouses with higher relative earnings do less housework net of hours of paid work, she finds a nonlinearity for men, such that as men's relative earnings go down, they do more housework up to some point, where the curve reverses as their housework begins to decline. This declining portion of the curve is not consistent with bargaining models; she attributes it to "gender display." It is as if men's sense of masculinity is threatened by financial dependence on their wives, so they shore it up by doing less housework. However, for most of the range of relative wages, the data fit a bargaining model.

16. Of course, if the increased marital power discussed previously made marriages sufficiently better for women, this might actually decrease women's desire to divorce. However, it is unclear what effect that would have on the divorce rate since it might also decrease the satisfactoriness of marriage to men and increase their desire to divorce.

17. The applicability of Hirschman's (1970) concept of "exit, loyalty, and voice" to marriage and divorce was independently suggested by Castles and Seddon (1988) and England and Kilbourne (1990).

Chapter Nine. Women and Union Democracy—Welcome as Members but Not as Leaders?

This research has been contracted by the Norwegian Federation of Labor (LO).

1. In this chapter, we will use "Scandinavia" as short for Norway, Sweden, and Denmark, as well as Finland, although Finland geographically is not part of Scandinavia as usually understood.

2. The national confederations of labor comprise unions that organize members in typical blue-collar working-class jobs as well as unions that represent workers within white-collar occupations. We therefore adopt a wide definition of the working class.

3. For a critique of class analysis for focusing on individual workers instead of working class capacities, see Lembcke (1991).

4. In Finland, Sweden, and Denmark, these figures also include the unemployed since the national confederations of labor in these countries also administer unemployment compensation.

5. In Finland, the association between SAK and the Finnish Social Democratic Party has been weaker than in the other Scandinavian countries. This is partly due to the strong position of the extreme left (Karvonen 1995).

6. Since the turn of the twentieth century, feminist organizations have disagreed on the best strategy to improve women's conditions, and these political divisions were also an expression of a class conflict: Working-class women have regarded capitalists and employers as their main opponents while acknowledging

the possibilities of solidarity with their fellow male workers, whereas middle-class women and their organizations have focused their attention on male resistance to women's work and liberation. In the 1970s, this conflict within the feminist movement was articulated as a conflict about class struggle versus women's liberation, as can be seen in the disputes on Marxism and feminism (Clayhills 1972).

7. A number of important historical and structural factors need to be added to this statement, such as economic growth (and stagnation), the emergence and development of the welfare states in Scandinavia, new types of technology, and political-ideological issues, such as second-wave feminism.

8. Approximately 40 to 50 percent of Swedish and Norwegian women work part time, whereas most Finnish women work full time. Part-time workers used to be less unionized, but today Norwegian data show that part-time workers are as likely as full-time workers to be unionized (Birkelund 1999).

9. In the United States, the proportion of male workers in unions has fallen since mid-1950, whereas the proportion of female workers has risen, reducing the gap in unionization rates. Therefore, the female proportion of union members has increased from 19 percent in 1956 to 36 percent in 1984 (Freeman and Leonard 1987: 180; see also Reich 1991: 212–15).

10. The absolute number of men within the Norwegian LO has declined since 1970, when 455,879 (of 594,380) members were men. In 1995, 444,898 (of 791,416 members) were men.

11. In Finland, SAK has for several decades faced competition from other centralized unions, whereas the Norwegian LO was the only possible central labor confederation in Norway until the 1980s.

12. The overall level of unionization is fairly stable. In 1989, 61 percent of Norwegian employees were unionized, in 1993 the figure was 64. Yet the LO's share decreased from 54 percent of all unionized workers in 1989 to 52 percent in 1993 (Øverås and Nergaard 1997).

13. The organizational structures of the Scandinavian confederations of labor are fairly similar.

14. These results confirm earlier research on the gender gap in authority within work organizations, which showed a large significant gender gap in Scandinavia (Wright, Baxter, and Birkelund 1995).

15. The statement refers to the female genitalia and certainly is very offensive in the Scandinavian languages as well.

16. The concept "Fittstim" was later used as a title of a book written by young female journalists in Sweden, arguing that it is time to revitalize the feminist movement again, thereby twisting the originally negative loading of the concept.

17. McCarthy (1977), writing in the perhaps more optimistic 1970s, argues that British trade unions ought to initiate societal changes in traditional attitudes toward women, whereas Hermansson, writing about the Swedish labor movement and feminism, argues that within the labor movement equal opportunity for women is subsumed under the (more important) class struggle (Hermansson 1993: 43).

REFERENCES

Abercrombie, Nicholas, and John Urry. 1983. *Capital, Labour and the Middle Classes*. London: Allen and Unwin.

Acker, Joan. 1973. "Women and Stratification: A Case of Intellectual Sexism." In J. Huber, ed., *Changing Women in a Changing Society*, pp. 174–183. Chicago: University of Chicago Press.

———. 1990. "Hierarchies, Jobs, Bodies: A Theory of Gendered Organizations." *Gender and Society* 4: 139–158.

Ahrne, Göran, and W. Clement. 1992. "A New Regime? Class Representation Within the Swedish State." *Economic and Industrial Democracy* 13, no. 4 (November): 455–479.

Akyeampong, Ernst B. 1996. "Another Measure of Unemployment." *Perspectives on Labour and Income* 8, no. 4 (winter): 9–15.

Aley, James. 1995. "Where the Jobs Are." *Fortune*, September 18, 53–56.

Atkinson, J. 1987. "Flexibility or Fragmentation? The United Kingdom Labour Market in the Eighties." *Labour and Society* 12: 87–105.

Atwood, Margaret. 1987. *A Handmaid's Tale*. New York: Ballantine Books.

Australian Bureau of Statistics. 1994. *Focus on Families: Work and Family Responsibilities*. Catalogue No. 4422.0. Canberra: Australian Bureau of Statistics.

———. 1997. *Australian Women's Year Book 1997*. Catalogue No. 4124.0 Canberra: Australian Bureau of Statistics.

Bahr, Stephen J. 1974. "Effects of Power and Division of Labor in the Family." In L. W. Hoffman and F. E. Nye, eds., *Working Mothers*, pp. 167–185. San Francisco: Jossey-Bass.

Barrett, Michele. 1984. "Rethinking Women's Oppression: A Reply to Brenner and Ramas." *New Left Review* 146: 123–128.

Baxter, Janeen H. 1988. "Gender and Class Analysis: The Position of Women in the Class Structure." *Australian and New Zealand Journal of Sociology* 24: 106–123.

———. 1991. "The Class Location of Women: Direct or Derived." In Janeen H. Baxter, Michael Emmison, John S. Western, and Mark Western, eds., *Class*

Analysis and Contemporary Australia, pp. 202–222. South Melbourne: Macmillan.

———. 1993. *Work at Home: The Domestic Division of Labour*. St. Lucia: University of Queensland Press.

———. 1994. "Is Husband's Class Enough? The Effect of Husband's Class on Women's Working Class Identity in the United States, Sweden, Norway and Australia." *American Sociological Review* 59: 220–235.

———. 1997. "Gender Equality and Participation in Housework: A Cross-National Perspective." *Journal of Comparative Family Studies* 28, no. 3: 220–247.

Beck, U., and Beck-Gernsheim, E. 1995. *The Normal Chaos of Love*. Cambridge: Polity Press.

Becker, Gary S. 1991. *A Treatise on the Family*. Cambridge, Mass.: Harvard University Press.

Behrman, J. R. 1992. "Intra-Household Allocation of Nutrients and Gender Effects: A Survey of Structural and Reduced-Form Estimates." In S. R. Osmani, ed., *Nutrition and Poverty*, pp. 287–320. Oxford: Clarendon Press.

Bell, Daniel. 1976. *The Coming of Post-Industrial Society*. New York: Basic Books.

Bendix, R., and S. M. Lipset. 1967. "Karl Marx's Theory of Social Classes." In *Class, Status and Power*, pp. 6–11. London: Routledge.

Berk, S. 1985. *The Gender Factory: The Apportionment of Work in American Households*. New York: Plenum Press.

Bernhardt, Annette, Martina Morris, and Mark S. Handcock. 1995. "Women's Gains or Men's Losses? A Closer Look at the Shrinking Gender Gap in Earnings." *American Journal of Sociology* 101: 302–329.

———. 1997. "Percentages, Odds, and the Meaning of Inequality: Reply to Cotter et al." *American Journal of Sociology* 102: 1154–1155.

Bianchi, Suzanne M., Melissa A. Milkie, Liana C. Sayer, and John P. Robinson. 2000. "Is Anyone Doing the Housework? Trends in the Gender Division of Labor." *Social Forces* 79, no. 1 (September): 191–228.

Bird, G. W., G. A. Bird, and M. Scruggs. 1984. "Determinants of Family Task Sharing: A Study of Husbands and Wives." *Journal of Marriage and the Family* 46 (May): 345–355.

Birkelund, Gunn Elisabeth. 1999. *Part-Time Work in a Welfare State*. Oslo: Fafo Institute for Applied Social Research.

Blau, Francine D. 1998. "Trends in the Well-Being of American Women. 1970–1995." *Journal of Economic Literature* 36 (March): 112–165.

Blau, Francine D., and Marianne A. Ferber. 1990. "Women's Work, Women's Lives: A Comparative Economic Perspective." National Bureau of Economic Research Working Paper No. 3447. Cambridge, Mass.: NBER.

Blau, Francine D., Marianne A. Ferber, and Anne E. Winkler. 1998. *The Economics of Women, Men, and Work*. 3rd ed. Upper Saddle River, N.J.: Prentice Hall.

Blau, Francine D., and Lawrence Kahn. 1996. "Wage Structure and Gender Earnings Differentials: An International Comparison." *Economica* 63 (Supplement): S29–S62.

———. 1997. "Swimming Upstream: Trends in the Gender Wage Differential in the 1980s." *Journal of Economic Literature* 15: 1–42.

Block, Fred. 1990. *Postindustrial Possibilities: A Critique of Economic Discourse.* Berkeley and Los Angeles: University of California Press.

Blossfeld, Hans-Peter, and Catherine Hakim, eds. 1997. *Between Equalization and Marginalization: Women Working Part-Time in Europe and the USA.* Corby, Northamptonshire: Oxford University Press.

Blumberg, Rae Lesser, ed. 1991. *Gender, Family, and Economy: The Triple Overlap.* Newbury Park, Calif.: Sage Publications.

Blumstein P., and P. Schwartz. 1983. *American Couples.* New York: William Morrow.

Bologh, R. W. 1990. *Love or Greatness Max Weber and Masculine Thinking.* London: Unwin Hyman.

Bourguignon, Francois, and Pierre-Andre Chiappori. 1992. "Collective Models of Household Behavior." *European Economic Review* 36: 355–364.

Bowles, Samuel, and Herb Gintis. 1990. "Contested Exchange: New Microfoundations for the Political Economy of Capitalism." *Politics and Society* 18, no. 2: 165–222.

Bradley, Harriet. 1989. *Men's Work, Women's Work.* Cambridge: Polity Press.

———. 1998. *Gender and Power in the Workplace.* Houndmills Basingstoke: Macmillan.

———. 1999. *Gender and Power in the Workplace: Analysing the Impact of Economic Change.* London: Macmillan.

Braverman, H. 1974. *Labor and Monopoly Capital.* New York: Monthly Review Press.

Brenner, Johanna, and Maria Ramas. 1984. "Rethinking Women's Oppression." *New Left Review* 144: 33–71.

Brines, Julie. 1994. "Economic Dependency, Gender, and the Division of Labor at Home." *American Journal of Sociology* 100: 652–688.

Brinton, Mary C. 1993. *Women and the Economic Miracle: Gender and Work in Postwar Japan.* Berkeley and Los Angeles: University of California Press.

Brodsky, Melvin M. 1994. "Labor Market Flexibility: A Changing International Perspective." *Monthly Labor Review* 117 (November): 53–60.

Browning, Martin, Francois Bourguignon, Pierre-Andre Chiappori, and Valerie Lechene. 1994. "Income and Outcomes: A Structural Model of Intrahousehold Allocation." *Journal of Political Economy* 102, no. 6: 1067–1096.

Bruegel, Irene. 1996. "Whose Myths Are They Anyway? A Comment." *British Journal of Sociology* 47: 175–177.

Burawoy, Michael. 1979. *Manufacturing Consent: Changes in the Labor Process under Monopoly Capitalism.* Chicago: University of Chicago Press.

Capowski, G. 1996. "The Joy of Flex." *Management Review* 85, no. 3 (March): 12–18.

Carchedi, Guglielmo. 1979. *On the Economic Identification of Social Classes*. London: Routledge and Kegan Paul.

Casper, Lynne M., Sara S. McLanahan, and Irwin Garfinkel. 1994. "The Gender-Poverty Gap: What We Can Learn from Other Countries." *American Sociological Review* 59: 594–605.

Castles, F. G., and E. Seddon. 1988. "Towards an Organisational Model of Marital Instability." *Australian Journal of Social Issues* 23, no. 2: 113–127.

Chafetz, J. S., and J. Hagan. 1996. "The Gender Division of Labor and Family Change in Industrial Societies: A Theoretical Accounting." *Journal of Contemporary Family Studies* 27, pt. 2: 187–219.

Cherlin, Andrew J. 1981. *Marriage, Divorce, Remarriage*. Cambridge, Mass.: Harvard University Press.

———. 1996. *Public and Private Families*. New York: McGraw-Hill.

Clark, S. C. 1995. "Advance Report of Final Divorce Statistics, 1989 and 1990." *Monthly Vital Statistics Report*, 43, no. 8 (Supplement). Hyattsville, Md.: National Center for Health Statistics.

Clarke, T., and S. M. Lipset. 1991. "Are Social Classes Dying?" *International Sociology* 6, no. 4: 397–410.

Clayhills, Harriet. 1972. *Kvinner og klassekamp*. Oslo: Tiden Norsk Forlag.

Clement, Wallace. 1994. "Exploring the Limits of Social Democracy: Regime Change in Sweden." In W. Clement and R. Mahon, eds., *Swedish Social Democracy: A Model in Transition*, pp. 373–394. Toronto: Canadian Scholars' Press.

Clement, Wallace, and John Myles. 1994. *Relations of Ruling: Class and Gender in Postindustrial Societies*. Montreal: McGill-Queen's University Press.

Cliff, Tony. 1987. *Class Struggle and Women's Liberation: 1640 to Today*. London: Bookmarks.

Cohany, Sharon R. 1996. "Workers in Alternative Employment Arrangements." *Monthly Labor Review* 119 (October): 31–45.

Coltrane, Scott. 1996. *Family Man: Fatherhood, Housework and Gender Equity*. New York: Oxford University Press.

Cotter, David A., Joann DeFiore, Joan M. Hermsen, Brenda Marstellar Kowalewski, and Reeve Vanneman. 1997. "Same Data, Different Conclusions: Comment on Bernhardt et al." *American Journal of Sociology* 102: 1143–1153.

Coverman, Shelley. 1985. "Explaining Husbands' Participation in Domestic Labour." *Sociological Quarterly* 26, no. 1: 81–97.

Coverman, Shelley, and Joseph F. Sheley. 1986. "Change in Men's Housework and Child-Care Time, 1965–1975." *Journal of Marriage and the Family* 48: 413–422.

Craib, I. 1987. "Masculinity and Male Dominance." *Sociological Review* 35, no. 4: 721–743.

Crompton, Rosemary. 1986. "Women and the "Service Class." In R. Crompton and M. Mann, eds., *Gender and Stratification*, pp. 119–136. Cambridge: Polity Press.

———. 1993. *Class and Stratification*. Cambridge: Polity Press.

———. 1995. "Women's Employment and the 'Middle-Classes.'" In Tim Butler and Mike Savage, eds., *Social Change and the Middle Classes*, pp. 58–75. London: UCL Press.

———. 1996. "Consumption and Class Analysis." In S. Edgell, K. Hetherington, and A. Warde, eds., *Consumption Matters*, pp. 113–132. Oxford: Blackwell.

———. 1997. "Women, Employment and Feminism in the Czech Republic." *Gender Work and Organization* 4, no. 3: 137–148.

———. 1998. *Class and Stratification*. 2nd ed. London: Polity Press.

Crompton, R., ed. 1999. *Restructuring Gender Relations and Employment*. Oxford: Oxford University Press.

Crompton, R., and F. Harris. 1997. "Women's Employment and Gender Attitudes: A Comparative Analysis of Britain, Norway and the Czech Republic." *Acta Sociologica* 40: 183–202.

———. 1999. "Employment, Careers and Families: The significance of 'Choice' and 'Constraint' in Women's Lives." In Rosemary Crompton, ed., *Restructuring Gender Relations and Employment*, pp. 128–149. Oxford: Oxford University Press.

Crompton, R., and G. Jones. 1984. *White-Collar Proletariat: Deskilling and Gender in the Clerical Labour Process*. London: Macmillan.

Crompton, R., and N. Le Feuvre. 1997. "Choisir une carriere, faire carriere: Les femmes medicins en France et en Grande-Bretagne." *Cahiers du GEDDIST*, no. 14: 49–75. Paris: Editions L'Harmattan.

Crompton, R., N. Le Feuvre, and G. E. Birkelund. 1999. "The Gendered Restructuring of the Medical Profession." In Rosemary Crompton, ed., *Restructuring Gender Relations and Employment*, pp. 179–200. Oxford: Oxford University Press.

Dahrendorf, Ralf. 1959. *Class and Class Conflict in Industrial Society*. London: Routledge and Kegan Paul.

Dale, Angela. 1996. *The Link between Educational Qualifications, Family Formation, Economic Activity and Occupational Attainment for Women in Britain*. Paris: Lasmas-IdL. Mimeographed.

Dale, Angela, Nigel Gilbert, and Sara Arber. 1985. "Integrating Women into Class Theory." *Sociology* 19: 384–408.

Davidoff, L., and C. Hall. 1987. *Family Fortunes*. London: Hutchinson.

Davies, C. 1996. "The Sociology of the Professions and the Profession of Gender." *Sociology* 30, no. 4: 661–678.

Delsen, Lei. 1998. "When Do Men Work Part-Time?" In Jacqueline O'Reilly and Colette Fagan, eds., *Part-Time Prospects*, pp. 57–76. New York: Routledge.

Deutschmann, Christoph. 1991. "The Worker-Bee Syndrome in Japan: An Analysis of Working-Time Practices." In K. Hinrichs, W. Roche, and C. Siranni, eds., *Working Time in Transition: The Political Economy of Working Hours in Industrial Nations*, pp. 189–202. Philadelphia: Temple University Press.

De Vaus, David, and Ilene Wolcott. 1997. *Australian Family Profiles. Social and Demographic Patterns*. Melbourne: Australian Institute of Family Studies.

Dill, Bonnie Thornton. 1988. "'Making Your Job Good Yourself': Domestic Service and the Construction of Personal Dignity." In Ann Bookman and Sandra Morgen, eds., *Women and the Politics of Empowerment*, pp. 33–52. Philadelphia: Temple University Press.

Dølvik, Jon Erik, and Arild H. Steen, eds. 1997. *Making Solidarity Work? The Norwegian Labour Market Model in Transition*. Oslo: Scandinavian University Press.

Duncan, Beverly, and Otis Dudley Duncan. 1978. *Sex Typing and Social Roles: A Research Report*. New York: Academic Press.

Eatwell, John. 1995. "Disguised Unemployment: The G7 Experience." United Nations Conference on Trade and Development Discussion Paper No. 106, November 1995.

Edmondson, Brad. 1996. "Work Slowdown." *American Demographics* 18 (March): 4, 6–7.

Edwards, Linda N., and Elizabeth Field-Hendrey. 1996. "Home-Based Workers: Data from the 1990 Census of Population." *Monthly Labor Review* 119 (November): 26–34.

Ehrenreich, Barbara, and John Ehrenreich. 1979. "The Professional-Managerial Class." In Pat Walker, ed., *Between Labor and Capital*, pp. 5–45. New York: Monthly Review Press.

Elster, Jon. 1989. "Wage Bargaining and Social Norms." *Acta Sociologica* 32, no. 2: 113–136.

Engels, Friedrich. 1884. *The Origin of the Family, Private Property and the State*. Reprinted in *Karl Marx and Frederick Engels: Selected Works in One Volume*. London: Lawrence and Wishart, 1968.

England, Paula. 1981. "Assessing Trends in Occupational Sex Segregation, 1900–1976." In Ivar Berg, ed., *Sociological Perspectives on Labor Markets*, pp. 273–295. New York: Academic Press.

———. 1992. *Comparable Worth: Theories and Evidence*. Hawthorne, N.Y.: Aldine de Gruyter.

England, Paula, and Michelle J. Budig. 1998. "Gary Becker on the Family: His Genius, Impact, and Blind Spots." In Dan Clawson, ed., *Required Reading: Sociology's Most Influential Books*, pp. 95–112. Amherst, Mass.: University of Massachusetts Press.

England, Paula, Karen Christopher, Tim Smeeding, Katherine Ross, and Sara McLanahan. 1998. "The Role of State, Family, and Market in the Gender Gap in Poverty in Modern Nations: Findings from the Luxembourg Income Study."

Paper presented at the annual meetings of the American Sociological Association, San Francisco, August.

England, Paula, and George Farkas. 1986. *Households, Employment, and Gender: A Social, Economic and Demographic View*. New York: Aldine de Gruyter.

England, Paula, and Barbara Stanek Kilbourne. 1990. "Markets, Marriages, and Other Mates: The Problem of Power." In Roger Friedland and A. F. Robertson, eds., *Beyond the Marketplace: Rethinking Economy and Society*, pp. 163–188. New York: Aldine de Gruyter.

Erikson, R., and J. H. Goldthorpe. 1993. *The Constant Flux*. Oxford: Clarendon Press.

Esping-Andersen, Gøsta. 1990. *The Three Worlds of Welfare Capitalism*. Princeton, N.J.: Princeton University Press.

———. 1992. "Postindustrial Cleavage Structures: A Comparison of Evolving Patterns of Social Stratification in Germany, Sweden and the United States." In Frances Fox Piven, ed., *Labor Parties in Postindustrial Societies*, pp. 147–168. New York: Oxford University Press.

———, ed. 1993a. *Changing Classes: Stratification and Mobility in Post-Industrial Societies*. London: Sage Publications.

———. 1993b. "Post-Industrial Class Structures: An Analytical Framework." In *Changing Classes*, pp. 7–31. Newbury Park, Calif.: Sage Publications.

Esping-Andersen, Gøsta, and Jon E. Kolberg. 1991. "Decommodification and Work Absence in the Welfare State." *International Journal of Sociology* 21, no. 1: 77–111.

Facteau, George. 1997. "T&A Notice #37—Expanded Family and Medical Leave." Washington, D.C.: U.S. Department of Agriculture.

Ferree, Myra Marx. 1990. "Beyond Separate Spheres: Feminism and Family Research." *Journal of Marriage and the Family* 52 (November): 866–884.

Figart, Deborah, Heidi Hartmann, Eleanor Hinton Hoytt, and Janice Outtz. 1989. "The Wage Gap and Women of Color." Proceedings from the First Annual Women's Policy Research Conference. Washington, D.C.: Institute for Women's Policy Research.

Finch, J. 1983. *Married to the Job*. London: Allen and Unwin.

Folbre, Nancy. 1994. *Who Pays for the Kids?* New York: Routledge.

Freeman, Richard B. 1994. "How Labor Fares in Advanced Economies." In *Working under Different Rules*, pp. 1–28. New York: Russell Sage Foundation.

Freeman, Richard B., and Lawrence F. Katz. 1994. "Rising Wage Inequality: The United States vs. Other Advanced Countries." In Richard B. Freeman, ed., *Working under Different Rules*, pp. 29–62. New York: Russell Sage Foundation.

Freeman, Richard B., and Jonathan S. Leonard. 1987. "Union Maids: Unions and the Female Work Force." In Clair Brown and Joseph A. Pechman, eds., *Gender in the Workplace*, pp. 189–212. Washington, D.C.: The Brookings Institution.

Friedson, E. 1986. *Professional Powers*. Chicago: University of Chicago Press.

Gallie D., P. White, A. Cheng, and M. Tomlinson. 1998. *Restructuring the Employment Relationship.* Oxford: Oxford University Press.

Geerken, M., and W. R. Gove. 1983. *At Home and at Work.* Beverly Hills, Calif.: Sage Publications.

Gershuny, Jonathan, Michael Godwin, and Sally Jones. 1994. "The Domestic Labour Revolution: A Process of Lagged Adaptation." In Michael Anderson, Frank Bechhofer, and Jonathan Gershuny, eds., *The Social and Political Economy of the Household*, pp. 170–192. Oxford: Oxford University Press.

Gershuny, Jonathan, and John P. Robinson. 1988. "Historical Changes in the Household Division of Labor." *Demography* 25 (4): 537–552.

Giddens, A. 1973, 1981. *The Class Structure of the Advanced Societies.* London: Hutchinson.

Ginn, Jay, Sara Arber, Julia Brannen, Angela Dale, Shirley Dex, Peter Elias, Peter Moss, Jan Pahl, Ceridwen Roberts, and Jill Rubery. 1996. "Feminist Fallacies: A Reply to Hakim on Women's Employment." *British Journal of Sociology* 47: 167–174.

Ginsburg, H. L., J. Zaccone, G. S. Goldberg, S. D. Collins, and S. M. Rosen. 1997. "Special Issue on: The Challenge of Full Employment in the Global Economy, Editorial Introduction," *Economic and Industrial Democracy* 18, no. 1: 5–34.

Glass, Jennifer, and Valerie Camarigg. 1992. "Gender, Parenthood, and Job-Family Compatibility." *American Journal of Sociology* 98: 131–151.

Glass, Jennifer, and Sarah Beth Estes. 1997. "The Family Responsive Workplace." *Annual Review of Sociology* 23: 289–313.

Glass, Jennifer, and Tetsushi Fujimoto. 1995. "Employer Characteristics and the Provision of Family Responsive Policies." *Work and Occupations* 22: 380–411.

Glenn, Evelyn Nakano. 1992. "From Servitude to Service Work: Historical Continuities in the Racial Division of Reproductive Labor." *Signs* 18: 1–43.

Glezer, Helen. 1991. "Maternity Leave." Papers from the Women's Consultative Council Conference on Workers with Family Responsibilities. Office of the Status of Women. Canberra: Australian Government Publishing Service.

Glucksmann, M. 1995. "Why 'Work'? Gender and the Total Social Organisation of Labour." *Gender Work and Organisation* 2, no. 2: 63–75.

Goldthorpe, J. H. 1980. *Social Mobility and Class Structure in Modern Britain.* Oxford: Clarendon Press.

———. 1982. "On the Service Class, Its Formation and Future." In Anthony Giddens and Gavin Mackenzie, eds., *Social Class and the Division of Labour: Essays in Honour of Ilya Neustadt.* Cambridge: Cambridge University Press.

———. 1983. "Women and Class Analysis: In Defence of the Conventional View." *Sociology* 17, no. 4: 465–478.

———. 1984. "Women and Class Analysis: A Reply to the Replies." *Sociology* 18: 491–499.

———. 1990. "A Response." In Jon Clarke, Celia Modgil, and Simon Modgil, eds., *John H. Goldthorpe: Consensus and Controversy*, pp. 399–440. London: Falmer.

———. 1995. "The Service Class Revisited." In Tim Butler and Mike Savage, eds., *Social Change and the Middle Classes*, pp. 313–329. London: UCL Press.

Goldthorpe, J. H., D. Lockwood, F. Bechhofer, and J. Platt. 1969. *The Affluent Worker in the Class Structure*. Cambridge: Cambridge University Press.

Goldthorpe, J. H., and Clive Payne. 1986. "On the Class Mobility of Women: Results from Different Approaches to the Analysis of Recent British Data." *Sociology* 20: 531–555.

Gornick, Janet C. 1999. "Gender Equality in the Labor Market: Women's Employment and Earnings." In Diane Sainsbury, ed., *Gender Policy Regimes and Welfare States*, pp. 210–242. Oxford: Oxford University Press.

Gornick, Janet C., Marica K. Meyers, and Katherine Ross. 1998. "Public Policies and the Employment of Mothers: A Cross-National Study." *Social Science Quarterly* 79: 35–54.

Gottfried, Heidi. 1992. "The Impact of Skill on Union Membership: Rethinking Gender Differences." *Sociological Quarterly* 33: 99–114.

———. 1997. "Duality or Dualism in German Industrial Relations?" *Organizations, Occupations, and Work Newsletter*, (winter/spring): 3–4.

Gouldner, Alvin W. 1970. *The Coming Crisis of Western Sociology*. New York: Basic Books.

Government of Japan. 1993. *Working Conditions and the Labor Market* 32, no. 6 (June).

———. 1994. *White Paper on Labor: Summary*. Tokyo: Ministry of Labor, Japan Institute of Labor.

———. 1995. *White Paper on Labor 1995—Summary*. Tokyo: Ministry of Labor, Japan Institute of Labor.

———. 1996. *Working Conditions and the Labor Market* 33, no. 6 (June); 35, no. 6 (June).

Gower, Dave. 1997. "Measuring the Age of Retirement." *Perspectives on Labour and Income* 9, no. 2 (summer): 11–17.

Greenstein, Theodore N. 1990. "Marital Disruption and the Employment of Married Women." *Journal of Marriage and the Family* 52: 657–676.

———. 1995. "Gender Ideology, Marital Disruption, and the Employment of Married Women." *Journal of Marriage and the Family* 57: 31–42.

Gross, E. 1986. "Plus Ca Change. . . ? The Sexual Structure of Occupations over Time." *Social Problems* 16: 249–264.

Grusky, David, and Robert M. Hauser. 1984. "Comparative Social Mobility Revisited: Convergence and Divergence in 16 Countries." *American Sociological Review* 49: 19–38.

Grusky, David B., and Jesper B. Sorensen. 1998. "Can Class Analysis Be Salvaged?" *American Journal of Sociology* 103: 1187–1234.

Haas, Linda. 1981. "Domestic Role Sharing in Sweden." *Journal of Marriage and the Family*, no. 43: 957–967.

———. 1992. *Equal Parenthood and Social Policy: A Study of Parental Leave in Sweden.* Albany: State University of New York Press.

Haas, Linda, and Philip Hwang. 1995. "Company Culture and Men's Usage of Family Leave Benefits in Sweden." *Family Relations* 44: 28–36.

Hakim, Catherine. 1995. "Five Feminist Myths about Women's Employment." *British Journal of Sociology* 46, no. 3: 429–455.

———. 1996. "The Sexual Division of Labour and Women's Heterogeneity." *British Journal of Sociology* 47: 178–188.

———. 1997. "A Sociological Perspective on Part-Time Work." In Hans-Peter Blossfeld and Catherine Hakim, eds., *Between Equalization and Marginalization: Women Working Part-Time in Europe and the USA*, pp. 22–70. Corby, Northamptonshire: Oxford University Press.

Hammonds, Keith. 1997. "A Close-up of Corning." *Business Week*, July 21, pp. 93, 96.

Hardesty, C., and J. Bokemeier. 1989. "Finding Time and Making Do: Distribution of Household Labor in Nonmetropolitan Marriages." *Journal of Marriage and the Family* 51: 253–267.

Hartmann, Heidi. 1979. "Capitalism, Patriarchy and Job Segregation by Sex." In Zillah Eisenstein, ed., *Capitalist Patriarchy and the Case for Socialist Feminism*, pp. 206–247. New York: MR Press.

Heath, Anthony, and Nicky Britten. 1984. "Women's Jobs Do Make a Difference." *Sociology* 18: 475–490.

Hermansson, Ann-Sofie. 1993. *Arbetarrorelsen och feminismen.* Stockholm: Utbildingstorlaget Brevskolan.

Hernes, Helga Marie. 1984. "Women and the Welfare State: The Transition from Private to Public Dependence." In Harriet Holter, ed., *Patriarchy in a Welfare Society*, pp. 26–45. Oslo: Universitetsforlaget.

Hill, Stephen. 1981. *Competition and Control at Work.* London: Heinemann.

Hinrichs, Karl, William Roche, and Carmen Siranni, eds. 1991. *Working Time in Transition: The Political Economy of Working Hours in Industrial Nations.* Philadelphia: Temple University Press.

Hipple, Steven, and Jay Stewart. 1996. "Earnings and Benefits of Workers in Alternative Work Arrangements." *Monthly Labor Review* 119 (October): 46–54.

Hirdman, Yvonne. 1998. *Med kluven tunga: LO och genusordningen.* Uddevalla: Atlas.

Hirschman, Albert O. 1970. *Exit, Voice, and Loyalty.* Cambridge, Mass.: Harvard University Press.

Hobcraft, John. 1997. "The Consequences of Female Empowerment for Child Well-Being." Paper presented at IUSSP Conference, Lund, Sweden, April.

Hobson, Barbara. 1990. "No Exit, No Voice: Women's Economic Dependency and the Welfare State." *Acta Sociologica* 33, no. 3: 235–250.

Hochschild, Arlie Russell. 1997. *The Time Bind: When Work Becomes Home and Home Becomes Work*. New York: Metropolitan Books, Henry Holt.

Hoffman, Saul D., and Greg Duncan. 1995. "The Effect of Incomes, Wages, and AFDC Benefits on Marital Disruption." *Journal of Human Resources* 30: 19–41.

Høgsnes, Geir. 1996. "Wage Distribution Conflicts in Norway—A Threat against the 'Solidarity Alternative.'" Working Paper No. 16, Center for Western European Studies, University of California, Berkeley, August.

Hossfeld, Karen J. 1990. "'Their Logic against Them': Contradictions in Sex, Race, and Class in Silicon Valley." In Kathryn B. Ward, ed., *Women Workers and Global Restructuring*, pp. 149–178. Ithaca, N.Y.: ILR Press.

Houseman, Susan N. 1997. "Temporary, Part-Time, and Contract Employment in the United States: New Evidence from an Employer Survey." Paper presented at the Sloan Foundation's Conference on Labor Market Inequality, Madison, Wisconsin, February 28–March 1.

———. 1999a. "Flexible Staffing Arrangements." Report to the U.S. Department of Labor.

———. 1999b. *How Children and Parents Cope with Divorce*. New York: Basic Books.

Hout, Michael, Clem Brooks, and Jeff Manza. 1993. "The Persistence of Classes in Post-Industrial Societies." *International Sociology* 8: 259–278.

Huber, J., and Glenna Spitze. 1983. *Sex Stratification: Children, Housework and Jobs*. New York: Academic Press.

Huffschmid, Jörg. 1997. "Economic Policy for Full Employment: Proposals for Germany." *Economic and Industrial Democracy* 18, no. 1: 67–86.

Humphries, Jane. 1977. "Class Struggle and the Persistence of the Working Class Family." *Cambridge Journal of Economics* 1, no. 3: 241–258.

Ingham, G. K. 1974. *Strikes and Industrial Conflict*. London: Macmillan.

Institute for Women's Policy Research. 1997. "The Wage Gap: Women's and Men's Earnings." Briefing Paper. Washington, D.C.: IWPR.

International Labour Office Geneva. 1995. *Conditions of Work Digest: Working Time around the World* 14: 301–317.

Jacobs, Jerry. 1989. "Long-Term Trends in Occupational Segregation by Sex." *American Journal of Sociology* 95, no. 1: 160–173.

———. 1992. "Women's Entrance into Management: Trends in Earnings, Authority, Values, and Attitudes among Salaried Managers." *Administrative Science Quarterly* 37: 282–301.

Jacobs, Jerry, and Kathleen Gerson. 1998. "Who Are the Overworked Americans?" *Review of Social Economy* 56: 442–459.

Japan Information Network. 1997, March. *White Paper on Labor*. Tokyo: Ministry of Labor.

Joshi, Heather. 1996. "Review of Catherine Hakim, Key Issues in Women's Work:

Female Heterogeneity and the Polarisation of Women's Employment." *British Journal of Sociology* 47: 330–332.

Kalleberg, Arne L. 1995. "Part-Time Work and Workers in the United States: Correlates and Policy Issues." *Washington and Lee Law Review* 52, no. 3: 771–798.

Kalleberg, Arne L., Edith Rasell, Naomi Cassirer, Barbara F. Reskin, Ken Hudson, David Webster, Eileen Appelbaum, and Roberta M. Spalter-Roth. 1997. *Nonstandard Work, Substandard Jobs: Flexible Work Arrangements in the U.S.* Washington, D.C.: Economic Policy Institute.

Kalleberg, Arne L., Barbara F. Reskin, and Ken Hudson. 2000. "Bad Jobs in America: Standard and Non-Standard Employment Relations and Job Quality in the United States." *American Sociological Review* 65, no. 2 (April): 256–278.

Kalleberg, Arne L., and Rachel A. Rosenfeld. 1990. "Work in the Family and in the Labor Market: A Cross-National, Reciprocal Analysis." *Journal of Marriage and the Family* 52 (May): 331–346.

Kanter, R. 1986. "The Reshaping of Middle Management." *Management Review*, January, 19–20.

Karvonen, Lauri. 1995. "Trade Unions and the Feminization of the Labour Market in Scandinavia." In Lauri Karvonen and Per Selle, eds., *Women in Nordic Politics: Closing the Gap*, pp. 133–153. Aldershot: Dartmouth.

Kelly, Joan Berlin. 1986. "Divorce: The Adult Perspective." In Arlene S. Skolnik and Jerome H. Skolnik, eds., *Family in Transition*, 5th ed., pp. 304–337. Boston: Little, Brown.

Kerbo, Harold R. 2000. *Social Stratification and Inequality: Class Conflict in Historical and Comparative Perspective*. 4th ed. New York: McGraw-Hill.

Kitson, Gay. 1992. *Portrait of a Divorce*. New York: Guilford Press.

Korpi, Walter. 1983. *The Democratic Class Struggle*. London: Routledge and Kegan Paul.

———. 1989. "Power, Politics, and State Autonomy in the Development of Social Citizenship: Social Rights during Sickness in Eighteen OECD Countries since 1930." *American Sociological Review* 54, no. 3 (June): 309–328.

Korsnes, Olav. 1981. "Fagbevegelse og konfliktregulering." In Tom Colbjørnsen, Olav Korsnes, and Odd Nordhaug, *Fagbevegelsen—Interesseorganisasjon og administrator*, pp. 133–156. Oslo: Universitetsforlaget.

Lembcke, Jerry. 1991. "Class Analysis and Studies of the U.S. Working Class: Theoretical, Conceptual, and Methodological Issues." In Scott G. McNall, Rhonda F. Levine, and Rick Fantasia, eds., *Bringing Class Back In: Contemporary and Historical Perspectives*, pp. 83–97. Boulder, Colo.: Westview Press.

Lerner, Gerda. 1986. *The Creation of Patriarchy*. New York: Basic Books.

Lewis, Jane. 1985. "The Debate on Sex and Class." *New Left Review* 149: 108–120.

———. 1992. "Gender and the Development of Welfare Regimes." *Journal of European Social Policy* 23: 159–173.

Lewis, S., and J. Lewis. 1996. *The Work-Family Challenge*. London: Sage Publications.

Lipset, Seymour Martin, Martin Trow, and James Coleman. 1956. *Union Democracy: The Internal Politics of the International Typographical Union*. New York: The Free Press.

LO Sverige. 1995. *Klass och kon*. Stockholm.

Lockwood, D. 1958. *The Black Coated Worker*. London: Allen and Unwin.

———. 1966. "Sources of Variation in Working-Class Images of Society." *Sociological Review* 14, no. 3: 244–267.

———. 1995. "Marking Out the Middle Classes." In Tim Butler and Mike Savage, eds., *Social Change and the Middle Classes*, pp. 1–12. London: UCL Press.

Mahon, Rianne. 1996. "Women Wage Earners and the Future of Swedish Unions." *Economic and Industrial Democracy* 17, no. 4: 558–562.

Marshall, Gordon, David Rose, Howard Newby, and Carolyn Vogler. 1989. *Social Class in Modern Britain*. London: Hutchinson.

Martin, Teresa Castro, and Larry L. Bumpass. 1989. "Recent Trends in Marital Disruption." *Demography* 26, no. 1: 37–51.

McCarthy, Margaret. 1977. "Women in Trade Unions today." In Lucy Middleton, ed., *Women in the Labour Movement: The British Experience*, pp. 161–174. London: Croom Helm.

McDonald, Gerald W. 1980. "Family Power: An Assessment of a Decade of Theory and Research, 1970–1979." *Journal of Marriage and the Family* 42, no. 2 (November): 841–851.

McGuire, Gail M., and Barbara F. Reskin. 1993. "Authority Hierarchies at Work: The Impacts of Race and Sex." *Gender and Society* 7: 487–506.

McLanahan, Sara S., and Kelly. 1999. "The Feminization of Poverty: Past and Future." In Janet Saltzman Chafetz, ed., *Handbook of the Sociology of Gender*, pp. 127–146. New York: Kluwer.

McLanahan, Sara S., Annemette Sorensen, and Dorothy Watson. 1989. "Sex Differences in Poverty, 1950–1980." *Signs* 15, no. 11: 102–112.

Meidner, Rudolf. 1997. "The Swedish Model in an Era of Mass Unemployment" *Economic and Industrial Democracy* 18, no. 1: 87–98.

Michael, Robert T. 1988. "Why Did the U.S. Divorce Rate Double within a Decade?" *Research in Population Economics* 6: 367–399.

Mills, C. W. 1951. *White Collar*. New York: Oxford University Press.

Moore, Kristin A. 1995. *Report to Congress on Out-of-Wedlock Childbearing*. Hyattsville, Md.: National Center for Health Statistics.

Myles, John, and Adnan Turegun. 1994. "Comparative Studies in Class Structure." *Annual Review of Sociology* 20: 103–124.

Nardone, Thomas. 1995. "Part-Time Employment: Reasons, Demographics, and Trends." *Journal of Labor Research* 16: 275–292.

National Women's Consultative Council. 1993. *Paid Maternity Leave: A Discus-*

sion Paper on Paid Maternity Leave in Australia. Canberra: Australian Government Publishing Service.

Negrey, Cynthia. 1993. *Gender, Time, and Reduced Work*. Albany: State University of New York Press.

O'Connor, Julia S. 1993. "Gender Class and Citizenship in the Comparative Analysis of Welfare State Regimes." *British Journal of Sociology* 44, no. 3: 501–518.

O'Connor, Julia S., and Gregg M. Olsen, eds. 1988. *Power Resources Theory and the Welfare State: A Critical Approach*. Toronto: University of Toronto Press.

Olsen, Gregg. 1994. "Locating the Canadian Welfare State: Family Policy and Health Care in Canada, Sweden and the United States." *Canadian Journal of Sociology* 19, no. 1: 1–20.

Oppenheimer, Valerie. 1997. "Comment on 'The Rise of Divorce and Separation in the United States, 1880–1990.'" *Demography* 34: 467–472.

O'Reilly, Jacqueline, and Colette Fagan, eds. 1998. *Part-Time Prospects*. New York: Routledge.

Organization for Economic Cooperation and Development. 1994a. *Employment Outlook*. Paris: OECD.

———. 1994b. *The OECD Jobs Study: Evidence and Explanations, Part I*. Paris: OECD.

———. 1995, July. "Long-Term Leave for Parents in OECD Countries." *Employment Outlook*. Paris: OECD.

———. 1996, July. *Employment Outlook*. Paris: OECD.

———. 1998, July. *Employment Outlook*. Paris: OECD.

Orloff, Ann Shola. 1993. "Gender and the Social Rights of Citizenship: The Comparative Analysis of Gender Relations and the Welfare States." *American Sociological Review* 58 (June): 303–328.

Øverås, Siv, and Kristine Nergaard. 1997. *Kvinner i fagbevegelsen*. Report No. 239. Oslo: Fafo Institute for Applied Social Research.

Pahl, R. E. 1989. "Is the Emperor Naked?" *International Journal of Urban and Regional Research* 13, no. 4: 711–720.

Pakulski, Jan, and Malcolm Waters. 1996. *The Death of Class*. London: Sage.

Parkin, Frank. 1979. *Marxism and Class Theory: A Bourgeois Critique*. London: Tavistock.

Pateman, C. 1989. "The Patriarchal Welfare State." In C. Pateman, ed., *The Disorder of Women*, pp. 179–209. Cambridge: Polity Press.

Pearce, Diana. 1978. "The Feminization of Poverty: Women, Work, and Welfare." *Urban and Social Change Review* 11: 128–136.

Peck, Jamie. 1996. *Work-Place: The Social Regulation of Labor Markets*. New York: Guilford Press.

Petersen, Trond, and Laurie A. Morgan. 1995. "Separate and Unequal: Occupation-Establishment Sex Segregation and the Gender Wage Gap." *American Journal of Sociology* 101, no. 2: 329–365.

Pfau-Effinger, B. 1993. "Modernisation, Culture and Part-Time Employment." *Work, Employment and Society* 7, no. 3: 383–410.

———. 1999. "The Modernisation of Family and Motherhood in Western Europe." In Rosemary Crompton, ed., *Restructuring Gender Relations and Employment*, pp. 60–79. Oxford: Oxford University Press.

Pfeffer, Jeffrey, and James Baron. 1988. "Taking the Workers Back Out." *Research in Organizational Behavior* 10: 257–303.

Pleck, Joseph H. 1984. "The Work-Family Role System." In P. Voydanoff, ed., *Work and Family*, pp. 8–19. Palo Alto, Calif.: Mayfield.

———. 1985. *Working Wives/Working Husbands*. Beverly Hills, Calif.: Sage Publications.

Polivka, Anne E. 1996a. "Contingent and Alternative Work Arrangements, Defined." *Monthly Labor Review* 119 (October): 3–9.

———. 1996b. "Into Contingent and Alternative Employment: By Choice?" *Monthly Labor Review* 119 (October): 55–74.

———. 1996c. "A Profile of Contingent Workers." *Monthly Labor Review* 119 (October): 10–21.

Portes, Alejandro, and Saskia Sassen-Koob. 1987. "Making It Underground." *American Journal of Sociology* 93: 30–61.

Poulantzas, Nicos. 1978. *Classes in Contemporary Capitalism*. London: New Left Books.

Presser, Harriet B. 1994. "Employment Schedules, Gender, and Household Labor." *American Sociological Review* 59: 348–364.

Raabe, Phyllis Hutton. 1996. "Constructing Pluralistic Work and Career Arrangements That Are Family—and Work—Friendly." In Suzan Lewis and Jeremy Lewis, eds., *Rethinking Employment: The Work-Family Challenge*, pp. 128–141. Thousand Oaks, Calif.: Sage Publications.

Raley, R. Kelly. 1996. "Cohabitation, Marriageable Men, and Racial Differences in Marriage." *American Sociological Review* 61, no. 6: 973–983.

Reich, Robert B. 1991. *The Work of Nations: Preparing Ourselves for 21st-Century Capitalism*. New York: Vintage Books.

Roberts, Helen. 1993. "The Women and Class Debate." In David Morgan and Liz Stanley, eds., *Debates in Sociology*. Manchester: Manchester University Press.

Robinson, Joan. 1937. "Disguised Unemployment." In *Essays in the Theory of Employment*, pp. 60–74. London: Macmillan.

Rosenberg, Samuel. 1989. "Labor Market Restructuring in Europe and the United States." In Samuel Rosenberg, ed., *The State and the Labor Market*, pp. 3–16. New York: Plenum Press.

Rosenfeld, Rachel A. 1996. "Women's Work Histories." *Population and Development Review Supplement (Fertility in the United States: New Patterns, New Theories)* 22: 199–222.

Rosenfeld, Rachel A., and Gunn Elisabeth Birkelund. 1995. "Women's Part-Time

Work: A Cross-National Comparison." *European Sociological Review* 11: 111–134.

Rosenfeld, Rachel A., Arne L. Kalleberg, and Ken Hudson. 1997. "The Good, the Bad, the Contingent." Paper presented at the annual meeting of the American Sociological Association, Toronto, August 9.

Ross, Catherine. 1987. "The Division of Labor at Home." *Social Forces* 65, no. 3: 816–833.

Rowntree Foundation. 1995. *Inquiry into Income and Wealth*. New York: Rowntree Foundation.

Rubery, J., ed. 1988. *Women and Recession*. London: Routledge and Kegan Paul.

Rubery, J., and C. Fagan. 1994. "Occupational Segregation: Plus ça Change?" In R. Lindley, ed., *Labour Market Structures and Prospects for Women*, pp. 29–42. Manchester: Equal Opportunity Commission.

Rudolph, Helmut. 1994. "Federal Republic of Germany: Change and Diversity." In O. Benoît-Guilbot and D. Gallie, eds., *Long-Term Unemployment*, pp. 79–91. London: Pinter Publishers.

Ruggles, Steven B. 1997a. "Reply to Oppenheimer and Preston." *Demography* 34: 475–479.

———. 1997b. "The Rise of Divorce and Separation in the United States, 1880–1990." *Demography* 34: 455–466.

Savage, Mike. 1992. "Women's Expertise, Men's Authority: Gendered Organization and the Contemporary Middle Classes." In Mike Savage and Anne Witz, eds., *Gender and Bureaucracy*, pp. 124–151. Oxford: Blackwell.

———. 1995. "Class Analysis and Social Research." In Tim Butler and Mike Savage, eds., *Social Change and the Middle Classes*, pp. 15–25. London: UCL Press.

Schein, Virginia. 1995. *Working from the Margins: Voices of Mothers in Poverty*. Ithaca, N.Y.: ILR Press.

Schellenberg, Grant. 1996. "Involuntary Part-Time Workers." *Perception: Canada's Social Development Magazine* 18, no. 3: 23–36.

Schmid, Günther. 1995. "A New Approach to Labor Market Policy: A Contribution to the Current Debate on Efficient Employment Policies." *Economic and Industrial Democracy* 16, no. 4: 428–436.

Scoon-Rogers, Lydia, and Gordon H. Lester. 1995. "Child Support for Custodial Mothers and Fathers: 1991." *Current Population Reports*. Series P-60. Washington, D.C.: U.S. Bureau of the Census, U.S. Government Printing Office.

Sinclair, Diane M. 1996. "The Importance of Gender for Participation in and Attitudes to Trade Unionism." *Industrial Relations Journal* 27, no. 3: 239–252.

Skjeie, Hege. 1989. *Rapport fra (d)en siste skanse: Kvinnerepresentasjon i fagbevegelsen*. Report 88:7. Oslo: Institute for Social Research.

Skolnick, Arlene S., and Jerome H. Skolnick, eds. 1986. *Family in Transition: Rethinking Marriage, Sexuality, Child Rearing, and Family Organization*. 5th ed. Boston: Little, Brown.

Smith, James P., and Michael P. Ward. 1994. *Women's Wages and Work in the Twentieth Century*. Report No. R-3119-NICHD. Santa Monica, Calif.: Rand.

Smith, Mark, Colette Fagan, and Jill Rubery. 1998. "Where and Why Is Part-Time Work Growing in Europe?" In Jacqueline O'Reilly and Colette Fagan, eds., *Part-Time Prospects*, pp. 35–56. New York: Routledge.

Smith, Vickie, and Heidi Gottfried. 1998. "Flexibility in Work and Employment: The Impact on Women." In Birgit Geissler, Friederika Maier, and Birgit Pfau-Effinger, eds., *FrauenArbeitsMarkt*, pp. 95–125. Berlin: Sigma.

Sorrentino, Constance. 1995. "International Unemployment Indicators, 1983–93." *Monthly Labor Review*, August, pp. 28–33.

South, Scott, and Glenna Spitze. 1986. "Determinants of Divorce over the Marital Life Course." *American Sociological Review* 51, no. 4 (August): 583–590.

Spain, Daphne, and Suzanne M. Bianchi. 1996. *Balancing Act: Motherhood, Marriage, and Employment among American Women*. New York: Russell Sage Foundation.

Spanier, Graham, and Linda Thompson. 1984. *Parting: The Aftermath of Separation and Divorce*. Beverly Hills, Calif.: Sage.

Spitze, Glenna. 1988. "Women's Employment and Family Relations: A Review." *Journal of Marriage and the Family* 50: 596–618.

Stafford, Rebecca, Elaine Backman, and Pamela Dibona. 1976. "The Gender Division of Labor in Two-Earner Families: Dimensions of Variability and Change." *Journal of Family Issues* 12: 158–180.

Standing, Guy. 1997. "Globalization, Labour Flexibility and Insecurity: The Era of Market Regulation." *European Journal of Industrial Relations* 3, no. 1.

Stanworth, Michelle. 1984. "Women and Class Analysis: A Reply to John Goldthorpe." *Sociology* 18: 159–170.

Stokke, Torgeir. 1998. *Utmeldinger i LO-forbundene på 1990-tallet*. Oslo: Fafo Institute for Applied Social Research.

Sundstrom, Marianne. 1993. "The Growth in Full-Time Work among Swedish Women in the 1980s." *Acta Sociologica* 36: 139–150.

Svedin, D. G. 1994. Mans och kvinnors syn pa skilsmassoorsaker och upplevda konsekvenser av skilsmassan: I Rapporten Hearing om Skilsm Ssor Och Familjesplittring. 1993. Dokument 1994:1. Fran Kommitten for FN:S Familjear. Socialdepartementet.

Taeuber, Cynthia. 1991. *Statistical Handbook on Women in America*. Phoenix: Oryx Press.

Takahashi, Yukichi. 1997. "The Labor Market and Lifetime Employment in Japan." *Economic and Industrial Democracy* 18, no. 1: 55–66.

Tam, May. 1997. "Demand for Part-Time Workers: An Assessment of Temporal Changes and Structural Features of Organizations." Unpublished manuscript, University of New South Wales, Australia.

Therborn, Gøran. 1983. "Why Some Classes Are More Successful Than Others." *New Left Review* 138 (March–April): 37–55.

Thomas, Duncan. 1990. "Intra-Household Resource Allocation." *Journal of Human Resources* 25, no. 4: 635–664.

Thompson, Linda, and A. J. Walker. 1989. "Gender in Families: Women and Men in Marriage, Work and Parenthood." *Journal of Marriage and the Family* 51: 845–871.

Thurow, C. 1996. *The Future of Capitalism: How Today's Economic Forces Will Shape Tomorrow's World.* St. Leonards: Allen and Unwin.

Tilly, Chris. 1996. *Half a Job: Bad and Good Part-Time Jobs in a Changing Labor Market.* Philadelphia: Temple University Press.

Tomaskovic-Devey, Donald, and Barbara J. Risman. 1993. "Telecommuting Innovation and Organization: A Contingency Theory of Labor Process Change." *Social Science Quarterly* 74: 365–385.

Trappe, Heike, and Rachel A. Rosenfeld. 2000. "How Do Children Matter: A Comparison of Gender Earnings Inequality for Young Adults in the Former East Germany and the Former West Germany." *Journal of Marriage and the Family* 62: 489–507.

Tzeng, Jessie M., and Robert D. Mare. 1995. "Labor Market and Socioeconomic Effects on Marital Stability." *Social Science Research* 24: 329–351.

Uno, Kathleen S. 1993. "The Death of 'Good Wife, Wise Mother?" In Andrew Gordon, ed., *Postwar Japan as History*, pp. 293–322. Berkeley and Los Angeles: University of California Press.

U.S. Bureau of the Census. 1988. "Characteristics of the Population below the Poverty Level: 1987." *Current Population Reports.* Series P-60. Washington, D.C.: U.S. Government Printing Office.

———. 1990a. *Current Population Reports.* Series P-60. Washington, D.C.: U.S. Government Printing Office.

———. 1990b. *Statistical Abstract of the United States: 1990.* 110th ed. Washington, D.C.: U.S. Government Printing Office.

———. 1991. "Poverty in the United States: March 1990." *Current Population Reports.* Series P-60. Washington, D.C.: U.S. Government Printing Office.

———. 1993. "Money Income for Households, Families, and Persons, in the United States: 1992." *Current Population Reports.* Series P-60. Washington, D.C.: U.S. Government Printing Office.

———. 1994. "Income, Poverty, and Valuation of Non-Cash Benefits." *Current Population Reports.* Series P-60. Washington, D.C.: U.S. Government Printing Office.

———. 1995a. "Poverty in the United States: March 1994." *Current Population Reports.* Series P-60. Washington, D.C.: U.S. Government Printing Office.

———. 1995b. *Statistical Abstract of the United States: 1995.* 115th ed. Washington, D.C.: U.S. Government Printing Office.

———. 1996. *Statistical Abstract of the United States: 1996.* 116th ed. Washington, D.C.: U.S. Government Printing Office.

————. 1998. *Statistical Abstract of the United States: 1998*. 118th ed. Washington, D.C.: U.S. Government Printing Office.

U.S. Department of Labor. 1989. *Handbook of Labor Statistics*. Bulletin 2340. Washington, D.C.: U.S. Government Printing Office.

U.S. Department of Labor, Bureau of Labor Statistics. 1998a. "Employment Characteristics of Families in 1997." *Bureau of Labor Statistics News*. USDL 98–217.

————. 1998b. "Work at Home in 1997." *Bureau of Labor Statistics News*. USDL 98–93.

————. 1999. "The Employment Situation: March 1999." *Bureau of Labor Statistics News*. USDL 99–81.

U.S. Department of Labor, Bureau of Labor Statistics, Office of Productivity and Technology. 1996, August. "Comparative Civilian Labor Force Statistics, Ten Countries, 1959–1995."

Wajcman, J. 1996. "The Domestic Basis for the Managerial Career." *Sociological Review* 44, no. 4: 609–629.

Waldfogel, Jane. 1998. "Understanding the 'Family Gap' in Pay for Women with Children." *Journal of Economic Perspectives* 12: 137–156.

Wallerstein, Judith S., and Joan Berlin Kelly. 1980. *Surviving the Breakup: How Children and Parents Cope with Divorce*. London: Grant McIntyre.

Ward, Kathryn B., ed. 1990. *Women Workers and Global Restructuring*. Ithaca, N.Y.: ILR Press.

Weber, Max. 1982. "Selections from *Economy and Society* vols. 1 and 2, and *General Economic History*." In Anthony Giddens and David Held, eds., *Classes, Power and Conflict: Classical and Contemporary Debates*, pp. 60–86. Berkeley and Los Angeles: University of California Press.

Wellington, Allison J. 1993. "Changes in the Male/Female Wage Gap, 1976–1985." *Journal of Human Resources* 28: 383–411.

————. 1994. "The Male/Female Wage Gap among Whites: 1976 and 1985." *American Sociological Review* 59, no. 6: 839–848.

Western, Bruce P. 1996. "The Puzzle of Australian Union Decline." *Australian and New Zealand Journal of Sociology* 32: 31–43.

Western, Mark. 1991. "The Process of Income Determination." In Janeen H. Baxter, Michael Emmison, John S. Western, and Mark Western, eds., *Class Analysis and Contemporary Australia*, pp. 105–138. South Melbourne: Macmillan.

————. 1994. "Class Structure and Intergenerational Class Mobility: A Comparative Analysis of Nation and Gender." *Social Forces* 73: 101–134.

Western, Mark, and Erik Olin Wright. 1994. "The Permeability of Class Boundaries to Intergenerational Mobility among Men in the United States, Canada, Sweden and Norway." *American Sociological Review* 59: 606–629.

Wickham, James. 1997. "Part-Time Work in Ireland and Europe: Who Wants What Where?" *Work, Employment, and Society* 11: 133–151.

Witz, Anne. 1992. *Professions and Patriarchy*. London: Routledge.

———. 1995. "Gender and Service-Class Formation." In Tim Butler and Mike Savage, eds., *Social Change and the Middle Classes*, pp. 41–57. London: UCL Press.

Wright, Erik Olin. 1977. "Class Boundaries in Advanced Capitalist Societies." *New Left Review* 98: 3–41.

———. 1978. *Class, Crisis and the State*. London: New Left Books.

———. 1985. *Classes*. London: Verso Press.

———. 1989. "Women in the Class Structure." *Politics and Society* 17: 35–66.

———. 1993. *Interrogating Inequality*. London: Verso Press.

———. 1997. *Class Counts: Comparative Studies in Class Analysis*. Cambridge: Cambridge University Press.

Wright, Erik Olin, and Janeen Baxter, with Gunn Elisabeth Birkelund. 1995. "The Gender Gap in Work Place Authority: A Cross-National Study." *American Sociological Review* 69, no. 3 (June): 407–435.

Wright, Erik Olin, Andrew Levine, and Elliott Sober. 1992. Re-*Constructing Marxism: Essays on Explanation and the Theory of History*. London: Verso Press.